What the Arabs Think of America

What the Arabs Think of America

Andrew Hammond

Greenwood World Publishing
Oxford / Westport, Connecticut
2007

First published by Greenwood World Publishing 2007

1 2 3 4 5 6 7 8 9 10

Copyright © Andrew Hammond

Andrew Hammond has asserted his right under the Copyright, Designs and Patents Act 1988 to be identified as the author of this work

This book is sold subject to the condition that it shall not, by way of trade or otherwise, be lent, resold, hired out, or otherwise circulated without the publisher's prior consent in any form of binding or cover other than that in which it is published and without a similar condition being imposed on the subsequent publisher

Greenwood World Publishing
Wilkinson House
Jordan Hill
Oxford OX2 8EJ
An imprint of Greenwood Publishing Group, Inc
www.greenwood.com

British Library Cataloguing-in-Publication Data: a catalogue record for this book is available from the British Library

Library of Congress Cataloging-in-Publication Data

Hammond, Andrew, 1970-
  What the Arabs think of America / Andrew Hammond.
       p. cm.
  Includes bibliographical references and index.
  ISBN 1-84645-000-4 (alk. paper)
  1. Arab countries – Relations – United States. 2. United States – Relations – Arab countries. 3. September 11 Terrorist Attacks, 2001 – Influence. 4. Iraq War, 2003–. 5. Arab-Israeli conflict. I. Title.

  DS63.2.U5H357 2007
  303.48'2174927073 – dc22
                                    2006039650

ISBN 978-1-84645-000-6

Designed by Fraser Muggeridge studio
Typeset by TexTech
Printed and bound by South China Printing Company

Contents

Preface vii

Chapter 1
America in the Arab World 1

Chapter 2
Domestic America 33

Chapter 3
The Palestinians 57

Chapter 4
The Iraq Project 87

Chapter 5
Peace with Egypt 119

Chapter 6
The House of Saud 151

Chapter 7
The Sudanese Card 179

Chapter 8
Conclusion 205

Chronology 211
Glossary 213
People 219
Notes 223
Bibliography 233
Index 237

Preface

Mecca, Saudi Arabia, January 2004.[1] At the narrow mountain pass known as Mina, hundreds of thousands of pilgrims following the hajj pilgrimage rites camp out for two days. During that time, according to the time-honoured tradition set out in the Muslim holy book the Quran, they visit the three pillars known as the *Jamarat* where the Devil is said to have appeared to the Prophet Abraham, the same biblical patriarch who all three of the Semitic monotheistic religions of Judaism, Christianity and Islam agree began life in the southern Iraqi town of Ur. Islam commands the pilgrims in Mecca, a dusty oasis town set in the mountains of southwest Arabia, to stone the pillars in a symbolic casting out of the Devil. The temptation to personify the evil force in question is great and this year many have fallen prey to it: amid the chaos of flying stones Egyptian peasant women take off their flip-flops and hurl them in anger against bad husbands or lovers, or others who have done them wrong. But, pushing through the crowds of pilgrims in white robes to get as close to the central *jamara* as possible in this hajj of the Muslim year 1424, one could discern a piece of graffiti across the pillar and part of its base. There, daubed in what appeared to be red spray paint, was the one clear simple word in four Latin letters, spelling out in English: BUSH. Against all theory on what the stoning rite was meant to represent, someone had taken it upon themselves to identify George W. Bush, the self-styled leader of the free world, as the Satan who God-fearing Muslims should cast out with their stones during hajj.

It would be difficult to find a more eloquent and succint statement of the anger and resentment felt by people throughout the Arab countries and wider Islamic world in the aftermath of America's invasion of Iraq. This momentous act of "preventive war" had as its stated aim the disarming of a Third World strongman whose country contained vast untapped reserves of oil, and bringing democracy and good governance to its long-suffering population. But in one fell swoop the military action ripped apart the fragile veneer of independence that Arab regimes had carefully constructed in the fifty-odd years since decolonization after the Second World War, with the help of complicit Western powers.

For the Arab world, the invasion was the culmination of years of growing hostility between the Arabs and America, as the contradiction between their hopes and dreams, on the one hand, and the realities of American foreign policy, on the other, had become painfully apparent.

Relations with the United States have gone from bad to worse in recent years. When the Palestinian uprising against Israel's occupation began in September 2000, public opinion blamed the United States for its moral, political, economic and military support for Israel and its domination of the indigenous Arab population in territories seized in 1967 without any offer of either independence or equal citizen status in the Jewish state. After the September 11 attacks in 2001, the United States pressured Arab countries to cooperate on security and to reform their Islam-loaded education systems in a move which appeared to be aimed at Egypt and Saudi Arabia in particular. Arabs also felt the chill winds of demonization of all things Arab and Muslim in the West, the intensification of an already existing disdain and contempt. The war on terror was in Arab eyes a war on Islam and a war on the Arabs.

It is a sobering fact that the official line of George W. Bush and Tony Blair, British Prime Minister at the time, that they were fighting a just war in Iraq which for that reason they must ultimately win, clashes not just with the thinking among the parties to the dispute itself – those Islamists, nationalists and others who have taken up arms in Iraq – but with the entire tenor of public discourse throughout the Arab world. Against such a backdrop, it becomes difficult to imagine a peaceful situation pertaining in Iraq as long as the United States and its allies pursue their current policies. The United States argues that anti-US Islamic violence is a malady that was not provoked by the United States. "We're not facing a set of grievances that can be soothed and addressed. We're facing a radical ideology with unalterable objectives: to enslave whole nations and intimidate the world. No act of ours invited the rage of the killers, and no concession, bribe or act of appeasement would change or limit their plans for murder," Bush has said. Some Arab writers have agreed with this view – but the majority argue that the Israeli presence in the West Bank and huge US political, economic and military presence in countries like Egypt and Saudi Arabia preceded September 11 and formed part of a wider intellectual and political approach to the region that sought to dilute its sovereignty and destroy its unity to serve American and Israeli interests. Public debate in the Arab world generally views Islamic radicalism as a response to Arab weakness and Western strength. Intellectuals argue that the Arab world does not need the United States or the West in general for it to learn democracy. They point to the experience of parliamentary democracy in pre-1952 Egypt as an example of how such meddling, in their eyes, subverts democracy and gives it a bad name.

PREFACE

Yet, while the Arabs suffer America's policies, they are also listening to its music, following its fashion, watching its TV shows, lapping up its gadgetry and inventions, and asking themselves how they can emulate all manner of American success. The United States has made considerable efforts to win the favour of the Arab world through projects such as Radio Sawa and Alhurra Television, but there was arguably little need, since the Arab world is for the most part happy to adopt the stuff of American popular culture anyway, such as it can hear on Radio Sawa, and hopes to have as much of its democratic political culture as possible, such as it can follow on Alhurra. But, as this book, hopes to show, there is little correlation, if any, between Arab attitudes towards American culture and American policies. "People appreciate American culture, entertainment and to some extent their values, concerning democracy," says media analyst Jihad Fakhreddine of the Pan-Arab Research Centre in Dubai. "But when it comes to attitudes towards the region it's a different story altogether. This is what the United States is not able to understand."[3]

The following pages aim to set out what the Arabs think and why. In doing so, I have used much material from the invigorating and informative new public sphere that has emerged in the Arab world over the last decade: that of the satellite television channels, where major political, religious and cultural issues are argued day-in day-out by writers, politicians and ordinary people from all over the Arab world. I have also used material from interviews I have conducted in my work as a journalist and news events and incidents I have witnessed, as well as writings by political analysts and novelists. Arabs consider that they have had huge difficulty in getting their viewpoint across in Western countries and in particular in the United States, where the media appears to be resistant to the views of Arabs themselves unless they are emigres such as Lebanese academic Fouad Ajami or Iraqi writer Kanan Makiya, who see very little positive in the Arab world and advocate nothing less than American-led radical change. US policy-makers have for some time been unconcerned about their lack of knowledge about what Arabs other than these US-based liberals think, partly because of a certain strand of opinion holding that the authoritarian nature of Arab governments means it does not matter, partly because of a sense that Arab views are often beneath contempt, or partly because America has its own analysts to elucidate what the barbarians have on their minds. After September 11 it was assumed, naively, that enforcing democratic change, after years of propping up dictatorships and cursory attention to the festering Israeli-Palestinian conflict, would do the trick. It will not.

While there have been plenty studies concerning American views of the Arabs – for example, Robert Kaplan's *The Arabists* – few works explain Arab views of the United States.[4] "Arab public opinion is a more complex phenomenon than conventional notions of a cynical elite and a passionate, nationalistic 'Arab street' suggest," political scientist Marc Lynch has written in a useful corrective. "But what matters more than the street, and sometimes even more than the rulers, is the consensus of elite and middle-class public opinion throughout the Arab world … It is here that the battle of ideas about internal reform and relations with the United States is already being fought, and here that it must be won."[5]

A word on style in this book: I have avoided the use of diacritical marks in transliterating Arabic names and kept to standard formats for many names and terms as they often appear in the media. Double consonants indicate that the emphasis in pronunciation is on that syllable, though I have tried to avoid this as much as possible. Finally, I would like to thank to the following people for their help: Simon Mason, Rola Mahmoud, Mahmoud Kassem, Amil Khan, Abdalla Hassan, Bharath Parthasarathy.

Chapter 1
America in the Arab World

Arab-American relations before 9/11

The Arab world has talked almost incessantly about America since September 11. What America thinks of the Arabs, who influences its thinking, how it can be made more disposed to listen to Arab concerns, how it can be shaken off altogether – all these have been obsessive themes of public discourse since the fateful day when nineteen young Arabs took nearly 3,000 people to their death in revenge for what they believed America had done to Muslims and the United States set out to wreak its revenge in return. The Arab world realizes as much as America does that their relationship has reached, if not its historical nadir, then at least a situation of raw, close-up anger. One might say that a bust-up that had been brewing for at least three decades has finally erupted and both parties have been forced to ask with brutal honesty what they want and what they expect to get from the other side. This troubled relationship, so irrevocably changed through the act of bringing down the Twin Towers and attacking Washington, is today characterized by conflicting attitudes towards a number of key issues: the American effort to promote democracy in the region, the war in Iraq, the "war on terror", and the Israeli-Palestinian conflict.

However, even before September 11, relations had deteriorated considerably since the relative innocence they knew in the immediate aftermath of the Second World War. Then, the emerging Arab states and their peoples hoped that the United States – a new superpower on the world stage who promoted grand visions of freedom and justice – would be a force for liberation that would help free them from the shackles of Old World imperial power. It was the key intervention of the United States during the Suez Crisis in 1956 that doomed to failure the invasion plotted by Britain, France and Israel to take back control of the Suez canal and bring down the charismatic pan-Arab leader Gamal Abdel-Nasser (usually known as Nasser). British and French control of the key international waterway through the Suez Canal Company was a relic of the colonial era, but their Suez trade concession was due to run out in 1968. Nasser decided to seize control of the company after the

United States informed him it would not fund his Aswan dam project. Britain and France knew that the nationalization sounded the death knell of their power and influence in the region, and Israel, only eight years old at the time and refusing to take back hundreds of thousands of Palestinian refugees, had its own reasons to want to see Nasser discredited and deposed. Thus the abortive invasion of the canal zone.

When the United States gradually took on the mantle of imperial power, it is important to realize what kind of Arab world it inherited. The basic map of the region had been drawn up by Britain and France. This was literally true of the borders of countries such as Jordan, Syria, Lebanon, Iraq and Palestine (present Israel plus the occupied territories), which had their origins in a secret agreement known as the 1916 Sykes-Picot accord to divvy up the region between British and French "spheres of influence". In 1917, war-pressed Britain sought to curry favour with the growing Zionist movement by promising a "Jewish national home" in Palestine, although Jewish settlers accounted for only 10 percent of the population at the time. In 1947, by which time Jews accounted for up to a third of the population, the United Nations voted to give the Jewish Zionist movement some 55 percent of the land – the objections of 13 non-Western countries were overruled by 33 Western nations (who between them ruled over some 120 future members that would quite possibly have voted against had they been able to). Britain allowed its ally, the Saudi family, to carve out a desert kingdom in the Arabian peninsula including the prestigious cities of the Red Sea coast, Jeddah, Mecca, Medina and Taif. All along the Gulf coast – a cultural backwater – Britain made treaties with a series of Bedouin families in order to secure its imperial trade interests. These countries are with us today in the form of the United Arab Emirates, Qatar, Bahrain and Kuwait, "the recent and monstrous spawn of Western politicking and the Western thirst for oil", as British travel writer Tim Mackintosh-Smith has said.[1] The three great political ideologies of the Arab world in the twentieth century, Islam, Arab nationalism and Communism, all sought to undo the work of the colonials in the independence period after the Second World War. Egypt united for three years with Syria, Syria and Jordan both considered union with Iraq, Iraq tried to seize Kuwait, Syria still smarts over the independence of Lebanon and many Westerners share the Arab intelligentsia's dismay at the survival of Saudi Arabia. These territorial state structures have clearly proved to be remarkably resilient, but transnational sentiments and links remain strong in the

Arab world and resentment lingers over what are perceived to be false borders imposed by outsiders.

By the late 1950s, the United States was already involved in the game of backing some regimes to the detriment of others. The primary motivation was to hold back Soviet influence in the region. It tried to guide and control Arab foreign policies away from the Soviets via the Baghdad Pact of 1955 (involving Britain, Turkey, Iran, Pakistan and Iraq). The CIA went on to prop up the Saudi monarchy, collude with Islamist forces against Egypt's Nasser, land troops in Lebanon to stop the country falling into the hands of Nasser supporters and promote two bloody coups in Iraq, the last of which was to eventually bring Saddam Hussein to power. American interest deepened with the development of Gulf Arab oil fields and the Palestinian and Arab challenge to the state of Israel. The United States became more deeply committed to Israel after the 1967 war – a policy crafted by veteran diplomat Henry Kissinger – but there was among Arabs themselves little popular awareness of the extent of American backing for the Israelis until the Arab media revolution of the 1990s, when satellite channels like al-Jazeera democratized access to information and promoted debate throughout the length and breadth of the Arab world.

The "Six-Day War" of June 1967 was a disaster for the Arabs, the repercussions of which are felt to this day. Not only did Egypt fail to challenge Israeli hegemony in the Levant and its waters – though the folly of the war was such that Egypt had no clear objections when entering into it – but Egypt lost control of the Gaza Strip and the Sinai peninsula, Jordan lost the West Bank and East Jerusalem, while Syria lost the Golan Heights. The Arab-Israeli was transformed into an international question where the major powers viewed Israel as the victim and Israel, with American backing, became the leading power in the Middle East. Washington rarely stood with the Palestinians, the great losers in the conflict. President Jimmy Carter made a valiant attempt to arm-twist the Israelis into giving the Palestinians a fair deal at the Camp David talks with Egypt in 1978, but his efforts, which eventually came to nothing, have gone practically unnoticed in the Arab world, surfacing only in a 1998 study in Arabic by Egyptian political writer Wahid Abdel-Meguid.[2]

In the 1990s, when American involvement in the Israeli-Palestinian conflict became more direct and public, there were periods when the United States was seen in a favourable light by the Arab public at large. This was the era of the high-profile diplomacy of former Secretary of State Madeleine Albright and special envoy to the Middle East Dennis

Ross, when the United States had sponsored the Declaration of Principles signed in Washington in 1993 in conclusion to the so-called "Oslo talks" between Israel and the Palestinian Liberation Organisation (PLO). This opening had only come about after the administration of George Bush took the step of reenergizing peace talks in the wake of the 1990–1991 Gulf war, when the United States led an international alliance to liberate Kuwait from Iraqi occupation. The administration appeared open to the idea that ending Iraq's occupation should be met by ending Israeli occupation of the Palestinians in the occupied territories. These events fell in the period of waning Soviet-Russian influence in the region, leaving the United States as the "sole superpower". Bush was briefly an Arab hero because of his administration's threat in 1992 to suspend some aid to Israel over its settlement building in the occupied territories. President Bill Clinton addressed the Palestinian National Council in Gaza in December 1998, where he even adopted the Palestinian language of "dispossession" by Zionism, and he tried to broker a deal to establish a Palestinian state between July 2000 and January 2001.[3]

Against that, when Palestinian suicide attacks had entered into the equation, Albright said bluntly in 1996 that building homes could not be compared to blowing innocent civilians in any register of crime and insult. Five years later, the administration of George W. Bush laid the blame for the state of violence that had gripped Israeli-Palestinian relations at the door of Palestinian leader Yasser Arafat and subsequently declared that there could be no Palestinian state without an end to the Palestinian armed struggle against Israel. In 2003, the Arab world was the helpless witness to the Israel-encouraged invasion of Iraq, an old and venerable civilization that figures prominently in the collective historical and cultural consciousness of the Arab world. Egyptian political commentator Hamdy Kandil described the invasion as the "biggest disaster for the Arabs since 1948" – the year of the fighting in Palestine that resulted in the exodus of up to one million of its native Arab population and the establishment of the Israeli state (estimates range from around 700,000 to one million).

Enter 9/11

After September 11, Arab societies and Arab mentalities suddenly mattered to the United States. Commentators such as Fouad Zakaria of *Newsweek* and Thomas Friedman of the *New York Times* talked of "virulent currents" that had taken hold of "dysfunctional" Arab societies such as Egypt and Saudi Arabia, two countries thought to be major American allies in the region, but which were the "breeding grounds" for the brain and the brawn behind al-Qa'ida.[4] "US policymakers and analysts now believe that the West is not fighting to eradicate terrorism. Terrorism is just a tool. It is fighting to defeat an ideology: religious totalitarianism", Friedman wrote.[5] The analysis was largely correct. The Arab world's festering problems became crucial to American interests because they had produced festering resentments. Since then American columnists have created a new vocabulary for the intellectual dissection of a region whose reconstruction has become the American project of the future. New words began to filter into mediaspeak, such as "jihadi" or "jihadist", a fine-tuning of the previously popular "militant" to describe the Islamist radicals who brandish a virulent anti-Western ideology that supports the use of violence. Bush has offered other fashionable epithets like "militant jihadism" and "Islamo-fascism".[6] With Radio Sawa, the State Department-funded radio station, and its sister Alhurra Television, Washington sought to present a news agenda and ethic that was emptied of the linguistic usage employed by Arab state medias and satellite channels like Hizbollah's al-Manar and Qatar's al-Jazeera and refocussed towards the aims of American policy. The State Department also set up Iraq's post-Saddam Hussein state television channel al-Iraqiya and the daily newspaper *al-Sabah*.

Following the Iraq war, the Bush administration embarked upon a drive to persuade Arab governments to democratize, allow more genuine popular participation in governance, ensure the rule of law and implement market economy reforms. The administration also wanted to encourage rapprochement with Israel. Many, if not all, Arab governments had little objection to this in principle, but public opinion was the complication. Arab commentators often suggest that the United States has little interest in the emergence of systems as democratic as those in Europe or the United States, since that would risk bringing anti-American and anti-Israeli forces to power. "I don't think the United States is serious at all about democracy in the Middle East. That would produce regimes much more able to say 'no' to the United States and challenge the United States, especially with regard to its policy towards Israel", Egyptian political scientist Hassan Nafaa says.[7] Indeed, some American commentators on the Middle East – many of them associated with the neo-conservative group of thinkers who are strongly pro-Israel – consider it imperative for Washington to impose its own solutions on the volatile Arab political culture, which they depict as too anti-Israeli, too shambolic and too important to be left to its own devices.

There is little faith among Arabs that the United States will deliver a fair deal over Palestine, while at the same time there is more awareness now than there has been since 1967 of the nature of American politics, the influence of Israel and the deep sympathy that many Americans feel for the Jewish state, be it as pioneering messianic project or a one-time place of refuge for the oppressed. Speaking at the Arab Strategy Forum in Dubai in December 2004, Ghassan Salameh, a politics professor in Paris and former minister of culture in Lebanon said: "If you have globalization across the Arab world, if you have democratic government, you will find that the normal Arabs are more interested in Palestine than the governments. The idea that it's because of the governments that most Arabs are interested in the Arab-Israeli conflict is not true. It's exactly the opposite. I know it's very fashionable at the moment in Washington to think that it will go away if you have democracy. Most Arabs are genuinely and legitimately concerned about this conflict ... the answer is not to say 'no, let's forget about Palestine' ".[8] The hope of American policymakers has been that the economic and lifestyle gains brought on by good relations with the United States will offset interest in "the resistance thing" and lessen pan-Arab obsession with Palestine by strengthening individual Arab state structures and their separate identities.

Iraq is something of a test case: remove a dictatorial Arab nationalist regime and who or what would step into its shoes? Those who promoted and prosecuted the war imagined a US-allied secular government coming to power, but the reality so far (March 2007) has been the creation of a new Shi'ite power allied to Iran. The Bush administration has been obliged to work with the unintended consequences of its actions, in the hope that pragmatism and the economic benefits of good ties with the United States will neutralize any impulse for anti-Western political radicalism. Yet, democracy properly applied could provide distasteful results for America across the Middle East. Much of the region is ruled by minority sects, such as Syria's Alawites, or minority military castes and associated elites, such as in Egypt, Algeria or Sudan, or tribal monarchies, such as Saudi Arabia where the Al Saud family rules in alliance with a puritanical Sunni Muslim religious sect known as the Wahhabis. Israel and the Palestinian territories, democratically reconstituted, could form one state with the Palestinian population gradually overtaking that of the Jews. Lebanon could be dominated by

Shi'ite Muslims (or at least Muslims), if it did not in fact merge with Syria. The United Arab Emirates would be ruled by Indians.

Arab regimes face US "democracy campaign"

The Iraq war was deeply worrying for all Arab leaders, but despite public warnings of the consequences, ultimately no Arab country stood in America's way to disrupt its Iraq plans. American air operations were conducted from the controversial US airbase in Saudi Arabia, which the royals had allowed Washington to maintain as part of a wider presence in the kingdom after the 1990–1991 Gulf crisis. The American military in Saudi Arabia caused deep resentment in Saudi society and gained the Saudi regime the opprobrium of Islamists and Arab nationalists around the region since Saudi Arabia contains Islam's holiest shrines and, with its oil wealth, has the potential to be a major political force challenging Western policy. Publicly, Riyadh opposed the war, but privately it was glad to see the back of Saddam Hussein. Other Gulf states with smaller populations and less sensitivities to consider were more upfront: Qatar housed the main command centre for the war and Bahrain remained home to the US Fifth Fleet. Kuwait was the launch pad of the land campaign and, as the country that American military action saved from Iraqi aggression in 1991, Kuwait is the most extreme case of an Arab regime that brazenly allies itself with the United States. Kuwait was the only country which appeared to be goading the United States publicly to invade and bring down the hated Saddam Hussein, who had sent their royal family fleeing to London when his troups stormed into the country in 1990. Elsewhere, Jordan appears to have allowed US special forces to operate from its territory; while Egypt allowed American vessels to pass through the Suez Canal on their way to the field of battle.

Arab leaders are resisting the external and internal pressures to democratize not only out of fear for the position of their own immediate family and ruling clique but also because they know that democracy would give political expression to the popular feeling against Israel and thus challenge the fundamental pro-Western orientation of their regimes. The nightmare scenario for these regimes of the masses, inspired by the decapitation of tyranny in Iraq, carrying out velvet revolutions across the length and breadth of the Arab world did not come to pass. American tanks also went no further than Iraq. But Arab leaders have been forced to engage in a dialogue on a democratic change with Washington. Through apparent political ineptitude, Syria lost its grip on Lebanon, which remains essentially no more democratic than it was in 1990 when the Taif Accords ended the civil war. Leading figures in the Syrian regime as well as Syrian-allied Lebanese have been implicated in the assassination of former prime minister Rafik al-Hariri in February 2005, prompting international pressure, led by the United States, to force Syria to withdraw its troops from Lebanon the same year. So far there has been little but window-dressing in Egypt, Saudi Arabia, Tunisia, Algeria and others. The real question is how much Washington wants to push them.

Arab rulers have talked doublespeak, on the one hand saying they will open up, and on the other claiming there are special cultural characteristics and sensitivities that somehow limit the potential for Western-style democratic political systems in Arab culture. Take the example of Sheikh Mohammed bin Rashid al-Maktoum, the crown prince of the freewheeling emirate of Dubai in the United Arab Emirates federation. At a special Arab Strategy Forum held in Dubai in December 2004, to which leading journalists like Fareed Zakaria, Thomas Friedman and Fouad Ajami were invited, he offered impressive soundbites on the need for reform: "I tell my fellow Arab leaders: 'If you do not change, you will be changed. If you do not initiate radical reforms that restore respect for public duty and uphold principles of transparency, justice and accountability, then your people will resent you and history will judge you harshly'".[9] With Iraq in mind, he also warned that change could not be imposed from outside: "We are indeed in need of help but reform cannot be realised by foreign projects and ready-made plans. And they cannot be realised by tanks and cannons and manipulating crises instead of solving them." But, in comments subsequently made in Arabic to the local media, he suggested that Western democracy is not compatible with Arab-Islamic culture. Egypt's Hosni Mubarak made similar comments before and after the Iraq war. "Arab nations are working hard to achieve democracy according to their own standards," he said.[10] Inspired by the fascist movements in Europe, Arab nationalism was led for decades by men who believed that "enlightened despots" were the best way to leapfrog to Western-standard economic progress and maintain political indepedence from predatory Western powers.

Under pressure from the United States and some calls for change from within, Saudi Arabia introduced limited local elections in 2005, though women could not vote or run as candidates and the king still chose half the council members. This was not even termed democracy – an alien un-Islamic import, in the Saudi view – it was rather "participatory government" (*al-mushaaraka fil-hukm*). As Saudi commentator Mai Yamani says: "Democracy is supposedly on the march in the Middle East. But Arab dictators are afraid of true democracy, with its civil liberties and competitive elections, so they conjure up potions that protect the status quo by selecting bits of Western political models and adding some religious interpretation to ensure a patina of Islamic legitimacy."[11] In Egypt, Mubarak promised democratic reforms, which began with his surprise move to amend the constitution to allow more than one candidate to run in the presidential elections. The rules meant he was still assured of victory in September 2005, but more importantly the reform did nothing to offset the rise of his son Gamal Mubarak, and in fact Gamal's position has been strengthened. As chairman of the ruling National Democratic party (NDP), Mubarak was able to appoint Gamal to a key role in the NDP in 2002 from where he acquired huge influence in government with the backing of the state media. (In 2006, Mubarak promoted him to the post of NDP assistant secretary-general.) The opposition fears that one way or another he will succeed his father, who has never appointed a vice-president. Numerous reports have suggested that, though they are not sure what to make of the rise of Gamal, the US administration is prepared to live with it should he eventually take over as president or prime minister.

Even bastions of Western rejectionism such as Saddam Hussein's regime in Iraq knew periods of harmony with the United States. The Bush administration was virtually silent at the time about the chemical weapons attack on the Kurdish village of Halabja in 1988 that left some 5,000 people dead. Arab commentators do not doubt that the Iraqi regime would have been prepared for a rapprochement at various stages since the Gulf war of 1990–1991 – Palestinian writer Said Aburish records such observations in his biography of Saddam Hussein.[12] Libya achieved this all-important dialogue with America when its leader Muammar Gaddafi agreed to renounce his nuclear and chemical weapons ambitions in the wake of America's invasion of Iraq in 2003.

Egypt was the pioneer in the field, winning American friendship and economic support through its peace with Israel in 1979. Maintaining good relations with Washington was important for the Egyptian government long before September 11. Politicians who have challenged this status quo have paid the price. Veteran Egyptian politician Amr Moussa was removed from his post as foreign minister not long after he stated bluntly at a press conference with then Secretary of State Colin Powell in early 2001 that he did not agree with the Bush administration's view of the Israeli-Palestinian conflict and its direction of blame towards the Palestinians. Moussa's frank approach towards the United States and Israel is one reason why he is so popular to this day, despite mixed results in his subsequent job as secretary-general of the decrepit Arab League. A website of Egyptians opposed to the presidency of Hosni Mubarak that sprang up in 2004 advocated Moussa as the people's choice in a free vote for the country's leader. The new rules approved in 2005 notably prevented the possibility of independent candidates running for president. "Why Amr?" the site, one of dozens opposed to the regime, asked rhetorically. "Because of his honorable stance on Arab and international issues, making him one of the few who have stood out in the way they have dealt with complex politics ... He is the best choice to face the government which will likely impose more restrictions on freedom and keep things as they are, and in the face of other candidates who the American government seems to support in order to maintain its interests in the region, even if that's at the expense of Egypt and its people, as always happens."[13]

The Israeli-Palestinian conflict

The Arab intelligentsia consider that it is not "regime change" that will bring democracy to the Arab world, but a just solution to the Israeli-Palestinian conflict. According to the predominant Arab thinking, Arab publics, ruling elites and intellectuals have accepted that their democratic rights are on hold pending a solution to the dispute. Once there is no conflict, it will be time to end authoritarian military rule, which has had as one of its main aims guarding against the transnational movements with pro-Palestinian sentiments that threaten the stability and order of the existing map of nation-states in the Arab world. The Iraq war marked a major upheaval for the Arab world because this assumption was turned on its head. The new message from Washington was that the Arab world, including the Palestinians, needed to democratize itself in order to deserve Palestinian statehood. The gulf between the Arab and American vision is huge. A US Senator could tell Arabs at a seminar of the 2005 World Economic Forum in Jordan: "It's a mystery to me why Arab countries can't work on their own countries before Palestine is fixed ... Obviously one of the greatest commitments that we have is to the Jewish people and the state of Israel, to try and manage the difficult process of the peace there and securing that nation, and doing so in a way that, if possible, is just to the Palestinians."[14] But Saudi diplomat Prince Turki al-Faisal sums up the Arab attitude thus: "In the West maybe freedom for the Palestinians comes second, third or fourth, but for us it is central. But this wound which is over more than 60 years old or more doesn't only affect us psychologically it also affects the way we behave [as political systems]." [15]

American attitudes towards the Arabs' focus on Palestine range from a certain sympathy, to surprise at this obsessive dwelling upon the past ("get over it"), to virulent assertions that nothing and nobody must be allowed to threaten the integrity of the state of Israel. After the September 11 attacks, *Newsweek* columnist Fareed Zakaria wrote in a discussion of Arab attitudes towards Israel: "It is obviously one of the central and most charged problems in the region. But it is a problem to which we cannot offer the Arab world support for its solution – the extinction of the state. We cannot in any way weaken our commitment to the existence and health of Israel." The article was titled "The Politics of Rage: Why Do They Hate Us?", but Arabs turn the argument around and ask why is it that the West hates them? "It has been 56 years since Israel was created. It has been a century or so since plans to create Israel were initiated. And yet, Israel's creation has triggered a conflict that is still causing immense havoc and likely to continue to do so," Egyptian political analyst Hassan Nafaa writes.[16] "The main goal of this project has been, and still is, the creation of a state in Palestine that any Jew in the world can 'return' to, inhabit, and enjoy its citizenship. This project is not yet complete, although it started over half a century ago. And those in charge of this project have not, and will not, give it up. They have used and will continue to use all available means, legitimate and illegitimate, to push this scheme through to the final end. They will use wholesale or piecemeal tactics, according to domestic, regional, and international circumstances."[17]

Zionism for the Arab world is a colonial movement, offering another fundamental clash with prevailing American attitudes. In 2004, the United States passed the American Anti-Semitism Law whose definition of anti-Semitism included "inciting anti-Israeli sentiment and harming Zionism". Since the late nineteenth century, Jewish settlers began moving in sizeable numbers to what the godfather of the movement Theodor Herzl called erroneously "a land without a people". It scored a major victory when Britain made support for the creation of a Jewish homeland in Palestine official policy without recourse to the views of the indigenous

Arabic-speaking population of Muslims, Christians, Druze and Jews. British Foreign Secretary Lord Balfour, after whom the Balfour Declaration was named, wrote in 1919 that: "For in Palestine we do not propose even to go through the form of consulting the wishes of the present inhabitants of the country ... The four great powers are committed to Zionism, and Zionism, be it right or wrong, good or bad, is rooted in age-long traditions, in present needs, in future hopes, of far profounder import than the desires and prejudices of 700,000 Arabs who now inhabit that ancient land."[18] For some decades before 1948, the numbers of European colonizers remained small in comparison to the indigenous Arab population, but their economic power was considerable. With a direct line to European finance and technology, they developed major towns like Tel Aviv. A failed uprising of the native Palestinians in 1936 led Britain to envisage a partition of the land which would grant the Jewish settlers around half of the territory, including most of the fertile coastal strip, a vision roughly mirrored in the 1947 UN Partition Plan which promised Israel around 55 percent of Palestine's total area. Only some 70,000 Jewish refugees managed to arrive in Palestine between the 1948 war and the end of the Nazis' attempt to annihilate European Jewry during the Second World War, but Israel's population of some 600,000 at its birth doubled within a year as the new state took in Jews from Europe and, more importantly, from surrounding Arab and Muslim countries. In fact, these latter, "Oriental" Jews may have been critical to the survival of the nascent state.

The Arab world, divided through various occupation stratagems such as "mandate" and "protectorate", watched helplessly as these events unfolded. Before the world war, Arab governments, such as they were at the time, were complicitous or silent, while opposition groups among the populace smouldered in anger. Egypt before the 1952 revolution had been reticently Arabist and sympathetic to the Zionists (who had chapters in Egypt in the 1920s and 1930s) for fear that the Palestinian nationalist movement would provoke anti-Jewish feelings in Egypt and ruin its multi-confessional social fabric. The Muslim Brotherhood, the pioneering Islamist group set up in Egypt in 1928, took up the cause in a grand fashion, organizing huge street protests in Cairo in the late 1930s and the Brotherhood managed to send a contingent to fight the Zionists during the 1948 war that led to Israel's creation. From this early stage, political Islam – the political movement calling for the Islamicization of public and private life – made Palestine as central an issue as Arab nationalism did, but it was Arab nationalism that was to have the first crack at doing something about it. From the 1950s to the 1970s, secular Arab nationalism was the most relevant political vocabulary in the Arab world. Things began to change after the disastrous war of 1967. Since then, political Islam has gradually come to take the centre stage – also encouraged by the Iranian revolution of 1979, when Muslim clerics seized power – and observers regard the ideology of a politicized Islam as the strongest political force in the Arab world today (for this reason, the trend is often referred to as "Islamist" and not "Islamic" – many, if not all, of its leaders are not religious scholars or clerics).

Palestinian society was ruined by the uprooting of over 700,000 people from their homes during the fighting that ensued when Britain evacuated the territory and by Israel's subsequent refusal to allow them back. For Palestinians it is their *nakba*, or catastrophe, commemorated every year on May 15. Though most of the refugees ended up in the surrounding countries of Jordan, Lebanon, Syria and Egypt, many Palestinians were geographically rearranged within historical Palestine itself, pouring into the Gaza Strip or the West Bank, which remained outside Israeli control until 1967. It is for this reason that so many living in these areas today are termed refugees who live in specific UN-funded camps. Critical to Israel's survival was the subsequent arrival of hundreds of thousands of Jews from Middle East countries, most of them Arab, such as Morocco, Yemen and Iraq. Facing persecution from the newly-independent Arab governments and encouraged by a clandestine Zionist campaign of bombs in public areas such as Jewish-owned cinemas in Egypt and Iraq, virtually all of these Jewish communities eventually left for Israel. Palestinians of the diaspora, now numbering around three million, remain in various states of national limbo in countries of the Middle East, while more than three million Palestinians live in cantons of Palestinian civil administration under the wider Israeli occupation of the West Bank, Gaza Strip and East Jerusalem, the 22 percent of mandate Palestine that Israel has ruled since 1967 (Israel removed its settlers from the Gaza Strip in September 2005). At the same time, more than one million Palestinians reside in Israel as citizens of a Hebrew-speaking state designed for Jews. One people, the Palestinians, has effectively been pushed back into the hinterland to make way for a new people, Jewish settlers, controlling the coastal plain where their major cities have been built. This century-old conflict is still in flux and it is not clear where it will end. While the Israelis hold all the cards politically and economically, the Palestinians retain a demographic edge, virtually their only remaining weapon.

There is a strong body of opinion in the United States that plays down the role of Israel in explaining anti-American sentiment in the Arab world. In a seminal article, Bernard Lewis argued over a decade ago that the origins of anti-Americanism do not lie in support for the State of Israel or US support for tyrannical regimes, but in pent-up anger and humiliation over the power of the "Christian West".[19] Regarding Israel, Lewis says the Arabs' one-time Soviet ally was one of the earliest supporters of Israel, while it was the United States that acted to force the tripartite alliance of Britain, France and Israel to withdraw from Egypt during the Suez crisis of 1956. In as much as they are aware of Lewis' arguments, Arabs would argue that in 1948 no one in the region imagined that fifty years later the Palestinian refugees would not have returned to their homeland, or that Jerusalem and the rest of the occupied territories would fall into Israeli hands nineteen years later. Neither was there the vigorous Arab satellite media that has today helped create and crystallize a clear and present Arab public opinion on these issues. In Lewis' post-September 11 bestseller *What Went Wrong?* Israel is listed a mere three times in the index of a book which sets itself the grand aim of answering the question "what went wrong?" in Arab-Islamic societies.[20] The idea of excepting the Zionist project from such a discussion is ludicrous to the Arab intelligentsia.

Arab opinion and the new Arab media

The Arab world has seen a media revolution since the mid-1990s when pan-Arab satellite channels – unshackled by state media constrictions and with the resources to match Western coverage in terms of extent and quality – took politics and media by storm. From a purely Arab perspective, the channels are by no means above reproach – al-Jazeera's Qatari ownership has been a factor in some of its coverage and al-Arabiya's Saudi ownership has been an even bigger factor guiding its output – but they have allowed a sharp and comprehensive Arab response to American policies affecting Muslims and Arabs around the world. They have played a crucial role in an Arab information revolution throughout a region where the internet has been slower to have an impact than in other regions of the world, and they have provided a forum for vibrant debate among commentators from across the political and ideological spectrum. Further, from an outsider's point of view, because of this media revolution, there is no secret any more about "what the Arabs think". Where once intelligence agencies, diplomats, journalists and academics would feverishly compete to deduce the attitudes and thought patterns of the Arab world, now all one has to do is switch on the television because it is there for everyone to see, 24 hours a day, 7 days a week.

The satellite media revolution has played a critical role in reinforcing a shared sense of Arab identity, and in engendering a bigger consensus than ever before across the Arabic-speaking world over foreign policy issues like the Israeli-Palestinian conflict and Iraq. Palestine was always a pivotal issue in modern Arab nationalism, but whereas in the past its influence was exercised on a political level from the top, today it is on the popular level, as governments are pressured to take public stands against Israel because of this powerful new media. When Palestinians began the Intifada in 2000, the uprising captured the popular imagination as the "Arab street" – grass roots public opinion and political activism – interracted in new ways with the Arab living room. Rarely did mass protests change an Arab political elite – most scenes involving the masses were manipulated. But policy makers are now aware that supranational satellite television, which circumvents the control that governments have over their own media, creates public opinion that those in power – American or their Arab allies – might not like.

The Arab media revolution has amplified the pro-American acts of governments and given voice to the majority who often disapprove or at least have reservations. The print and visual media has been dominated by governments since independent Arab states emerged in the era after the Second World War. While there was virtually no space whatsoever for independent television, there was a vigorous opposition press in some countries; but even in Egypt, which has the largest press, its ability to change policy was limited, operating within strict red lines and governed by draconian laws that often saw journalists tried and imprisoned. Beirut served as a centre within the Arab world for opposition publications from other Arab countries. Pan-Arab newspapers based in London have served to provide a fair semblance of comprehensive and unbiased coverage for the region, in the form of *al-Hayat* and *Asharq al-Awsat* newpapers, although both are Saudi-owned and avoid dissident news and views about Saudi Arabia.

The equation was rocked in the mid-1990s, however, with the emergence of the Arab satellite media led by al-Jazeera. The battle between official and unofficial opinion in the realm of print media has since been undercut by satellite channels that individual Arab governments are essentially powerless to stop or gag. That is not for want of trying. Governments have made war on al-Jazeera in various ways, depriving the channel of advertising revenue, closing its offices or launching campaigns to discred its coverage. Yet, in the end, they have been left with no choice but to engage politically on this new playing field. The Saudi-owned MBC channel struck back in 2003 with al-Arabiya, a news competitor to al-Jazeera; Egypt set up its own satellite news channel (the Egyptian Satellite Channel); post-Saddam Iraq was given al-Iraqiya by the United States, which entered the fray alongside the American government's Alhurra Television. Opposition commentators also accuse Egypt, Saudi Arabia and other governments allied to Washington of trying to divert the public's attention from politics with a plethora of entertainment channels.

Al-Jazeera and al-Arabiya, which came on air just in time for the Iraq war of 2003, have become important opinion-makers in the region and one can gauge their impact alone by the attention the Bush administration has given them. Though both were attacked for a while as promoting "anti-American hate", the Bush administration eased up on al-Arabiya, granting it two exclusive interviews with President Bush, while al-Jazeera was consistently rubbished as, variously, the mouthpiece of Osama bin Laden, staging scenes of destruction during the Iraq war to make the United States look bad, and providing a media forum for Iraqi insurgents in order to promote rebellion against the US-backed authorities in Baghdad. Within the political dynamics of the Arab world, al-Arabiya is an "appeaser" of the United States, which promotes dialogue with the Bush administration, while al-Jazeera is a classic "radical hardliner", promoting the politics of resistance. This difference of emphasis reflects each channel's ownership. Saudi Arabia is hated by al-Qa'ida and other Islamists for its close alliance with the United States, thus al-Arabiya promotes moderation; al-Jazeera's Qatari owners have given the channel free rein to tell like it really is the Arab world – bar attacking Qatar – and that means reflecting the extent of opposition to American policies, no matter who leads that opposition.

As much as al-Jazeera has annoyed Washington, it has offended just about every Arab government too. In the immediate years after the channel's inauguration in 1996, Jordan once closed down its offices for four months because a talk show host mentioned collaboration between the late King Hussein and Israel. Opposition politicians said Algeria shut off electricity in parts of the country so people would not see a debate on the country's conflicts. The channel was banned from reporting in Kuwait for a month after an Iraqi viewer insulted the late Emir Sheikh Jaber al-Ahmed al-Sabah during a telephone call from Norway on a live program. These are just some of dozens of examples. In more recent years, al-Jazeera was banned from working in Iraq in August 2004 for its coverage of the insurgency against the American-backed authorities, and Saudi Arabia continues to operate an informal ban on advertising on the channel because it airs criticism of the kingdom and gives radical Islamists like bin Laden the time of day.

Despite this, both channels are staffed by teams as Arab nationalist in political orientation as the other – reflecting the kind of knee-jerk, natural Arab nationalism one would find among the educated in any Arab country. Rather than create anti-American sentiment in the region, as Washington claims, it is perhaps more accurate to say these channels reflect the bad feeling that is already there. "In modern Arab history, including during the revolutionary period of the 1960s and 1970s, there has been nothing to equal the power of the Arab satellite channels to change the nature of popular consciousness and perhaps in the political attitudes of popular forces in the Arab world," says US-based Palestinian academic Hisham Sharabi.[21] The satellite media with their unifying power across the Arab region offer an Arab view for the Arabs, contrary to past reliance on the BBC World Service radio or CNN television. They have been critical in formulating the debate on the American presence in Iraq by providing the forum where all Arabs can come together to argue about it, and they bear witness to the fundamental reality that the Arab world regards solving the Arab-Israeli conflict as a prerequisite for moving from authoritarian military states to democratic systems.

The leading Arab political trends

Most of the constituencies taking part in the public debate about the United States have far more critical views than do the governments, who in fact fear the wrath of America. Politicians and intellectuals today tend to fall into three categories according to the ideologies within which they primarily operate: Islamists, Arab nationalists and liberal democrats. These are not mutually exclusive categories. Islamists usually argue today that they are democrats, and many of the Arab nationalists are as secular in outlook as liberals. The liberal democrats are sceptical about how far the nationalist and Islamists are commited to democracy and human rights, and the Islamists suspect that both the nationalists and liberal democrats are prepared to compromise on the central role of traditional Islamic values when it comes to governance. Communism was a powerful force in the Arab world in the 1950s and 1960s – fear of their strength led Syria's Baath Party into union with Egypt in 1958 to form the United Arab Republic that broke up acrimoniously three years later – but the rise of political Islam and the fall of the Soviet Union has reduced the left in general to a shadow of its former self. Although there are still many political parties nominally appealing to socialism, most leftists are counted as either secular nationalists (with their preference for state-control in the economy) or liberal democrats today. Business entrepreneurs are also a powerful force in politics, but they are usually associated with the pro-American regimes, forming a class of what is often termed "crony capitalists".

The Islamists

Political Islam is a huge movement with roots in Arab societies that go back to two key historical developments: the establishment of the Muslim Brotherhood in Egypt in 1928 and the radical movement of mainstream Sunni Islam known as Wahhabism, which the Saudi family used as the ideological gel for the desert kingdom they pieced together in the early twentieth century in the Arabian peninsula. Wahhabism and the Brotherhood have coalesced since the 1970s when thousands of Brotherhood cadres found work in Saudi Arabia during that country's first major oil-boom – at the time Islamists considered this black gold to be a blessing from God in Islam's holy land – and with the brains of the Brotherhood's thinkers and the brawn of Saudi capital, these two trends have made Islamic fundamentalism the powerful force that it has been in Arab politics and society over the last three decades. Together these Sunni Islamist movements seek a return to the ways of the early Muslims during the period of the Prophet and the first four caliphs, or leaders of the Islamic *umma* ("community", "nation"). Thus, their own preferred term for what they represent is *al-Salafiyya*, or Salafism – following the ways of the ancestors.

The Sunni Islamic groups who promote violent struggle against Western influence and the Western-oriented governments are offshoots of this mainstream current of Salafi thought in Egypt and Saudi Arabia. This violent trend has its origins in Egypt with the radical theorizing of Brotherhood ideologue Sayed Qutb. It was Qutb who first advanced the argument that the post-colonial Arab regimes – virtually all of which were secular Arab nationalist in orientation – were godless, despotic monstrosities created by a cruel convergence of circumstances, but, crucially, that Arab societies ruled by these regimes were just as much *kafir*, or infidel. Qutb reached these conclusions as the victim, like thousands of other Egyptian political activists, of Nasser's brutal regime, which was merciless in its treatment of Islamists and communists. Modern technology and modern methods of political organization in the twentieth century allowed a brutality of scale that appalled Qutb, as did the insistence of these Arab nationalist military regimes on aping the secularism of the West. "The world was not cleansed of the Byzantines and the Persians to pave the way for the authority of the Arabs – it was for the sake of the authority of God ... Infidel societies include those which claim to be Muslim but give authority to other than God," he wrote.[22] Since Qutb was put to death by Nasser's regime in 1966, this use of *takfir*, or deeming nominal Muslims as apostates from Islam, has developed a whole complex ideology of its own at the hands of myriad radical groups, including today's al-Qa'ida.

It is these groups that commentators and politicians such as George W. Bush are now terming "jihadists" and "Islamo-fascists". Their followers justify killing Muslims in attacks on Western targets (such as the foreign residential compounds bombed in Riyadh in 2003) and justify killing Shi'ite Muslims in Iraq, arguing that their acquiescence and complicity in the American invasion project confirms the heresy of their Shi'ite beliefs – an idea developed specifically by Wahhabism and employed with brutal force in Iraq since the invasion of 2003. In the first instance, their argument is that God must have chosen the innocent victims as unwitting martyrs to the cause who will have their place in heaven (an argument occasionally aired publicly in the pan-Arab television discussions by figures such as Egyptian Islamist Hani al-Sibai). Regarding the second case, the original al-Qa'ida leader in Iraq Abu Musab al-Zarqawi (killed by US forces in 2006) often warned ordinary Iraqis to keep their distance from foreign forces or official offices such as police stations, ministries and army recruit centres. The group announced open warfare against Shi'ites simply for being Shi'ites in September 2005, killing hundreds of ordinary Iraqis in suicide attacks, though it made special allowance for Shi'ite militias that had taken a stance against the American occupation, such as Moqtada al-Sadr's Mahdi Army.[23] Zarqawi's group was initially called the Organization for Monotheism and Jihad, but the Jordanian later allied himself with the al-Qa'ida leaders bin Laden and Zawahri and switched the name to "the al-Qa'ida Organisation for Jihad in the Land of the Two Rivers [Iraq]". The reference to monotheism reflects the Wahhabi penchant for regarding the Shi'a as not true monotheists because they worship the Prophet Mohammad's cousin Ali and his descendants as semi-divine figures. Islam in general regards Jews and Christians as wayward monotheists who have strayed from the original faith set out by Abraham and corrected by Islam.

Shi'ite Islamist groups such as Lebanon's Hizbollah and both the Supreme Council for the Islamic Revolution (SCIRI) and Da'wa Party in Iraq – all militias-cum-political parties – are just as opposed to Western influence as the Sunni Islamists. How long SCIRI and Da'wa remain American allies in Iraq is questionable. The Sadr group has already blazed a stridently anti-American trail. Among the Palestinians there is Hamas, which though Sunni Muslim, is quite different from al-Qa'ida in that it is the product of a specific nationalist context as a form of resistance to an alien invading power. Iran's Shi'ite theocracy has long been recognized by political scientists as a response to Western interference in the country's political life, a kind of counterpoint to the CIA-organized coup to bring down the nationalist government of Mohamed Mossadegh in 1953 (though there is considerable debate over whether Mossadegh's domestic opponents would have brought him down anyhow).

While on one level the rise of political Islam in the Arab world was a response to the dominance of Western politics, commerce, consumerism and thought, America had only a peripheral role in its evolution into a radical force among Sunni Muslims in its early stages. Commentators such as Egyptian writer Salah Issa, who has researched the growth of Islamist movements in the Nasserist period, say it was the systematic brutality of Nasser's secular-national regime in its treatment of the Islamists that nudged Qutb and his acolytes into radicalizing their ideology. Interestingly, the United States did have one backstage role: as the foil for Qutb's opinions. Qutb's intellectual journey into radical politics began with a sojourn in the United States that apparently very much shocked him, and this partly accounts for his diatribes against what he saw as the crass consumerism, selfishness and the worthlessness of modern civilization in general. "The world now is in a 'state of ignorance' which is in no way eased by the formidable materialistic comforts of today ... Arab society is one of the worst in terms of the distribution of wealth and justice. A small minority has wealth and business and increases its wealth through usury, while the majority has only hardship and hunger," Qutb wrote. "Yet we have something to give to mankind [Islam] which it does not have, something that isn't one of the 'products' of Western civilization or East or West European genius."[24]

During the period when Qutb wrote this work, the United States was promoting pan-Islamism against communism and Arab nationalism, and maintained close relations with both Saudi Arabia and the Brotherhood.[25] This Islamic fringe received more solid support from the United States towards the end of the Soviet era, when it funded the Arab mujahideen army that gathered in Afghanistan to fight the Soviet occupation in the 1980s. Government officials in Egypt and Saudi Arabia have often talked bitterly of the CIA support for these revolutionary Islamic idealists who came back to launch a major insurgency in Egypt and Algeria in the 1990s before they struck at the United States in September 2001. They turned their attention more sporadically to Saudi Arabia in the 1990s, and, after the Iraq war of 2003, an indigenous home-based group claiming allegiance to al-Qa'ida launched an open battle against the Saudi regime. Their rallying cry was a commonly-cited saying of the Prophet, "get the polytheists (*mushrikeen*) out of the Arabian peninsula" – their slogan for war on the Americans and other Westerners whose military and civilian presence in the kingdom they perceived as supporting a corrupt monarchy which relied on the United States to survive.[26]

Debate swirls around the question of the extent to which these people despise the West because of Islamist ideology or have found the ideology that best fits their desire to resist foreign intervention in the Arab world. Western governments and a small group of Arab intellectuals argue the former, but most writers in the Arab world tend to favour the latter view, even if they find Islamist uber-violence distasteful or counter-productive. Lebanese novelist and historian Amin Maalouf writes: "In observing militant Islamist movements today, I can easily see the influence of the Third World-ism of the 1960s, as much in the discourse as in the methods. At the same time, no matter how hard I look into Islamic history, I can find no precedent for them. These movements are not the pure product of Muslim history, they are the result of our era, its tension, its distortions, its practices, its despairs."[27] Similarly, Abdel-Rahman al-Rashed, the manager of Saudi-owned al-Arabiya television, says: "Unless I hear someone directly alluding to Marx or quoting [medieval scholar] Ibn Taymiyya, you can't tell sometimes are they radical Islamist or radical Marxist and/or radical Nationalist."[28] Yet, against that, we have opinions expressed in English-language media, such as this editorial comment in Beirut's *Daily Star*: "There was a time not long ago when Al-Qaeda might have been analyzed or interpreted as a manifestation of Arab discontent, a violent quest for political reform or an aggressive statement against American or Zionist domination ... In declaring war against Iraqi Shi'ites, Al-Qaeda has proven itself to be nothing more than a ruthless, sectarian gang."[29]

Interestingly, Zarqawi himself jumped into this debate in one of his taped sermons released on the Internet where he criticized the lumping together of Sunni Muslims, Shi'ites and secular nationalists as different facets of the one, insoluble resistance to the West. "Many Muslims have been affected by this campaign and they began shying away from using this term [jihad] for fear of being accused of terrorism. They instead replaced it with the term 'resistance' ... This has tarnished jihad and its supporters and led to the inclusion of factions that have nothing to do with jihad, such as the rejectionist [Shi'ite] Hizbollah, Fatah movement and the Popular Front for the Liberation of Palestine," he said, referring to the Lebanese and Palestinian guerrilla groups. "All this has been done under the pretext that whoever defends his country against the enemy and fights an occupier is involved in resistance. But jihad is much deeper than that."[30] Yet Zarqawi often betrayed his essentially nationalist-inspired interests. In one sermon which was posted on Islamist websites accompanied by images of Israeli soldiers abusing Palestinians and Iraqis suffering under American military operations in Iraq, he waxes lyrical: "I am still haunted by the pain of the *umma* [Islamic nation], a great *umma* which has been poisoned by treacherous and evil traitors, so that the blanket of humiliation and shame has darkened and the dreams have been put aside, and illness spreads throughout the body which has been nailed to the ground as the beasts gather around and torn its limbs."[31] Because "jihadism" is not framed in the language of Palestinian or Arab nationalism does not mean that its central concerns are not "nationalist" in the sense of opposing foreign control and neo-colonialism. Arabs will automatically understand the reference to Palestine in bin Laden speeches that make no explicit mention of the issue; and the claim, often heard after the 9/11 attacks, that bin Laden had never evidenced any particular concern for the Palestinian issue is entirely erroneous. Palestine is the wound that cuts to the heart of all anti-Western resistance movements in the Arab world over the last century, be they Islamist or secular Arab nationalist.

Resistance in Iraq has become a *cause celebre* throughout the Arab world, and many Arab nationalist and Islamists who would be regarded as moderates barely conceal their readiness to accept the methods of the Islamists who have decapitated foreigners, as well as Iraqis who cooperate with the Americans, and randomly murder the Shi'a. Al-Jazeera often runs talk shows where guests openly defend the Zarqawi tactics. Jordanian Islamist Marwan Shehadeh said in one such discussion: "The fundamentalist [*al-salafi al-jihadi*] movement of which al-Qa'ida and al-Qa'ida in Iraq are part is managing to win people over because it represents the living conscience of the Islamic nation and can return Islamic life to the world."[32] Two years after the September 11 attacks, and in the aftermath of the Iraq invasion, there was a marked shift in the manner in which commentators talked about al-Qa'ida. Sympathizers with bin Laden felt sufficiently confident to refer to him reverentially as "Sheikh Osama". The al-Jazeera website Aljazeera.net even ran a vote in August 2004 asking "Do you support al-Qa'ida's war on the Europeans?" (60 percent answered no, 40 percent said yes). Hassan Hanafi, a renowned Egyptian philosophy professor who is regarded as having Islamist leanings, wrote on the anniversary of the attacks: "September 11 was a scream against tyranny and slavery: the World Trade Centre towers, the White House and the Pentagon ... Despite scenes of destroying land, demolishing homes, killing women, children and whole families [in the Palestinian territories], most Arab capitals saw no movement. Someone had to scream in the face of this world which does such injustice."[33] He concluded: "September 11 in my opinion, although it harmed us in that it connected Islam with terrorism and violence, showed that there are people who can deal with America with the same language of force."

Figures from the Muslim Brotherhood, the great standard-bearers of moderate political Islam, stridently defend "resistance", though they are more careful to avoid praising the actions of the al-Qa'ida groups as such. They argue that fighting the US occupation of Iraq and the Israeli occupation in Palestine is legitimate by any means. Their moderate opponents in these satellite TV discussions are invariably on the defensive. In one such debate, Abdel-Moneim Abul-Fotouh, a leading Brotherhood member, closed his argument with a quote from former President Richard Nixon's book *Seize The Moment*, "just so we know who are our real enemy is, whether you're an Islamist, a nationalist or a leftist", Abul-Fotouh said. "The American President Richard Nixon wrote in his book that the only interest America has in the East is oil and Israel, and that 'Muslim fundamentalists' who are moved by extreme hatred for the West are determined to regain their former Islamic civilization by reviving the past. He said that they aim to implement Islamic law and call for Islam as religion and state, and while they look to the past, they do so as guidance for the future, so they are not conservatives, they are revolutionaries'".[34]

Islamists have made clever use of the internet to promote their agenda. There are numerous Islamic Web sites, and one of the most successful is www.IslamOnline.net, an English-language site overseen by Brotherhood-associated cleric Sheikh Yousef al-Qaradawi and other scholars. Representing the Islamic mainstream, it was set up in Qatar and Cairo in 1999 and now has around 2.8 million hits a day for news and views on Islam and politics. Islamist radical groups disseminate their opinions on dozens of websites, partly in the hope that the Internet will do for bin Laden what cassette tapes did for Ayatollah Khomeini in Iran. Supporters of the insurgents in Iraq, Saudi Arabia, Afghanistan and Chechnya filled the chatrooms of dozens of popular Islamic websites where reports and statements could be disseminated. But the insurgent groups became more sophisticated, setting up their own sites or using special sites with limited membership and access where they would post videotapes of the murder of foreign hostages, including grisly beheadings, and audiotaped sermons by their leaders. Web magazines appeared such as the Saudi *Sawt al-Jihad* (*Voice of the Holy War*) and *al-Bitar* and, in September 2005, a group of al-Qa'ida supporters began a weekly internet TV broadcast called *Sawt al-Khilafa* (*Voice of the Caliphate*). Chatroom strings even carried links to web pages with training manuals on bomb-making, weapons handling and how to stage an assassination. These groups have had to engage in a game of hide-and-seek with Internet providers, but there is too much space in the vastness of the World Wide Web to keep them down. Ever resourceful, they have been known to choose an innocuous chatroom of, say, an Arabic pop music site to announce a kidnapping or murder of a hostage, then simply wait for a sympathizer to find the statement and post it in the regular Islamist chatrooms for the world to see.

Political Islam in general was quick to make use of modern technology. When the Egyptian government first began a crackdown against them in 1995, the interior ministry would relay breathless reports to the state press listing the computer equipment and other demonish modern devices, generally not to be found in tired and dusty government offices, that were uncovered among the allegedly radical pamphlets and books seized at the homes of Muslim Brothers – displaying a certain paranoia over what one paper jokingly referred to as the "Cyber Brother".[35] Compared to the government, Islamists seem more attuned to the modern world, a continuing element of their appeal to young people today.

The Nationalists

Arab nationalism developed as an ideology in the early twentieth century. Definitions of who constituted the Arabs were debated and disputed until by the end of the Second World War the term *al-qawmiyya al-arabiyya* (Arab nationalism) had been coined in reference to all those countries that spoke the Arabic language, though some of its earliest proponents had excluded Egypt, Sudan and North Africa. During this period, the colonial powers introduced limited democratic experiments to their Middle East dominions. But democracy did not serve the cause of independence, creating instead an elite that benefited from its close ties with the colonial powers. As the British and French resisted completely letting go, military cadres took centre stage and set about removing the foreigners and the political systems they had help build. These military revolutionaries blamed their democratic semi-independent governments for the failure of Arab armies to prevent the birth of Israel in the 1947–1949 fighting in Palestine. Egypt took centre stage with a military coup in 1952 and Egypt's revolutionary system – Arabist, socialist and totalitarian – inspired similar changes in Algeria, Libya, Sudan, Syria, Iraq and Yemen. The political systems in place in most Arab countries today date back to this period and retain its mindset.

Political Islam has come to eclipse secular Arab nationalism as the ideology of resistance. The reference point for this major ideological shift in the Arab world is the crushing Arab defeat to Israel in 1967, an event that deeply effected the collective Arab psychology for a whole generation. Completely unprepared for war and largely aware that victory was unlikely, yet trapped by the false hope spun by their own nationalist rhetoric, the Arab leaders hurled themselves into what writer Said Aburish has called "an act of mass suicide" by engaging Israel in a war that was neither coordinated, nor planned nor had united goals behind it on the

Arab side. Guided by Nasser as he flew off on the "magic carpet of pan-Arabism", as one observer has said, Arab nationalism had charmed and hypnotized the peoples of the region.[36] No one imagined that the Arabs could not defeat this little country, Israel. The shock of defeat has had inordinate consequences on political and cultural life, which are still with the Arab world to this day. Termed euphemistically, the *naksa*, or "setback", this comprehensive defeat for the Palestinians, Egypt, Jordan and Syria has spurred political Islam to the heights of popularity it enjoys today. It presented Israel with the poison chalice of territories that it coveted as part of its purported "biblical birthright" but which were peopled by a large non-Jewish population. In the Arab view, undoing the damage remains the elusive key to resolving the Arab-Israeli conflict.

Its reverberations have been felt in other fields of life. Tunisian film director Nouri Bouzid discerns enough in Arab cinematic output since that date to dub it "post-defeat cinema". Many intellectuals who had given their talents to the regimes discredited by 1967 never recovered from the blow. Willingly drafted into the service of Nasser's Egypt, they range from poet and cartoonist Salah Jahine to heart-throb singer Abdel-Halim Hafez, who had sung the praises of Egypt's Aswan High Dam, Nasser's socialism, and the dream of Arab unity in intoxicating songs that have remained part of the modern Arab cultural canon. Many associates say Jahine, who committed suicide in 1987, never fully recovered from the shock, but it was the shock of an entire generation. Some briefly thought they had found their new Nasser: When Iraq emerged as a powerful force in the 1970s under Saddam Hussein's leadership, many Arab professionals put themselves at the service of his regime, including Egyptian nuclear scientists and Palestinian poets and writers. Versus Egyptian director Yousef Chahine's epic *Saladin* (1963), a veiled paean to Nasser as the new Saladin who would repel the Israeli Crusaders, there was Egyptian director Saleh Tawfik's *The Long Days* (1980), a dramatization of Saddam's revolutionary younger days.

In a 2003 study called *The Culture of Defeat,* German historian Wolfgang Schivelbusch examined how Japan and Germany dealt with military-political collapses of such moral and material magnitude after the two world wars that they were forced to engage in a process of radical reinvention that enabled them to rise anew.[37] In the Arab world, where most of the territories seized are still occupied, the only successes to speak of have been those of small states that have managed to keep their distance from the Arab-Israeli conflict and the revolutionary dynamics of

Arab nationalism, such as Tunisia, Oman or the United Arab Emirates. To compensate for the trauma of 1967, Egypt has created a glory cult around the 1973 war, when Egypt and Syria launched an offensive against Israel to regain the territories they lost six years before. Neither Egypt nor Syria gained anything directly through the war. Egypt's President Anwar Sadat chose to use the stunning success Egyptian forces achieved in its early days to launch a long diplomatic process that aimed to win massive American financial support in return for a negotiated peace with Israel. The state media has exploited President Hosni Mubarak's role as air force commander-in-chief in that war as his prime claim to merit leading the nation since 1981. The war even played a role in his campaign for a fifth term in office in 2005, over three decades after the war in question. Nasserists nurtured their own "stab-in-the-back" legend – like Germany's after the First World War – to exonerate their hero Nasser. The treacherous womanizing of air force chief Abdel-Hakim Amer is known throughout the Arab world, the stuff of TV dramas, films and novels. The conventional view is that his dereliction of duty meant Egypt's military was in no state of readiness for the war. Amer committed suicide in strange circumstances some months after the June 1967 defeat and debate continues to rage over whether it was Amer or Nasser who was to blame for the dismal performance of Egypt's military.

Both Iraqis, after the American invasion, and Palestinians under Israeli occupation have employed the psychological device of heroic but ultimately futile military postures to ease the acceptance of gains that have come at a cruel price. Foreigners achieved what Iraqis could not do for themselves during some three decades of cruel dictatorship by removing the regime of Saddam Hussein through a lightning invasion of the country. Shi'ites with a strong distaste for America's gift to Iraq can console themselves with the repeated revolts of the Moqtada al-Sadr movement against the American forces. Palestinians negotiating their future with Israel are arguably no better off for the uprising they began in 2000, but at least when the talking is done they can say they fought for what they have. These tendencies are occasionally noted in the Arab media.

The forces of resistance, be they Islamist or nationalist, are attempting to get over the crushing culture of defeat that has gripped the Arab world since 1967. Both Islamists and Arab nationalists argue vociferously that Arab countries have the power to stand up to the American-Israeli reality, if only they stop believing the narrative of weakness and powerlessness that the West has entangled them in. Mohammed Hassanein Heikal, an

Egyptian writer who was once Nasser's right-hand man and now is one of the most respected intellectuals in the Arab world, has repeatedly called for the Arabs to conduct a critical reappraisal of their links with the United States so that the main Arab powers, in his view Egypt and Saudi Arabia, join together to mobilize Arab countries against Washington's pro-Israeli policies. The American-Israeli plan, as he has argued in prominent appearances on al-Jazeera and in his recent books, is to "bury" the Palestinian issue for Arab countries, so that all the Palestinians get in the end is a weak state on bits of the West Bank and Gaza that is incapable of supporting a growing population, thus leaving Israel the main political and economic power-broker in a new Middle East and solving Israel's demographic problem. This in large part is in fact the stated aim of the neo-conservatives in the United States, who seek the neutralization of Syria and Iraq as radical forces giving sustenance to the Palestinian will to resist and for whom the paramount importance of the US alliance with Israel is a given.[38]

The Liberal Democrats and Minorities

The liberal democratic trend largely developed in Egypt out of the human rights movement of the 1990s, which attracted many political activists who were disillusioned by the opposition parties. But, as with the rights movement, they have been compromised by the support they garner from Washington and US organisations and individuals, support which makes it easy for governments and state-controlled medias to discredit them in the eyes of the public. The democrats traditionally looked to the West and the United States for support and inspiration and the Iraq war has created a new battleground where, in Egypt for example, they hope to reap benefits from the new American interest in the region and desire to impose democracy; yet they risk the vitriol of Islamists and nationalists with whom they find themselves in uneasy alliance against the regime. At least some of the new democrats secretly supported the American invasion of Iraq and their greatest fear was that Washington was not serious about democracy in the region, believing that countries like Egypt and Saudi Arabia were safer bets under their current leaderships. The democrats, with a strong presence in satellite television debates, argue that lack of democracy has critically affected the Arab world's ability to challenge Israel, politically and economically, and help the Palestinians. Citing damning evidence such as the United Nations Arab Human Development Reports, they say that the Arab world, where under-14s form some 38 percent of a population of nearly 300 million people, is in a crisis of such proportions that democracy at the level of individual Arab states must be made the priority. Their Islamist and nationalist detractors accuse them of promoting the "culture of defeat" (*thaqafat al-istislam*), to quote the title of *al-Hayat* op-ed writer Bilal al-Hassan's latest book – propagating the idea of the futility of opposing American hegemony.[39]

Some have paid dearly for their association with the United States. Egyptian academic Saadeddin Ibrahim, an Arab darling of the American media, experienced first-hand the attitudes towards those who have foreign backing to promote democracy. In 2000, he was arrested on suspicion of sullying Egypt's reputation with his critiques of Egypt's political system and intention to monitor parliamentary elections, charges which led to a trial in which he was eventually acquitted. But he was viciously attacked in the press, which focused on his dual nationality. One writer said in an independent newspaper: "Saad the American, aka Saadeddin Ibrahim, was caught red-handed trading in the honor of the nation ... when he said he had decided – no kidding, he 'decided'! – to form a committee to monitor the next parliamentary elections ... I hope Saad the American understands well that he no longer has any future on the land of this nation, or in any home or grave in the soil of Egypt. Great Egypt ejects all those who violate its honor and trades in its pride and is biased towards its enemies. The reason for that is that Saad the American, even if he was born in Egypt, receives his instructions from the American embassy and intelligence agencies."[40]

Many of the democracy activists see Islamist violence as a greater danger to the Arabs than American foreign policy or Israel. Mamoun Fandy, an Egyptian academic based in the United States with a regular column in *Asharq al-Awsat* daily, has been a prominent voice in this regard. Fearing the latent sympathy for al-Qa'ida around the region and in its media, he says clerics have to take a stronger position: "The time has come to issue a fatwa to excommunicate bin Laden and his followers from the world of Islam. In fact, as terrorism rages in cities from New York to Casablanca, Cairo to London we need a stream of solid counter fatwas from the Muslim community. Thus far we have heard Muslim fatwas telling us that Islam does not condone violence against the innocent or Islam condemns these actions. This is not enough. We need to exclude those among us who make it necessary to defend Islam in such a way. As a Muslim, I think that we need to be absolutely clear. We need to respond to the fatwas that are issued in our names."[41]

The Egyptian commentator Abdel-Moneim al-Said, another prominent proponent of democratic reform, says that uniquely among colonized peoples Arabs and Muslims have reacted with senseless violence that knows no bounds and recognizes no statute of limitations on perceived wrongs done. "India offers a prime example of a country with a history steeped in colonialist oppression, economic subjugation, colonialist settlement expansion and geographic partition. Nevertheless, not a single Indian is to be found among the groups that bombed London, New York or Madrid, among the ranks of the 'resistance' in Iraq or Chechnya, or anywhere else in the known arenas of the 'jihad'," he says. Also comparing Japanese and Chinese responses to colonialism, he adds: "In none of these nations do we find that morbid sense of isolation and that destructive desire to be rid of the world, which has long inflicted pain on other human groups, both Muslim and Christian."[42] His detractors would respond that while India has been left alone by the foreigners since 1947, the Arab countries have not.

Apart from rights activists and democratic reformers, there are certain minority groups in the Arab world who have openly strived to persuade Washington to intervene on their behalf. They hope to mirror the success of the Israelis in the United States, where the American-Israeli Public Affairs Committee (AIPAC) is rated as one of the most powerful political lobby groups. (Arabs, who are weaker in number than Jews, are served by the Arab-American Institute, though there are a host of others, such as the American-Arab Anti-Discrimination Committee (ADC).) In Iraq, groups of various persuasions including Kurds, Shi'ites and democracy activists had America's ear throughout the 1990s because of the regime's interest in nuclear weapons and its challenge to American policy in the region, to the extent that the United States eventually invaded the country in 2003. After civil war began in 1982, the Sudan People's Liberation Army (SPLA) found a willing audience in the United States, sympathetic to stories of Muslim persecution of Christians and Arab abuse of black Africans. During her tenure as Secretary of State from 1997 to 2001, Madeleine Albright made no secret of her admiration for SPLA leader John Garang. The southerners gained a powerful new friend in Christian conservatives, also supporters of Israel, who had the ear of the Bush administration when it came to power in 2001. American pressure was instrumental in forging a final peace deal in 2005 that guaranteed the southerners the right to vote on secession. The Khartoum government did itself no favours by adopting radical Islamist ideology and even hosting Osama bin Laden for a period in the early 1990s. Minority groups will often help each other. Ali al-Ahmed, a dissident from Saudi Arabia's maligned minority Shi'ite population, testified before a subcommittee of the US Congress on human rights in the Middle East. Discussing the Darfur conflict in west Sudan, he accused Arab governments of "silence and media blackout". "Darfur has not been the exception, but rather the rule. There are many non-Arab cultures and peoples that are persecuted in the region over their faith or ethnicity," he said.[43]

In Lebanon, American help was courted in order to force Syria to relinquish its grip on the country. France has been the traditional friend of Lebanon's Maronite Christians, for whose sake the former colonial power helped create the Lebanese state in the inter-war period. The struggle for Lebanon's heart and soul has been long and bitter. After a fifteen-year civil war that ended in 1990, Maronite Christians have seen their power and influence wane as their numbers have also lessened in proportion to other denominations, mainly the Shi'ite Muslims who are now thought to be the largest group. Together Sunni and Shi'ite Muslims likely outnumber the Christians in Lebanon today, though a census to establish the matter is politically impossible. The Christians have traditionally looked to the West for support and inspiration, while the Muslims have looked to the Arab world. Both France and the United States were behind UN Security Council Resolution 1559 passed in September 2004, which required Syria to end its occupation of Lebanon. After the assassination of former Prime Minister Rafik Hariri in February 2005, one of a series of attacks on those campaigning to end Syrian control, Damascus was forced to remove all its troops. But Islamist and nationalist forces, led by Hizbollah, are opposed to what they see as an attempt to make of Lebanon some kind of American, pro-Israeli protectorate, citing the doomed peace treaty with Israel that Maronite Christian president Amin Gemayyil signed at the height of the civil war in May 1983. It was abrogated in March 1984 because of opposition from Sunnis, Shi'ites, Druze, some Maronites, and Syria.

Egyptian Coptic Christians in the United States have had limited success in winning American help to pressure the Egyptian government over the status of the Coptic minority. Groups such as the American Copic Association have made a point of staging protests against President Hosni Mubarak during his visits to Washington, but despite some grand gestures from US administrations they have obtained few results on the ground. Congress established in 1998 the US Commission on International Religious Freedom, which has conducted fact-finding trips to Egypt to investigate the position of Copts, though the commission was mainly focussed on Sudan, China, Iran, Iraq and Myanmar. Saudi Arabia, oddly, considering the persecution of local Shi'ites and banning of churches despite hundreds of thousands of Christian expatriates, was not in the commission's sights. The commission, born of the International Religious Freedom Act (IRFA), travels the world investigating areas deemed "trouble spots" with regard to religious freedom. But the Egyptian government, aided by Islamist and Arab nationalist opposition voices, has managed to neutralize the commission's impact. When three members visited Egypt in March 2001, even prominent public figures who agreed to meet them, including the Coptic Orthodox leader Pope Shenouda III himself, rebuked them for their efforts and underplayed Coptic problems. Most politicians, clerics and activists refused to meet them and some who did tried to keep it secret. Yet the problems of the Copts remain, including the trouble they have in obtaining permits to build or expand churches, their token representation in government and occasional violent flare-ups with Muslims.

Two major groups in the Arab world stand out for their abject failure to promote their cause in the United States – the Berbers of North Africa and the Assyrian Christians of Iraq. Ravaged by emigration to the West, the Assyrians form barely one percent of the Iraqi population, but they retain their ancient language which is in fact a dialect of the same Aramaic tongue spoken by Jesus Christ. The Berbers, who make up around 50 percent of Morocco and a fifth of Algeria, have also failed to make waves in America. They have traditionally looked to former colonial power France, whose language and culture many happily embraced at the expense of Arabic after independence. Hollywood films have often pushed the popular Zionist line that it was the Jews who built Egypt's Pyramids, but 2001's Oscar-winning film *Gladiator* by contrast did not know its Berbers from its Arabs – it depicted Roman-era North Africans as speakers of Iraqi Arabic. Berbers consider themselves the original inhabitants of North Africa, where the Arabs were not to arrive until the late seventh century AD, though the Phoenicians who earlier colonized Tunisia and sent Hannibal with his elephants to war with Rome were a Semitic people, the ethnic and linguistic brothers of the later Arabs.

Chapter 2
Domestic America

The Arab obsession with American culture

The Arab world is obsessed with America. Even Islamists who have no love for the American way of life want to have a fair amount of the freedoms as well as the technology that have enabled the United States to become the powerful nation that it is. There is no truth to the belief that has been popular in the aftermath of September 11 that the Arab world and Muslims in general "hate" America and all it stands for. It is true that there is a strong body of Islamist and Arab nationalist opinion that is dismayed by a perceived American cultural invasion – the spread of American music and cinema, for example, among young people who show less interest in the Arab cultural canon of poetry, literature, music and film – and among these people one could talk about a certain disdain for much of what America represents. But modern democracy and political pluralism is generally admired in the Arab world and many are prepared to associate it specifically with America, although Europeans have as much of a claim to these ideas as anyone else. Public rhetoric in the Arab world never tires of arguing that the Arabs' problem with America is its foreign policy – the perceived double standard in its treatment of the Israeli-Palestinian conflict, prizing Jewish rights above those of the dispossessed indigenous Arab population, and, since 2003, intervention in Iraq for the sake of oil and Israel, not for democracy.

American-style consumer culture is now all the rage in the Arab world. Arab societies are rapt by what Americans do and agonize over the question of how far their own cultural values allow them to ape them. But the intellectuals are pining over a process they have had little power to stop. American magazine *Readers Digest* twice suspended its Arabic editions because of enmity over the 1948 Arab-Israeli war and the 1967 Arab-Israeli War, when it was viewed by intellectuals as "a pulpit for spreading the American way of life".[1] Yet, when Newsweek introduced an Arabic-language edition in 2000, newspapers could only joke that after "Coca-Cola-ization" and "McDonaldization" (coined in Arabic as *kawkala* and *makdana*), now the Arabs have *nawzaka*, "Newsweekization".[2]

For the most part, the Arab world makes a clear distinction between American culture and American politics. What rankles the Arabs is the American foreign policy, and there is remarkably little rancour towards various elements of American life as they effect or are reflected in the region. The icons of Western culture that have been role models and heroes for youth in the United States and elsewhere in the world have been no less influential here. They include Michael Jackson, Madonna, Demi Moore (in her time), Bryan Adams, Shakira, Sylvester Stallone and Bruce Willis. Youth culture in the Arab world never had a radical moment to match the 1960s in the West – in 1996 in Egypt and in 2003 in Morocco police arrested fans of heavy metal, the genre which wealthy, elite kids tend to go for, on suspicion of "devil-worshipping" – and the population demographic across the Arab world is heavily tilted towards young people. At least 38 percent of the Arab League member states' near 300 million people are minors, according to the UN Arab Human Development Reports. This vast age group's exposure to and large-scale embracing of all things American has been a marked feature of the cultural landscape over the last decade, despite the concurrent nosedive in sentiment towards the United States as it is represented by its politics on the world stage.

American commentators who talk of "virulent currents that are capturing Arab culture" make a serious mistake when they conflate attitudes towards American foreign policy and attitudes towards American life.[3] Radical Islamists despise both, and old-style Arab nationalists have resented the latter because US-allied regimes have been unable to challenge the former, but the depoliticized masses hold American culture in high esteem, as do secular liberals and human rights activists who retain faith in American politics to deliver them from the region's autocrats and dictators, whatever their feelings about US policy on Palestine. In other words, when many, if not all, Arabs listen to Radio Sawa on their car radio, they will enjoy the latest hip-hip hits in American slang but, for all that, come away no less convinced that Washington is biased towards Israel or that suicide bombings could be a legitimate response from the oppressed in the face of overwhelming power, no matter how much they admire or envy that power. Jihad Fakhreddine, media research manager for the Dubai-based Pan Arab Research Center, which monitors the Arabic media, wrote in the Beirut-based *Daily Star*: "… a visit to any affluent Arab home in the Gulf, especially those of Arab expatriates, shows how the global, or more specifically the US culture, is shaping the lifestyles and attitudes of young and teen generation alike. The affluent Gulf nationals are catching up very fast. Similar cultural manifestations could also be seen in the Levant." Yet, despite his own children's Western cultural outlook – the Oprah they watch or the McDonald's they eat – they now harbour an animosity towards the United States because of "uncalculated American policies in the region", Fakhreddine wrote.[4]

American television on Arab TV screens

This ardour for American culture is nowhere more apparent than in the current fad for US programmes on Arab television. American television has stormed the Arab small screen with a vengeance, with free-to-air satellite channels airing little else but US sitcoms, chatshows and even real-time news broadcasts and discussion shows such as ABC's Primetime and World News Tonight, the CBS Evening News and 60 Minutes, Inside Edition and star gossip such as Entertainment Tonight and The Insider. Since 2002, Saudi-owned Middle East Broadcasting has expanded its main Arabic news and entertainment channel, MBC 1, to include a channel dedicated to Hollywood movies, MBC 2 and another given entirely to US sitcoms and talk shows, MBC 4. Dubai emirate in the United Arab Emirates followed suit in late 2004 with One TV, which offers the same Americana mix at a cost that, as with all the new Arab channels, has not been disclosed. All three channels have become hugely popular across the Arab world and advertisers are chomping at the bit to buy air-time on them because they are popular in the affluent Gulf Arab countries in particular. Their management argue that they offer a window on the world for Arabs at a crucial time when the region, because of the al-Qa'ida phenomenon, has been held up in the West as dangerously out of touch with the modern world in its politics, culture and religion. "We are a platform. We give you the privelage of having a view on the world and knowing what the Western view is," says Mohammed Al-Mulhem, public relations director for MBC. "Western entertainment appeals to youth. Consumers are getting more sophisticated and getting demanding. We are trying to spot trends."[5] MBC conducts monthly marketing reports on viewing trends in Saudi Arabia, in particular. With a high per capita income, a population of 24 million and a consumer culture that places high store on shopping as a pasttime, Saudi Arabia is a prime target for advertisers on the phethora of Arabic satellite television channels out there. In Saudi Arabia, the country which produced fifteen of the nineteen September 11 suicide hijackers, viewers have the freedom to flick from Islamic stations to dreary state television to the entertainment channels featuring chat show queen Oprah Winfrey and repeats of sitcoms like *Friends*.

Dubai's One TV is even less abashed about its America admiration. In promotional segments between programmes, presenters effuse in Arabic about Hollywood stars who are depicted as giant cardboard cut-outs against a Dubai skyline that seems to equate the ambitious city with Manhattan. In another promotion segment, a young Lebanese woman gushes in a Hollywood-obsessed monologue: "How could I forget that film?! The face, the look – Brad Pitt! Sean Penn, Andy Garcia!" A male voice-over cuts in: "Demi Moore, Sandra Bullock, Monica Belluci!" Then back to the thrilled afficionado of American glitter: "I was frightened, I was really moved, I laughed! I mean, I really got into the film! And even if they showed it a thousand times, I'd watch it – in order to see ... John Malcovich, Denzil Washington, Tom Cruise!" Male voice-over again: "Sharon Stone, Penelope Cruz, Nicole Kidman." Woman: "The colours, the camerawork – amazing! The lights, the décor, the music – and George Clooney, Kevin Spacey, Ben Affleck!" Man: "Lucy Liu, Meg Ryan, Angelina Jolie." Woman: "Isn't that right? The acting was unbelievable! And the action, suspense, comedy, Jim Carrey, Johnny Depp" – as the tinseltown music comes to an end. These PR montages form a striking contrast to the news channels like al-Jazeera and al-Arabiya and the between-programme montages the Arab viewer sees there – the voice of former Israeli Prime Minister Ariel Sharon announcing he "comes in peace" against a backdrop of Israeli soldiers and tanks in the Intifada, or guests from noted past shows who came out with memorable soundbites such as "Why do they think their blood is worth more than ours? What makes us cheaper than them?".[6]

"We researched what our viewers would like to see and what would attract more commercial activity," says Rashid Murooshid, One TV's manager. Britain and other English-language entertainment industries hardly get a look in, Murooshid admits; the shows are almost entirely American.[7] "We have to admit that Hollywood is one of the biggest and best producers of movies, sitcoms and popular shows. Their standard is high and can be easily accepted in this part of the world, since it's in English," he says. The irony of the viewers' distaste for the foreign policy of the country producing the material is by-the-by for Murooshid. "I'm not in a situation to decide which culture people should watch, that's up to the people, but ... advertisers like it because the viewers like it. The intention is to provide the favourite choice to our viewers, shows that they like and will be happy to watch. But we are not intending to get into cultural bridges," he says.

The Dubai skyline is a projection of what the government plans for the city to look like in several years time once a raft of construction projects are complete, including two towers competing for the title of the tallest building in the world. In a word, Dubai leads the Arab world in its desire to emulate American capitalist cosmopolitanism and Dubai's success in mimicking this explains much of its allure for Arabs from countries like Egypt, Syria and Lebanon, which are failed states by comparison. Dubai is bold, brash and new, with clean streets, rule of law, personal freedom and no hang-ups about following America. Dubai is a haven for Arabs who want to leave behind the corruption, the unemployment, the poverty, the pollution and the despair. Dubai also wants America's attention. Its international film festival has succeeded where Cairo's long-established version has failed in bringing Hollywood stars. Sarah Michelle Gellar told reporters in December 2004: "I love it here, I have to tell you. I think the region is absolutely beautiful, and I can't believe how clean the city is."[8] She confessed she had not managed to see a single Arabic film, but Dubai does not mind – the next target is to persuade Hollywood productions to shoot in the Emirates in a tax-free studio complex under development. When Emirates airline launched direct daily flights from Dubai to New York in 2004, it did so with a huge lifesize advertising poster of the Statue of Liberty covering the entire face of a highrise looking down upon the city's main highway. Nearby, a billboard announces that the area, witnessing massive and ambitious construction projects that Dubai government hopes will turn the city into a global playground of the rich, is "the most prestigious square kilometer on Earth" – a catchphrase one might associate with Manhattan.

Some commentators have seen in this binge on American television pop culture an expression of the very same political and social crises decried by American writers such as Thomas Friedman and Fareed Zakaria in their pronouncements about Arab dysfunction and expanded on by Arab writers themselves in the celebrated UN Arab Human Development Reports of recent years. Media analyst Jihad Fakhreddine says the owners of these Western entertainment channels have chosen ready-made foreign programmes over putting up the money for developing more Arabic-language entertainment of different forms, for which there is huge demand. "It shows the total bankruptcy of the Arab entertainment industry. It's cheaper for them to buy ready-made products, be it cars, fridges, or entertainment," he says.[9] Other commentators suggest the public is seeking refuge in US entertainment as an escape from the region's political problems, much of them ironically involving the United States. "Because of the political situation in the region, people don't want just political news," says Tarek Sheikh-Shabab of market researcher Ipsos-Stat in Dubai.[10] Most of the executives running the new stations are Saudis who are in fact American-educated. "MBC was thinking of Saudis who had American culture. Young Saudis are educated in the United States and they come home wanting the same series, movies and talks shows," Sheikh-Shabab says.

Arab entertainment apes America

The Arab world has tried to mimic American television, music and cinema with varying degrees of success. Reality TV hit the Arab world during 2002 and 2003. Most of the reality programs were copies of internationally patented shows such as *Star Academy* and *Big Brother*. Although *Big Brother* was forced off the air after one week because of MBC's mistake of hosting it in Bahrain, where the Islamist opposition is growing in strength, *Star Academy* was a huge success. Alarmed by its popularity in Saudi Arabia, the country's leading religious figure condemned it as "an open call to sin", but the kids were still mobbed whenever they headed into Beirut malls. Pierre Dhaher, the chief of Lebanon's entertainment channel LBC, has said he thinks it's the future of Arab television in the coming years and Dubai entrepreneur Mohammed al-Abbar, the head of construction firm Emaar who went to Israel in February 2005 to discuss buying Israeli settlements in Gaza, hopes to do an Arab version of Donald Trump's *The Apprentice*.[11] As yet, it is hard to imagine a show on Arab pop channels like MTV's *Dismissed* promoting lesbianism as a mainstream phenomenon where young women will have to choose between dating a young guy or a young girl and intimately kiss both in the process of finding out who she prefers.

Arabic pop music has frantically aped Americana since the late 1990s. There are now a plethora of satellite music channels a la MTV, mixing Western and Arab pop videos, such as Rotana, Melody, Mazzika, M-Plus, Zain, which some commentators think could herald the arrival of a youth-led Arab liberalism. America is the backdrop to the cultural war-of-the-era in the Arab world between youth finding their own voice and pushing the boundaries in music and fashion, and a motley array of retrograde forces, including governments, nationalists, leftists and Islamists, underpinned consciously or otherwise by the seminal views of Sayed Qutb. "More and more Arab women singers are presenting themselves in provocative terms, as figures who express and assert themselves erotically through fashion, movement, expression, and voice," writes Charles Paul Freund in Reason.[12] "The Arab world will eventually achieve its long-delayed goal of liberalized modernity; it might just as well dance itself there." Lebanon has generally led the way in introducing Western, and specifically American trends, to the Arab world, a sort of clearing house where these foreign influences are filtered and repackaged for an Arab audience.

There have been roughly two stages in Arab music history over the past half century – the "golden age" of classical singers associated with the period of Arab nationalist hope, singers whose style placed them as part of a renaissance of an ancient Arab heritage, and the pop music revolution since the 1980s. Islamist and nationalist culture critics view the first group as authenticly Arab and the second as dupes of American cultural imperialism. The dominance of the second group has become so complete in recent years, through the synergy of Arabic satellite channels and video clip productions, so as to provoke alarm among intellectuals. In a critique of a video by Lebanese popstar Nawal al-Zoghy, Egyptian academic Ashraf Galal noted an "absence of Arab identity and positive values and a clear approval of Western values – the Arab environment is absent and there is a complete cancellation of higher meanings and values".[13] In Lebanese singer Nancy Ajram's first videoclip, 2002's *Akhaasmak Aah* (*I Would Fall Out with You*), she belly dances her way through a men's coffee shop in a tight-fitting dress, thus provoking protests when she performed in Bahrain and calls in numerous Arab parliaments for a ban on broadcasting her video. Egyptian singer Ruby provoked a similar outcry with her 2004 song *Leih Byidaari Kida* (*Why Does He Hide Like That?*), where she engages in a fair bit of bottom and breast-wiggling to camera. "Songs today lack any real value, in the voice that sings it or the composer who wrote it. It's all about the look. But songs should be about more than just sticking your bottom out," rued composer Hilmy Bakr.[14] Lebanese DJs have even scored hits by rejigging classical Arabic songs in hip-hop formats, but again opposition has been expressed. "This trend to take the classics and modernize them is deforming our heritage," writer

Ibrahim al-Arees complained.[15] How to make it big in America is the question racking the brains of the biggest Arab pop stars and their managers. Arabic music has had limited success. There was an expectation in the international music industry that it would finally make a breakthrough into the mainstream, like Latino music, after Sting's hit Desert Rose, with Algerian singer Cheb Mami, but the suspicion of all things Arab after September 11 put paid to that.

The indigenous Arab cinema industry, centred in Egypt, has engaged in tortured attempts to replicate liberal American popular culture since the more open 1960s. Filmmakers and actors across the region are constantly testing the waters to see what public opinion, critics and Islamist opposition groups will make of their treatment of sexual issues. Many have fallen foul of the prevailing social sentiment. In Egypt, actress Yousra was taken to court in 1995 over a scene in *Tuyour al-Zalam (Birds of Darkness)* because her bare legs offended Islamic fundamentalists and Maali Zayed received a prison sentence in 1997 because a bedroom scene in the film *Abu Dahab* (1996) disgusted one moviegoer who saw it with his little boy. Legal action has been taken against a number of films by Egyptian director Inas al-Degheidy, who delights in pushing the boundaries: "I don't recognise the word *ayb* [shame] in art. Unfortunately, people are judging art as *ayb*, *haram* [morally wrong], *halal* [morally right], God said this, God didn't say that. I have faith, but cinema has nothing to do with religion. Religion is one thing, art is another. The artist should be able to realize everything that he imagines ... There are many things I'd like to be able to do."[16] Morocco saw similar problems throughout the 1990s, with Abdel-Qader Laqtaa's *Love in Casablanca* (1991) and *The Closed Door* (1995), and Mohamed Lotfi's *Rhesus* (1995), which stood out for its scenes of French-kissing. Egyptian director Yousef Chahine's *The Emigrant* (1995) was banned for a while in both Egypt and Morocco. Directors rue the restrictions placed on them and will go to extraordinary lengths to maintain the semblance of American-style libertarian cinema – the 2001 Egyptian film *Muwatin wa Mukhbir wa Harami (Citizen, Informer and a Thief)* contained a scene where a maid revealed herself topless, but with clear use of papier-mache to represent her bust. The camera angle was not in any case fully frontal.

Ali Abu Shadi, Egyptian film critic and former head of the state censorship office, argues that up to the 1960s and the sexual revolution in the West, the Arabs and Hollywood had a similar balance between modesty and freedom. For the Arab world, this was a time of Egypt-led renaissance. "It was a time of freedom in the arts. We were moving in the same direction as the rest of the world then," he says.[17] "Maybe we can get back to where we were in the 1960s, but even that's being ambitious." Only in the rarefied atmosphere of film festivals, cultural foundations or seminars can the real thing be seen, with bad language or nudity, in most of the Arab world – Lebanon and Tunisia are occasional exceptions. The 1998 film *Beirut al-Gharbiya* (*West Beirut*) was the first Arabic-language movie to go on general release in the North America. It showed in Beirut, but in Cairo only aired once at the Cairo International Film Festival where the audience loved its racy language. "People can like many things, but they will still walk out of a film like that and say confidently that it shouldn't be shown in public. It's a form of schizophrenia, but it's a natural, inherited instinct in this culture. It touches on a very fundamental problem we have in this culture," says Abu Shadi.[18] One TV, MBC 2 and MBC 4, the prime purveyors of Americana, have a policy of editing out scenes of kissing in American sit-coms and drama.

One thing cinema has done, though, is offer a critique of Arab obsessions with America. There is an attitude of awe towards America perhaps best captured in a popular Egyptian film of the 1990s *Amreeka Shikabeeka!* (*America, Abracadabra!*) starring pop star Amr Diab. Ironically, director Khairy Beshara wanted to suggest that going to America might not be all it's cracked up to be. Yousef Chahine's 2004 film *Alexandria ... New York* offers an interesting contrast between that era of awe and admiration and the current air of disillusion. An aging Arab filmmaker returns to New York after some years, meets an old lover and discovers that he had fathered a son by her. But the son rejects the father and, in the end, the father rejects the son in a metaphor for relations between the Arabs and the United States. "The violence which started in Hiroshima ends with you!" the father cries at the son at one point, referring to America's use of atomic weapons in Japan. When Chahine began his movie career in the 1940s studying in Pasadena, he was in love with the country. It was the American backing for Israel's often brutal treatment of Palestinians under occupation – beamed relentlessly into Arab living rooms by the satellite channels – that seems to have tipped the balance for him, though the way for divorce was prepared by the display of American power shown in the bombing of Baghdad during the 1991 Gulf War. Come the Iraq war in 2003, for Chahine, as for most admirers of America, the high-tech pummelling of an Arab capital confirmed their belief that America has become an uncompromising, violent force in the world. Chahine first ventured down this path in his 1999 film *al-Akhar*

(*The Other*), in which actress Nabila Ebeid is the Egyptian protagonist's American mater, presented as a predatory computer-whizz mom who drinks, interferes in his life and ridicules his Arab identity. Similar populist themes abounded in the autobiographical *Alexandria ... New York*, which traced this development from admiration to disillusion with America. Chahine was also involved in the French-produced omnibus of eleven short films called 11'09'01': *September 11*, released in 2002, in which eleven directors from around the world each contributed a submission that was eleven minutes, nine seconds, and one frame long, intended as a personal response to the September 11 attacks. Chahine's input presented a filmmaker who becomes flustered at a news conference when he hears reports of the 9/11 attacks, and who then enters into a dialogue with the ghosts of an American marine killed in the Hizbollah suicide attack in Beirut attack 1982 and a Palestinian suicide bomber killed during the second Intifada. Chahine is no fundamentalist. Most of his work of the last decade has pilloried political Islam and its deleterious effect on the secularism of the Arab 1960s that he idolizes.

Arabs attitudes towards American democracy

America's democracy, its openness and its strength are admired throughout the Arab region. For most Arabs, living in countries where political freedoms are restricted, rule of law is often arbitrary, and economic elites, religion, tradition and bureaucracies conspire to stifle creativity, social mobility and business opportunity, America is a country that "works". Though there is a considerable Arab-American community in the States who could have helped do the job of cross-cultural understanding itself, the satellite channels have had to make an effort to inform the Arab world what America is all about. Al-Jazeera and al-Arabiya both have weekly political talkshows featuring Arab journalists and academics based in the United States as well as Republicans and Democrats who as Arab-Americans are often able to communicate in Arabic. Democracy means a media in general more free than anything found in the Arab world, and this is something that has struck Arab commentators time and again, from Watergate to the Abu Ghraib scandal. When the images of American military personnel abusing Iraqi prisoners first came to light in 2004, one Egyptian editor wrote: "The American media may have supported Israel against the Arab countries, but on the Iraqi question it has taken a different view. They have called the

American crimes in Iraq 'abhorrent' and 'inhuman' and written in a clear, objective manner. American writers and intellectuals have been shocked by events in Iraq and condemned American policy."[19]

Like Dubai, America is viewed as a country where the "dream" of starting all over again comes true, and, for all their criticisms of its global politics, many middle-class Arabs hope their children can be educated there. American education is a commodity in demand for those who can afford it, either through American University branches in Arab countries or the real thing in the States. Samir Khader, the Jordanian producer who features in *Control Room*, an acclaimed documentary about al-Jazeera's operations during the Iraq war, admits to the camera in one of the film's more poignant moments that he hopes that one day he can live in America and his kids can study there to "exchange the Arab nightmare for the American dream." He says this despite his deep cynicism over how decades of Western intervention have ravaged the Arab world and created deformed societies. "Between us, if I am offered a job at Fox News, I'll take it," he adds, referring to the right-wing US television station. "You don't have to justify once you're victorious. That's it," he says in his last confessional piece to camera at the film's end.

Escape to America has been more difficult since September 11. The flow of Arab tourists, businessmen and students has slowed considerably because of the difficulties in obtaining visas, and a certain amount of Arab money invested in the United States has returned to the region. "Being an Arab in North America is not easy today. Three-and-a-half years after the September 11, 2001, attacks on the US and two years since the US-led invasion of Iraq, if you have not been interned at the pleasure of the American government as an Arab or Muslim, you are likely to have faced obstacles in everything from applying for a driver's license to depositing a check in your name in a bank," Beirut's *Daily Star* says.[20]

While America's separation between state and religion has been a certain source of inspiration for the secular Arab nationalists and liberal democrats, many Islamists curse America as a godless society and not a model for the Arab world. According to Yousef al-Qaradawi, an Egyptian independent cleric who has a weekly show on al-Jazeera: "Islam must take on board Western scientific developments. But we don't want their values, their understandings and their philosophy. We just want their mechanisms so that we know how to achieve at what they achieved."[21] As for the often-cited secular Muslim "model states" of Turkey and Tunisia, Qaradawi wrote them off as examples of "secular extremism" that ape the West at the expense of Islamic cultural specificity. "That's not the mix that we want," he said. Egypt's Brotherhood, the trend-setter for Islamists across the Arab world, only reconciled itself with the idea of parliamentary democracy in the 1980s. Their decision under the leadership of the late Omar al-Tilmissani to take part was so troubling that it had Islamists "throwing themselves off their balconies" in angst, quips Egyptian rights activist Hisham Kassem.[22] For them, ultimate authority lay in God's law as revealed in the Quran and through the living example set by the Prophet Mohammad. It did not lie in a popularly-elected parliament with the theoretical power to enact whatever it saw fit, such as gay rights or abortion laws. In Saudi Arabia, the "parliament", or Shura Council, is considered merely an "advisory" not "legislative" (*tashri'i*) body that issues "organising statutes" (*nuzum*) not laws, since Sharia law (*al-Shari'a*) already exists and is only for clerics to interpret, not to add to or amend.

Many Islamists and Arab nationalists think too much democracy has made America soft. They also think, or hope, that it is only America's wealth that holds it together and eventual collapse and internal strife between ethnicities and regions is inevitable. Al-Qa'ida statements in Iraq accuse Americans of hiding beyond technology to defend themselves because modern comforts have made them soft. When US troops opened fire on prisoners in Basra in February 2005, Zarqawi's group responded: "What was the fault of defenceless prisoners with nothing but God to protect them, that you should treat them like this? Tyrants of the age, we will not let these crimes of yours pass – we will settle the score ... We will come at you with brothers who love death just as you love life, monks by night and knights by day, who protect the book of God and dedicate themselves to pleasing Him."[23] The same rhetoric is often encountered concerning Israel. Israel was perceived to have withdrawn from south Lebanon in 2000 because its modern society, in which people follow Western trends of marrying late and having fewer children to allow more "quality of life", could not handle the relatively few deaths caused by Hizbollah's pot-luck katyusha rocket attacks on Israeli settlements near the Lebanese border. Israel's failure to crush the guerrilla group in the war of July and August 2006 merely confirmed this view.

Islamists often argue about democracy and the evils it can lead to in Internet chatrooms. "What's wrong with there being an opposition? And freedom of opinion? And a salary for the ruler, specifying his term of office, and legislating that he cannot appoint a successor? Where's the apostasy in calling for any of this?" wrote one user on a popular site.[24]

"Brother," someone calling himself "A Muslim from Egypt" replied: "Democracy in Holland has approved marriage for homosexuals and light drug addiction such as hashish, while Canada has also approved homosexual marriage and America approved war on Afghanistan and Iraq. After all this, you still want to come and defend it?" Another calling himself "Ibn Amr" added: "It's democracy that planted Israel in our lands in the name of the historical rights of Jews, and do you know that Israel is the most successful democracy in the Middle East according to human rights groups? If we look at the second most successful democracy, which is Morocco, isn't it odd that it is the regime that has done the most for Israel and Francophone culture and is the regime that has spread prostitution and drugs despite the opposition of the Moroccan people?"

America's democracy has allowed Christian fundamentalists to gain influence, they also argue. Interestingly, one commentator has suggested that Egypt's Brotherhood has taken heart from the rise of Christian right and, following their example, is less convinced of the advantages of being allowed to operate as an official political party – a long-time goal of the group, which has been technically banned since Nasser's day. "In the United States, Christian fundamentalism attained its highest level of political influence after having evolved into a movement that acquired momentum and a mass following on the basis of systematic campaigns against certain social and moral conditions. These fundamentalist movements were thus able to accomplish most of their objectives without running afoul of government authorities, the constitution or political party traditions. They certainly did not attempt to form a political party on religious lines, which would have shaken the foundations of the American system," Gamil Matar says.[25] "… developments in the United States have increased the confidence of political Islamists in the Arab world that they stand a greater chance of augmenting their influence if they abandon the idea of founding a religious political party. Their thinking probably runs that as long as political party life is in decline anyway there is little point in risking confrontation with the authorities for the sake of an objective that has lost the appeal and value it held in past decades."

Views on America's "promiscuous" culture

American democracy never looked more silly or effete to some Arabs than during the Monica Lewinsky scandal. The promiscuity in itself did not surprise people, but the fact that the president had no ability to prevent his affair with a White House intern becoming public knowledge or threatening his presidency was astounding, that Bill Clinton could have appointed a special prosecutor to an independent post who subsequently turned against the president, and that America's media and political culture was so willing to embarrass itself before the world by dwelling on what should have remained in the private domain. It is really only political Islam that looks down on American society as promiscuous, though nationalists, humiliated by America's ability to keep Arab nations divided and nourish Israel, also saw in the scandal a chance to score points and assert the higher morals of Arab culture.

While American liberals saw a right-wing conspiracy, many Arab commentators saw an Israeli plot to bring down Clinton because he backed the Oslo peace process, which was intended to lead to a Palestinian state led by Yasser Arafat. All this because Lewinsky was Jewish. Others wondered at the rights of women in the American workplace, and the fact that it was Clinton and not Lewinsky who was taking the blame and the flack. There was not much sympathy for the girl but a lot of it for Clinton. This commentary from a Bahraini newspaper captures it all in one passage: "What kind of a girl is Monica Lewinsky? She entered the White House as an unknown trainee and overnight has been changed to a girl after whom every TV network is running to get inside information ... Is she a prostitute looking for a market after she failed to find it at the White House? Is she a bait dropped by the CIA to damage the picture of the president because he crossed the red line? Is she an element of a foreign intelligence party, perhaps Israel, recruited to shake the white house because its occupant said no to something it asked for? It is difficult to imagine how the president will survive the allegation of this frivolous girl. No one knows how much she is getting for her disgraceful role in this well-prepared and well-designed play."[26] And there were popular plays – two in fact. Typically bawdy Cairene affairs, one of them, *Me, My Wife and Monica*, went on tour around the Arab world. It was a big hit in pre-war Iraq, where UN sanctions and international isolation had all but snuffed out cultural life.

Israel is depicted in the Arabic press as an oasis of American-style promiscuity that follows the garish Western insistence on celebrating in public what goes on in private. A favourite target is homosexuality. One Egyptian tabloid paper wrote: "Gays and lesbians are everywhere. More than 10,000 Israelis of both sexes have revealed this deviancy at a festival held in Tel Aviv. Israel showed its filthy social face during this odious festival. Male youths were keen to exchange kisses, engage in obscene acts and take commemorative pictures. There is a statistic that shows that homosexuality in Israel represents 25 percent of the population of the Jewish state!!"[27] Israeli transsexual singer Dana International was briefly popular in Egypt in the mid-1990s and even made a surreptitious trip to Cairo. A tabloid journalist published a book about the affair which said the singer, who went on to with the 1998 Eurovision Song Contest, had been sent to Egypt by Israeli spy agency Mossad "to unleash her moans and shameless words from the city of a thousand minarets".[28]

Israel is depicted in the media as dissolute and artificial, in contrast to an Arab self-image of moral uprightness and richness of history and tradition. America is seen to beas lacking in cultural depth and strength as Israel. At a more serious level of discussion, former Egyptian diplomat Mustafa al-Fiki suggests that Americans have found the perfect foil in Israel's ancient history and religious mythology. "Behind the decisions of the United States is the knowledge that is a very strong nation, very rich and way ahead of everyone else. But it does not have much history or cultural heritage behind it, thus it finds in Israel a model where history and politics are entwined with religion. American support for Israel has taken on a sacred status and has gone beyond the merely political to reflect a more emotional link," he says.[29] The dissolute and empty nature of American society is of course a theme developed by Islamists in particular, taking their cue from Sayed Qutb in his writings. For them, America is the leading force in the deconstruction of the faith-based society that "the West" once was – even if it was centred on wayward Christianity. "Modernity", never mind "post-modernity", is a dirty word for many purists (Saudi Arabia's state media imposed a ban on use of the word "modernity" – *hadatha* – in the 1980s). Nothing really shocks these conservatives; everything confirms. A former translator who worked at Guantanamo Bay, the US prison in Cuba where al-Qa'ida suspects have been held without the full protection of the US justice system or the Geneva Convention compact on treatment of prisoners of war, relates in his book *Inside the wire* how women interrogators would employ the so-called "sex-up" approach to get information.[30] In one incident, the interrogator wiped what she pretended was menstrual blood on the face of a Saudi detainee, saying, "Does that please your God, does that please Allah?" then leaves him with parting words: "Have fun trying to pray tonight without water in your cell." The thinking behind such behaviour,

Saar says, is to break the detainee's will by denying him the ability to draw strength from his direct link to God through prayer. Ultimately, this type of behaviour would not shock an Islamist, since for him it simply proves what he knew all along, that America is a godless abherration.

In Egyptian novelist Sonallah Ibrahim's 2004 work *Amrikanli*, the Egyptian protagonist who teaches at an American university finds one of his students comparing Cairo to San Francisco. The professor responds derisively: "I made a disdainful sign with my hand and said, 'this is a comparison that might work in newspapers, but the history of the two cities is different. Of course, the difference itself could be your subject but it has to say something. What do you have? An ancient city over 1,000 years old which rests on the remains of an ancient civilization which is another few thousand years old – and a modern city no older than two centuries'."[31] Later, Ibrahim's protagonist is taken on a walkabout by an American friend through a rough district of San Francisco where they pass by all manner of social deviants. "He took me to streets full of cheap shops and massage parlours, Vietnamese grocers, shops with old and ruined things, young people who had pierced their ears, lips and eyebrows with various kinds of rings, people living inside their coats on the sidewalks. I was attacked by the smell of cat piss from the entrace of one house, mixed with curry, and the noise of an old opera from the house next door. I almost tripped up on a sleeping bag wrapped up and leaning against a wall, underneath the poster of a child furiously eating a hamburger. I noticed that every shop was surrounded by strong iron bars," he writes.[32] The professor, who is a visiting scholar teaching history, passes no comment on all he sees. With dark humour stalking the text, Ibrahim sets American urban reality against stereotypes he knows exist in America of the sexually obsessed Arab and the anti-Semite. The professor leaves his students lost for words as he merges tales of his sexual exploits with intellectual musings on Egyptian, Arab and American history.

The Arab world and American Muslims

On 18 March 2005, New York City witnessed a major event in the history of modern Islam: for the first time a woman publicly led the service at Friday prayers and her congregation was of mixed gender. Men traditionally lead prayers, and men and women sit in separate areas of the mosque or are separated by a partition so that no sexual tension can interfere with moments of communion with God. It is for this reason too that women in prayer are veiled or choose to veil during the course of their daily lives – the same reasons, in essence, why women of other faiths cover their hair. The landmark event provoked a huge controversy that engulfed Muslims in the United States and Islamic scholars in the Middle East, and it set the scene for a major debate over the coming generation between "progressive Islam" in the United States, led mainly by black, non-Arab Americans, and traditional or mainstream Islam, led by Arab scholars in the Arab world and Arab (and sub-continent) immigrant communities in the United States. The prayer was even broadcast live on the internet. The organizers said the event was about "Muslim women reclaiming their rightful place in Islam" and creating Muslim communities that "reflect the egalitarian nature of Islam".[33]

Opponents of the prayer, which was led by a lady called Amina Wadud, an American Muslim convert of Indian origin, argued that there was no textual basis in Islamic law and that if the law and its stipulations, which are based mainly on the Quran – as the revealed word of God – and the Sunna, or way, of the Prophet and his early followers (including the hadiths, or recorded sayings, of the Prophet and his companions), are ignored, deconstructed, or reinvented then Islam ceases to be Islam. Extracting principles and rules from this ancient legal and behavioural corpus is called *ijtihad* in Arabic. Hina Azam, a sympathetic American Muslim and professor of Islamic law at the University of Texas, wrote: "The proposed ruling – that women may lead men in salat al-jumu'ah (Friday prayer) – violates several basic texts and classical interpretive principles, and its proponents provide neither a sound critique of the traditional legal methodology or nor an improved one to replace it. The impression one gets is that there is no consistent methodology, that in fact, the desired ruling (the permissibility of women leading mixed-sex congregations for *salat al-jumu'ah* [Friday prayer]) dictates their use of texts and of interpretive method. Heaven knows I have wished for women to be able to lead *salat al-jumu'ah*. But wishful thinking is not a sound methodology."[34] In response, other American scholars suggested that by that reasoning one might as well reintroduce slavery since it is mentioned in the Quran. Another writer, Hussein Ibish is Vice-Chair of the Progressive Muslim Union, suggested that this slavish attitude to Islamic law was "an expression of deep arrogance, a marshaling of elite academic training in an effort to limit other peoples' choices" – language and thinking which is distinctly American and which is diametrically opposed to the dominant traditionalist Islam of the Arab world, as espoused and promoted on television by mainstream Sunni scholars like Yousef al-Qaradawi. In fact, al-Qaradawi is a figure of scorn for Ibish, a counterpoint to all that progressive Muslims in America want to be. "If this is what Hina Azam has to offer, we can just go back to Yusuf Qaradawi and dispense with her altogether," Ibish says.[35]

The reaction in the Arab world to Wadud's prayer itself was one of outrage. Only in America would such an abomination happen, was the general tenor of public debate. Egypt's state-owned *al-Messaa* newspaper called Wadud "the deranged woman" and proclaimed in a front-page headline: "They are tarnishing Islam in America!"[36] In Saudi Arabia, the government's highest appointed cleric Grand Mufti Abdel-Aziz al-Sheikh told worshippers: "Those who defend this issue are violating God's law. Enemies of Islam are using women's issues to corrupt the community." Egypt's independent *al-Osboa* newspaper talked of "the American conspiracy to Americanize Islamic religious discourse via turning mosques into social centres that engage in all sorts of activities, allowing worshippers to engage in a dialogue with the imam at Friday prayers to allow all opinions, and for America to be a central player in developing Al-Azhar's syllabus by organising training sessions for preachers in Washington to teach them the basics of religion ... This is part of a plot to destroy Islam and efface it from the hearts of Muslims."[37] It was commonly argued that a woman leading prayers, which involve prostrations – bending over – would prove distracting to male worshippers. But there was some sympathetic treatment – Wadud was invited to appear on al-Jazeera – and what was striking in fact was that the Arab world was obliged to engage seriously in a debate generated by Muslims living in the West. Wadud's colleague Asra Nomani, an American Muslim of Pakistani origin who has organized women prayer sessions through her Muslim Women's Freedom Tour, has also been hosted on al-Jazeera, though the presenter of one show commented on what he considered to be the sensationalist cover to one of the English editions of her book *Standing Alone in Mecca*.[38] Nomani, a former *Wall Street Journal* reporter, says mosques in North America are dominated by Saudi Wahhabi-style Islam.

Opponents in the Arab world and in the West offered compromises whereby women could lead other women in prayer and have their own special mosques, a position backed by Qaradawi himself. Islamic tradition cites the Prophet's wife Aisha as sometimes leading women in prayer and elaborates on situations where this would be possible; there is also one hadith in which a woman is advised to lead her household in prayer, including one man, because she was the most knowledgeable about the Quran (in the hadith collection of Abu Dawoud). Britain already has such as a woman *imam* (prayer leader), Salma Qureishi.

The woman imam controversy was the first major encounter the Arab world has had with the new currents in American Islam. America over the last century has its own particular history of Islam, through black, African American movements such as the Moorish Orthodox Church of Timothy Drew, or Noble Drew Ali (1886–1929) and the Nation of Islam founded by Wallace Fard Muhammad in 1930. Informed and driven by the persecution and dispossession of black Africans in America, these movements involved beliefs that were heretical in the eyes of most mainstream Muslims. Ali claimed to have knowledge of a "lost Quran" and the Nation of Islam believes its founder was the latest in a series of God incarnates on Earth. The primary concern of these groups has been black empowerment, through an Islamic – non-white – paradigm. When the doors to immigration were thrown wide open in the 1960s, black Islam was to find itself marginalized by the growing Muslim immigrant communities who imported their own Islamic social values and Islamic hierarchies and structures with them. The immigrant communities tended to look down on the indigenous Muslims as part of a wider Western cultural corruption, and the American Muslims looked down on the immigrants in return. The black American Muslims had their own more liberal practices and doctrines, and some have even argued there must have been a "corrupted transmission" of the Quran in order to explain the text's apparent approval of practices such as slavery and wife-beating in the time of the Prophet. "These interpretations are likewise threatening to mainstream Islam in America because they respond to indigenous Islam's radical critique of white culture and resistance to the exclusionary claims of 'orthodox' Islam," writes Laury Slivers, Assistant Professor of Religion at Skidmore College.[39]

The Arab world had its first introduction to black American Islam in the 1990s when Louis Farrakhan launched his Million Man March in 1995, a campaign to encourage African Americans to make their voice heard in American politics and society through, for example, registering to vote, and to change the image of black men through more concern for women and family. He subsequently toured the world, including Sudan, Libya, Egypt, Jordan, Iraq and the Palestinian territories, making common cause with issues ranging from Aboriginal rights in Australia, to Libya and Iraq under United Nations sanctions, to Sudan's dream of becoming an Islamic power in Africa. His central theme was a strident criticism of American foreign policy and subjugation of non-Western, non-white peoples.

There appears to be a convergence of these different Islams in the emergence of the new progressive trend in the United States, often led by younger Muslims who are Arab or African American in origin. In 2004, a US-based web site *Muslim Wake Up!* was set up to promote a modern, "reform" Islam which, its founders said, represents the silent majority among the seven million or so Muslims in North America. Its ethos runs counter to much of the dominant discourse in the Arab world. In a bid to improve Muslim-Jewish relations, the site encourages readers to "hug a Jew", runs articles pleading the cause of black African Muslims persecuted in the Sudanese region of Darfur, promotes an Islamic feminism and publishes satire against traditionalist thinking and clerics. The site's mission statement says that "Muslim Wake Up! champions an interpretation of Islam that celebrates the Oneness of God and the Unity of God's creation through the encouragement of the human creative spirit and the free exchange of ideas, in an atmosphere that is filled with compassion and free of intimidation, authoritarianism, and dogmatism. In all its activities, *Muslim Wake Up!* attempts to reflect a deep belief in justice and against all forms of oppression, bigotry, sexism, and racism."[40] Minus the references to belief in God, perhaps, the generation of the sixties could not have put it better. An online poll it ran in October 2005 asked readers to vote on whether "Most Muslim religious leaders are corrupt, irresponsible, ignorant or all of the above". Over 58 percent chose "all of the above". Other prominent internets forums for American Muslims include *AltMuslim* (www.altmuslim.com), which is more focussed on the political problems facing American Muslims after September 11, and the slightly more academic *The American Muslim* (www.theamericanmuslim.org). Muslims in the Arab world who try to push similar thinking invariably run into trouble, facing courts, jail, book-banning, ostracization and even death.

Attempts to "understand America"

Since September 11 and the Palestinian uprising in 2000, "understanding America" has become a major theme of public debate in the Arab world. Commentators who have experience of the country are constantly exhorting Arabs to better understand the nature of American politics and society. There has been been a marked effort to connect Arabs in the Middle East with those living in America via programmes like al-Jazeera's *From Washington (Min Washington)* and al-Arabiya's *Across the Atlantic ('Abra al-Muheet)*. The media is constantly arguing that the Arab world and Arab governments should do more to make their "causes" (*qadaya*) known to the American public. The Arab League came up with a plan in 2001 to spend $1 million on print advertisements in major world newspapers. More of a sop to public opinion than a real project, this metamorphosed into an idea to finance visits to major Western capitals and American cities by ordinary Palestinians – doctors, students, unemployed labourers, priests – wounded during the Intifada. This was to be part of a $25 million blitz over two years in cooperation with Arab-American advocacy groups in the United States and spearheaded by media-friendly Palestinian politician Hanan Ashrawi, who was appointed to a new post called Arab League Media Commissioner. Hopes were high at the time that this was the beginning of a new attitude towards making the Palestinians' case in the West, but Ashrawi remained in Ramallah, the finance and organization required to get things moving failed to materialize, and then Arab political attention switched focus to the Iraq crisis and futile Arab attempts to prevent the war.

Possibly the single most effective piece of propaganda was the time out taken by Saudi Arabia's Crown Prince Abdullah – who became king in 2005 – at a meeting with President Bush on his Texas ranch in April 2002 to show him photographs of Palestinians killed or maimed by the Israeli army and the destruction of their homes and towns. "I felt it was my duty to spend as long a time as possible to brief him on the facts directly and without an intermediary," Abdullah said later, claiming to have sensed that Bush was deeply moved by what he saw.[41] He said of Bush: "He has noble qualities. He is honest, courageous and highly compassionate. These are all good news for the Palestinians. He listens and debates politely, but was not fully informed about the real conditions in the region, especially the conditions suffered by the Palestinian people."[42] Brave and innovative as the effort might have been, it pales in comparison with the non-stop lobbying of Israel's supporters in Washington. Fareed Zakaria admitted to an Arab audience in 2004: "The Zionist lobby is very powerful. It's well-organized, it knows how to be effective, and to be effective at a society-to-society level rather than a state-to-state level. If you want to contrast two methods of going about it, look at how the Saudis conduct their relationship with the United States and how Israel goes about it. The Saudis believe that as long as they have good relations with 25 people in Washington, and wine and dine them and do certain other things, all will be well. The Israelis believe that what you have to create is more links [between] the American public [and] the Israeli public. It's very different."[43]

Some individual efforts to improve the Arab image and promote Arab issues have fallen flat on their face. One was Saudi Prince al-Walid bin Talal's donation of $10 million to the families of victims of September 11. New York mayor Rudolph Giuliani turned it down because of a statement Prince Walid issued linking the attacks to what he called pro-Israel bias in American Middle East policy. "The government of the United States of America should re-examine its policies in the Middle East and adopt a more balanced stance toward the Palestinian cause. Our Palestinian brethren continue to be slaughtered at the hands of Israelis while the world turns the other cheek," the prince said after touring the site of the destruction in New York just days after the attacks. Guilani responded: "Not only are those statements wrong, they are part of the problem ... There is no moral equivalent to this attack. There is no justification for it ... One of the reasons I think this happened is because they were engaged in moral equivalency in not understanding the difference between liberal democracies like the United States, like Israel, and terrorist states and those who condone terrorists."[44] The Bush administration backed Guiliani.

The Arab media was indignant about the incident, which did indeed confirm how unimportant the Palestinian story of dispossession and suffering was to Americans, but no one managed to suggest a more effective way of addressing the United States. "Rudolph Giuliani's unexpected behaviour serves warning about the level of hatred caused by merely talking about the suffering of the Palestinians," the UAE paper *al-Khaleej* said.[45] "We have a clear case and we must transfer our media battle to Washington, the centre of the United States and the centre of its political decision-making," al-Walid himself later said.[46] In the days immediately following the attacks, many in the region were holding their breath to see if they would perhaps sway the Bush administration towards the Palestinians rather than away from them. After all, in the Arab thinking, the Islamic extremism of al-Qa'ida is the rejoinder of a proud world culture with a series of historical gripes against the West and the United States, at the centre of which is the pain, physical and psychological, surrounding the loss of Palestine. The attacks could have been read in Washington as the result of excessive support for Israel and ignorance of Palestinian suffering, or they could have been viewed as evidence that Islamist violence among Palestinians was one facet of the wider al-Qa'ida threat, an example of how to operate. Yasser Arafat's donation of blood before the world media in a statement of solidarity with Americans paled before the Israeli media onslaught to convince Washington that Palestinian suicide bomb attacks were as morally repugnant as the September 11 suicide plane hijackers. In hindsight, perhaps there was no question which view would prevail. A strong Israel protected from Palestinian existential threat was a central concern of the neo-conservatives who built the ideological edifice on which the Iraq project was based, and the invasion and occupation were the Bush administration's great riposte to September 11. The framework subsequently established by President Bush to bring the Israeli-Palestinian conflict to an end held as a core value the idea that the Palestinians would only get a state if they put an end to the cult of the suicide bomber.

The desire to better understand America is driven by an awareness of the chronic naivete that has consistently dominated Arab attitudes towards the United States. Politicians and commentators had been hopeful that the Republican government that succeeded Bill Clinton's tenure as president would be more pro-Arab. Partly because of such assumptions, Arab governments backed by the Arab media did not consider it essential for the Palestinian leadership to obtain a peace agreement with Israeli governments during the Oslo era, although there was less indication that the Palestinian leadership held this view. The Arabs ended up with simultaneous Israeli and American rightwing administrations, and the American administration formed in 2001 reflected the dominant right-wing pro-Israeli thinking in American politics, which does not want a solution based on the 1967 borders that obliges Israel to roll back entirely its encroachments into the territory occupied in 1967. Israel has effectively said this would provoke civil war in the Jewish state. "The Palestinian leadership has done well to stick to the principles of its people and to give itself more time so that new developments will hopefully make the Israelis and their supporters understand that there can be no solution other than one based on United Nations resolutions," op-ed writer Maher Osman said in the pan-Arab *al-Hayat* a month before rightwing champion of the settler movement

Ariel Sharon was voted into office in February 2001.[47] He was referring to the last-ditch efforts to reach a deal sponsored by US President Bill Clinton in his final days in office, efforts involving take-it-or-leave-it ultimatums which in the Arab view were too vague and too rushed. Egyptian state-owned paper *al-Gomhouriya* gushed at the time: "Congratulations to the Arabs on this new victory. They refused to surrender and be subjugated to a race against time and showed courage in facing America and 52 countries who wanted to impose a *fait accompli* on the Palestinians which is completely incongruous with their future and 50 years of struggle."[48]

Chapter 3
The Palestinians

Palestine and Arab views of America

Arab views of the United States today are first and foremost conditioned by American policy vis-à-vis the Israel-Palestinian conflict and the degree to which the United States is seen as backing Israel to the detriment of the Palestinians. The United States was looked upon favourably in the aftermath of the Suez war in 1956, since it had intervened to end the British, French and Israeli military intervention to wrest the Suez canal from Egyptian control. But 1956 in fact marked the replacement of Britain and France as the predominant foreign powers in the region with the United States, and the United States was inexorably drawn towards the Israeli camp. The Arab-Israeli wars in 1967 and 1973 were to bear this out, wars that although left Israel in control of Arab territories they had not won in the 1947–1948 fighting nevertheless further harnessed Israel's image in Western eyes as a brave, beleaguered state standing its ground in a hostile environment. This was largely the image in Europe too, and in fact the two countries that went on to style themselves as "friends of the Arabs" played key roles backing Israel: Russia was the first country to recognize Israel at the United Nations and the communist bloc was a key arms supplier of the Zionist movement, while France conspired to help Israel achieve nuclear weapons capability. The image of "the Arabs" in Western popular culture was overwhelmingly negative in the aftermath of the 1967 conflict and worsened when Saudi Arabia used the oil embargo during the subsequent 1973 conflagration, when Egypt and Syria launched a surprise attack on Israel in an attempt to retake the territories they lost in 1967. The cause was seen in the region as the fight of all the Arabs, not just the countries involved in the war. English travel writer Jonathan Raban wrote: "Arabs were a remote people who were either camping out in tents with camels and providing fodder for adventurous photographers, or a brutish horde threatening the sovereignty of the state of Israel."[1] Now they were walking the streets of London and buying up property.

What diversified the picture somewhat was the growth of the Palestinian liberation movement, as the Palestinian Liberation

Organization (PLO), an umbrella movement of Palestinian groups of different political persuasions, came together in 1964. In Europe and areas of Asia and South and Central America where third world development and liberation from colonialism were popular and vibrant themes, the Palestinians emerged as a distinct people, with an identity of their own and a cause to shout about. In Europe, the more sour image of "the Arabs" shifted specifically to the Gulf Arabs, while the Palestinians – even despite the campaign of aircraft hijackings and bombings carried out by some fringe groups in the European arena – acquired an audience and respect among many on the Left.

But this did not happen in the United States. As Palestinians gained a hearing in Europe, America secured its alliance with Israel in the post-1967 period and Israel came to be seen by the Arabs as an American proxy in the Middle East preserving a regional balance of power in America's favour and battling Arab radicalism. "In contrast to its perception in the 1950s, the United States now perceived Israel as a bastion of regional order and as a strategic asset in the Middle East," historian Avi Shlaim says.[2] Shlaim says the State Department, with its army of Arabists, had believed that Israel should be prodded into peace on the principles of UN resolution 242, the post-1967 UN document which became the basis of peace negotiations in the decades to follow. The text talks of Israel's withdrawal "from territories occupied in the recent conflict", which to the State Department Arabists, as well as the Arabs, meant all the territories it did not possess on the eve of the Six-Day War. The State Department was prepared to consider proposing moves such as threatening to withhold arms to get Israel to return the lands. But national security advisor Henry Kissinger, architect of the current era of US policy towards the conflict, won out in the 1970s with his view that Israel should only ever compromise from a position of strength and should not therefore be subject to American pressure. Despite occasional exceptions, American diplomacy has held to this principle for a generation. During the Camp David talks in 1978, President Carter sought a promise from Israeli Prime Minister Menachim Begin to stop settlement building in the West Bank, a project of colonization which Likud governments championed after coming to power in 1977, and President George Bush's secretary of state James Baker threatened to withhold aid money over settlements in 1992. But, in 2004, President George W. Bush unilaterally announced that an Israeli return to the borders of 1967 was "unrealistic", as was the idea of any Palestinian refugees returning to land in what is now Israel. These comments form the broad outlines of American policy in the current, post-Intifada stage of the conflict.

Since Israel is the biggest recipient of annual aid from the United States, the Arab world considers that the United States has bankrolled the settlements and the occupation. Total military, economic and other aid from 1948 to 2006 has been estimated at over $99 billion, hitting an annual high of $4.9 billion in 1979 and coming close to that again in 2000 at $4.1 billion – around a third of the US foreign aid budget to Israel accounts for well under less than one percent of the world's population.[3] Over half of the total is military, a third is economic. Since 2000, annual military aid has gone up ($2.28 billion in 2006, $1.86 billion in 1999), while economic aid has gone down ($240 million in 2006, $1.08 billion in 1999). These figures do not include the tax-deductible donations that go to Israel from Americans each year. It has also provided the weaponry to get the job done. The Arab world saw simple hypocrisy when the United States was alarmed by an intercepted arms shipment, valued at $10 million, which Israel said was sent to the Palestinian Authority from Iran with Hizbollah help.[4] It is assumed that American aid money is funding the controversial Israeli wall, or security barrier, under construction since 2002 around Palestinian areas in the West Bank. Israelis say it aims to keep out suicide bombers, but Palestinians say that, since it snakes deep into the West Bank and does not stick to the pre-1967 border, it amounts to one last land-grab before unilaterally fixing borders. A team of American Anglican Christians who led a fact-finding trip to the West Bank in 2005 were disturbed to hear that this is the general impression among Palestinians. "What the commission members found the most shocking of all was that the Wall or Separation Barrier or Fence, as it is variously called, is perceived by all parties as being almost entirely underwritten by the American taxpayer," commission member Michele Spike said of the wall, which encircles Palestinian towns and cuts through villages and fields.[5]

Between Suez in 1956 and the Intifada in 2000, the United States became identified in the minds of the Arab public at large as an enemy of their aspirations for Palestinian independence. But it is a complicated relationship in two senses: judging the extent of actual US support for Israel against sometimes different public perceptions of that support in the Arab world, and judging US positions against the shifting parameters of the conflict itself since 1948. American policy in the region after World War Two was driven mainly by oil interests. Before 1967, "the Palestinian issue" was of less public concern for Arab and Western publics because the West Bank and Jerusalem remained in Arab (Jordanian) control. The refugee problem was a real one but it was drowned out by the general euphoria in the West over the fledgling Israeli state and its Utopian visage, while the state-controlled media in the Arab world focussed more on the abstract idea of Israel than the concrete reality of a million dispossessed Palestinians. With the Israeli occupation in 1967 of the rest of historical Palestine and the birth of the Palestinian nationalist movement, a more clearly defined "cause" emerged for the United States, and the Arab world, to put their minds to. It still took some two decades for the Palestinians, under Yasser Arafat's guidance, to form a concensus around the idea of a "two-state solution", concentrating their efforts on liberating the West Bank, Gaza Strip and East Jerusalem and ditching the idea of one shared, secular state for the Jewish incomers and the native Arab population, the vision originally championed by the Palestinian nationalist movement. Even after the peace deal of 1993, which specifically concerned the territories under Israeli occupation, the fact that the refugee question was still alive continued to limit American support for the Palestinians in the evolving conflict because the refugees' rights, if realized, would make the Jewish state less Jewish and more Arab by default. Yet, the Israeli settlement project in the West Bank and Jerusalem has in fact brought the one-state-for-two-peoples solution more close to reality than ever. Many intellectuals on both sides now see it as the only hope.

Israeli statistics in June 2005 put the number of settlers in the West Bank at 246,000, but to this figure should be added some 190,000 Israelis who now live in East Jerusalem in neighbourhoods, on annexed territory, which are part of the Jerusalem municipality.[6] Israel says it wants to draw borders including the large settlement blocs in the West Bank, as well as East Jerusalem neighbourhoods and the border territory with Jordan, by 2010. For Israel, this West Bank presence not only fulfils a "biblical birthright" claimed by some religious right-wingers, but makes up for the one-fifth of Israel's own population which is Arab.

Within Arab societies, there are three relevant sectors forming opinions on American policy on the conflict – the governments, the opposition and "public opinion". After Egypt's peace with Israel in 1979, the Arab government's relationship with Washington generally began to improve across the region, but among opposition groups and the public at large things were moving in another direction entirely. One of the key moments in this deterioration was the American involvement in the Lebanese civil war after Israel invaded the country in 1982 to destroy the PLO, which moved there after being ejected from Jordan in 1970. The United States led a multinational force, including French, Italian and British troops, that deployed to oversee the evacuation of PLO guerrillas and restore stability. In the eyes of most Arabs, bar Lebanon's Christian militias for whom the Palestinian presence signalled the end of Christian domination, this was an American effort to consolidate the achievements of Israel's invasion and deliver the country back into the hands of the pro-Western Christians who were prepared to live in peace and alliance even with Israel. In other words, the United States was perceived to have taken sides. In 1983, the Shi'ite guerrilla movement Hizbollah organized spectacular suicide bomb attacks against the US Marines in Beirut, killing 241 Marines and more than 50 French paratroopers. This was the dawn of a new era of Islamist resistance and heralded the arrival of the Arab suicide bomber. Before the attack, US forces had pounded Shi'ite villages, and, in their aftermath, had struck at anti-Israeli Shi'ite and Druze targets in the mountains.

In Arab eyes, the United States was also indirectly implicated in the massacre of Palestinian refugees at Sabra and Shatila camps on the outskirts of Beirut in 1982. Israel's Defence Minister Ariel Sharon had given Israel's Christian militia allies the green light to enter the camps to root out Palestinian gunmen, thinking, Sharon later said, that he had an American green light to do so. The camps were defenceless and the Christian Lebanese Forces were out for revenge for the assassination of President-elect Bashir Gemayyil, who was idolized by his followers. For letting the militia in and, later testimonies have suggested, actively facilitating days of carnage, Sharon was forced to resign in disgrace. Sharon had masterminded the Israeli invasion as part of a grand plan to force the Palestinian revolutionary movement out of Lebanon and back to Jordan, with its Palestinian majority population, where they would overthrow the ruling Hashemite family and establish the state of "Palestine". It was primarily the Lebanon debacle which made of Sharon a hate figure in the Arab world, someone who on his return to politics in the late 1990s Arab cartoonists would regularly depict with devil horns and a tail.

America and Israel: cultural soul-mates

The existence of a special relationship between the United States and Israel has never been lost on Arab political classes but in recent years the information has been revolutionized, consumerized and made available to all by the new Arab televisual media. The Arab media age means that much of what was once the stuff of legend and conspiracy theory is now a quantifiable fact: the long era of suspicion over whether and why the United States likes Israel so much has given way to a clearer picture of the facts, however displeasing they may be for Arabs.

Now that Arab publics are more aware of the extent and nature of American thinking and politics, they are hardly any less convinced that Washington's political culture is more sympathetic to the Israelis than the Palestinians. Arabs are often pilloried for their conspiracy theories, but influential American writers have been quite blunt about the United States' backing for the Israelis over the Arabs. "Indeed, while the US public is skeptical about foreign aid in principle, a review of 40 years of history shows that 'most Americans strongly support' economic and military aid to Israel. Conspiracy theorists tend to ignore these inconvenient details," writes Daniel Pipes in *The Hidden Hand*.[7] He continues: "Middle Eastern perceptions of Israel's place in the world suggests that, even after a century of Zionist enterprise, Muslim peoples cannot understand the Jewish state's relations with the Western world. As Muslims, they fail to understand the emotional resonance of a common Bible and a host of Judeo-Christian features. As Middle Easterners, they cannot see beyond the clash of nationalisms to comprehend shared interests between countries. As citizens of authoritarian states, they miss the importance of personal, cultural, and political bonds between free peoples."[8] A strong supporter of Israel and *bete noire* of Arab-American and Muslim groups, Pipes is an influential figure among the constellation of experts forming opinion in the United States about the Arab world. Controversially, he was appointed by Bush in 2003 to the board of a federal think-tank, the US Institute of Peace. The peoples of the region do not have to look far back into the past to recognize the hand of foreign nations in their affairs; in fact, most Arab countries have school history curricula that glorify the act of throwing off this foreign yoke and employ it as a legitimator of current regimes. As veteran American diplomat William Polk has written: "When outsiders sneer at Middle Eastern paranoia, Iraqis, Iranians, and others speak of history."[9]

The Arab world has plenty of responses to the arguments used to justify the close American link to Israel. From an Islamic perspective, the sense of common bond of history and tradition between Christianity and Judaism is hard to understand, since Islam emerged from the same Semitic, monotheistic tradition as its two predecessors, and in fact from a purely theological perspective, Islam and Judaism are considerably closer to each other than either are with Christianity (in the primacy of religious law). Yet, culturally, European Christianity and European Jewry were forged in the same crucible, and both can claim a central role in the march of modern science in the West and the victory of secularism. There was dismay in the Arab world when then Secretary of State Colin Powell described the United States as "Judaeo-Christian" in an American television interview in 2003, and the comments served to confirm the view, proffered publicly by the likes of Pipes, that the United States was not an impartial player in its efforts to mediate an end to the Israeli-Palestinian conflict.[10] Some Arab commentators had hoped that when the Bush administration came to power in 2001 its close personal and political bonds with the government of Saudi Arabia would have a positive impact on its attitude towards the conflict. Even American commentators expressed concern at the time that an administration with crude oil connections to the Saudis could signal a pro-Arab shift away from the Clinton administration's approach. The fact that it did not just proved that America was biased and Arab rulers treacherous. Arab regimes, essentially weak before American power, would rather their peoples were kept in the dark about the complex political web connecting themselves, Washington and Israel. When Egyptian novelist Ahdaf Soueif was commissioned by Britain's *The Guardian* to visit the occupied territories a few months into the second Palestinian uprising, it was a voyage of discovery for Soueif into the heart of a dispute about which she in fact knew very little, as she confessed in subsequent articles which were directed at a British audience.[11]

Intellectual debate in the Arab media has delved a little further into the ideas put forward by Pipes to ask what lies at the root of the American sympathy with Zionism. On one level, they see a skilful and orchestrated long game played by Israel and its supporters over many decades to entrench their views in American politics and public consciousness: If Bernard Lewis has posed the question "where did they go wrong?", the Arabs are asking themselves "what did Zionism do right?" But beyond that, something about Zionism must resonate with America's own historical experience, intellectuals wonder. The answer is that the United States too began life as a settler society with a set of Utopian aims guiding its spirit. As the biblical tale depicted Jewish tribes fleeing tyranny in Egypt and streaming into their promised land, the new Israel, the settlers abandoned Europe with its class division, social iniquity and political tyranny to establish a new society guided by British rule of law and a Protestant work ethic where hard graft and whatever God-given ability the individual was blessed with would reap their rewards. As Samuel Huntington starkly puts it in his 2004 examination of America's changing identity *Who Are We?*, "nothing was allowed to come in the way of the dream and the desire for land, long inhabited by others, that it inevitably entailed". The native Indian population of America was decimated as the United States formed and expanded and pushed westwards throughout the nineteenth century. "The settlers concluded that expulsion and/or extermination were the only policies to follow in the future. The possibility of a multicultural society in America was extinguished and was not to be revived for three hundred years," Huntington writes.[12]

When Arabs look at the Zionist movement that began over a century ago, they see the history of European colonization of America and destruction of the weaker indigenous society, so they also see the reasons why America would sympathize with Israel. Thus, the Palestinians have been dubbed bitterly "the Red Arabs". "What is happening is frightening, and it is the natural consequence of a state established on ethnic-religious lines whose representatives think they are the best and the closest to God, and those who do not belong to them must be removed en masse for them to take their place … Isn't this what lay at the core of Hitler's Nazism? Isn't this the essence of the war of extermination [Ariel] Sharon, his government and the Israeli war machine is waging now?" celebrated Egyptian novelist Gamal al-Ghitani has written, coining the phrase "Red Arab".[13] In this analysis, which was elaborated by the late Palestinian-American academic Edward Said, the Arabs have been systematically devalued through a derogatory discourse about their culture, propagated by Israel's American supporters, a discourse which has laid down the ground for the further physical removal of Palestinians one day, should the situation demand it. Israeli historian Benny Morris has also drawn the comparison to the fate of the indigenous Americans, saying: "Even the great American democracy could not have been created without the annihilation of the Indians. There are cases in which the overall, final good justifies harsh and cruel acts that are committed in the course of history."[14]

When mass immigration to America began in the latter nineteenth century, those immigrants were expected to adapt to Anglo-American culture and its Anglo-Protestant political and cultural values. White immigrants became Anglo-Saxon by default. In Israel, Jews from around the world are fed into a society with a particular political and cultural mould, held together by the resuscitated Hebrew language, Jewish religion and a historical memory of persecution in Europe nursed with cultic devotion. Where America's white intellectual elite, of whom Huntington is a good example, fear that the multi-culturalism dominant since the 1960s could allow Hispanic culture to challenge their country's Anglo-Protestant identity, Israel fears that the Arabs in its midst – both the citizens and the occupied – are a threat to its defining Jewish identity. The Arabs who remain could well prove to be Israel's Achilles' heel. It is a fear the Israeli Right in particular has focused on in its relations with American politics since the second Palestinian uprising launched in 2000. The Palestinian claim to a right of return in particular is seen as an attempt to dismantle the state of Israel as it is currently constructed. In fact, for the Israeli Right, the precept of the Olso peace process – that all the territories occupied in 1967 could theoretically be given over to a Palestinian state – is in itself a threat to Israel's survival. Not only because the return of the settlers to Israel proper could provoke a civil war but also because such a Palestinian state, swollen by millions of Arabs and Muslims pouring into East Jerusalem to visit its holy sites, would possess far too much dynamism and confidence vis-à-vis a cowed and rather depressed Israel, whose own Palestinian regions form a smooth geographical continuum with the northern end of the West Bank. White America's fear of being swamped by Mexican immigrants reflects Israel's fear of being swamped by Palestinians who are already 20 percent of Israel proper and 40–45 percent of the whole population of historical Palestine, all of which is under Israeli control. If Spanish-speaking Mexicans are "a major potential threat to the cultural and possibly political integrity of the United States", to quote Huntington, the Palestinians are a far worse threat to Israel. They do not seek assimilation and, if they did, they would not get it.[15] There are even striking similarities in the cliches employed by Anglo-Americans about Hispanics and by Israelis against Palestinians. While Arab culture is characterized by IBM – "inshallah", "bokra" and "mumkin" ("God-willing", "tomorrow" and "maybe") – the Mexicans have "the *manana* syndrome".

For Arabs, Israel remains intent on depopulating historical Palestine of its Palestinians and with American complicity, and if Israel had the Peel Commission as a framework for action before 1948 (the British Commission proposed moving Arabs to allow a Jewish state in part of Palestine), now it has Bush's road map. Arabs suspect in American support for Israel admiration for a perceived proven racial superiority, a sense that if Palestinian-Arab society and culture has shown itself to be the weaker, then it does not deserve to impede the inexorable march of the superior Israeli society. In other words, might is right. If Zionism had managed to organize the growth of a successful urban society in Palestine under British Mandate control, and then succeeded in developing a modern, democratic state, then it deserves American support. Selama Nemat, a well-known Jordanian op-ed writer in *al-Hayat*, writes: "Israel, the regional superpower, thinks that just like Washington, the global superpower, it does not need to convince international opinion of its point of view. Why shouldn't Israel, just like America, change ruling regimes and redraw political maps so long as it has the power to do so? And just as Washington helps keep Israel above the law, it might also allow it to apply the law of the jungle, so long as its behavior doesn't undermine or detract from American interests."[16] Israel has in fact borrowed much from the conquered, in terms of food, language and popular culture. The Arab media often pines over the "Israelization" (*asrala*) and "Hebrewization" (*'abrana*) of Palestinian youth inside Israel proper and puts Israel's absorption of Arab elements down to simply a process of "theft" in tune with the loss of territory to the settler state.

The cult of the suicide bomber

When the first Intifada broke out in 1987, the Palestinians' front line of defence was nothing more than teenagers wielding stones, and it was the power of this striking image of weak versus strong and of Israel as a human rights abuser of an oppressed people – soldiers breaking teenagers arms to stop the stones – that brought huge international attention to the conflict, and even some White House sympathy for the Palestinians. But the entry of the suicide bomber into the equation was to monumentally change the face of the conflict. While it was part of a wider movement of socio-political action that obliged the international community to address the situation of the Palestinians, the suicide bomber came to define American attitudes to the conflict itself. Hamas developed the tactic in order to create what they considered a "balance of terror" before Israel's huge military machine. Palestinian researcher Khaled Hroub explains their thinking: "In order to justify the logic of targeting civilians, Hamas repeatedly asserts that the balance of power has always been in favour of Israel because of American backing and that there is no comparison between its military might and Palestinian weakness."[17] Hroub cites one Hamas leader who offered a comparison to Britain's justification for carpet bombing of German cities during the Second World War, which the allies resorted to because they could not confront Hitler conventionally, army against army.

There are three levels of controversy involved in Hamas tactics: attacking civilians, attacking inside Israel proper and the use of suicide bombers. Most operations have involved all three aspects, in order to generate maximum impact. Hamas, which Israel had encouraged at the outset of the Intifada to counter Palestinian secular-nationalist groups, was to become Israel's *bete noire* and the two parties engaged in a tit-for-tat war that ultimately played into Israel's hands. The Israeli Right condemned Hamas' tactics as motivated simply by hatred for Jews and the idea of a Jewish state, and while in the first months of the second Intifada of 2000 international media coverage generally recognized the tit-for-tat nature of suicide attacks, Washington gradually moved towards the Israeli view (and the international media in turn stopped citing the Palestinian justifications). The use of suicide attacks inside Israel itself, not Israel inside the territories occupied in 1967, allowed Israel to present the entire Intifada as a revolt against Israel itself – a valid interpretation of Hamas policy, though not an explanation of why many, if not all, bombers are ready to give their life in this manner – and not an uprising against Israel's occupation of territory outside its internationally recognized borders. This, again, has come to be the dominant view among America's political class concerned with the conflict.

With the US administration taking this position, the brutality of the conflict has in effect brutalized Arab attitudes towards the United States. The second Intifada marked the coming of age of the independent Arabic satellite media. It was the first chance for this media, led by al-Jazeera, to put to use its newly acquired techniques and capabilities when faced with a major political event in its own backyard. It did so with great gusto, bringing home the reality of a regional war situation in a way that had never been done before. The conflict itself was one at the heart of Arab political consciousness, and it also happened to have scaled new heights of ferocity and destruction. The Intifada was urban, communal warfare comparable to the Balkans conflicts of the mid-1990s, the Chechen war and the Lebanese civil war in 1982–1983. What Arabs saw from the comfort of their living rooms (or the discomfort of slums) was one of the world's most technologically advanced armies embark upon an orgy of violence and destruction against a poorly armed people whose weapons included their own bodies and stones. That Israeli policy began in earnest in March 2002 when the army laid seige to entire towns, including Jenin. The Israeli army's policy of house demolition – long used against Palestinians for building violations, appropriation of land for military purposes or as revenge against the families of suicide attackers – took on a larger dimension, as one psychology of annihilating the enemy met another. Israeli home demolitions set the tone. From 1987 to 2005, 1,115 homes were destroyed as punishment for armed operations against Israelis, at least 1,425 homes were destroyed for military purposes in 2004–2006 and 4,148 homes from 1987 to 2005 for failing to have a permit.[18] In March 2006, the number of Palestinians killed by Israelis in the Intifada was 3,436 (not including several hundred suicide bombers) and the number of Israelis killed by Palestinians was 994. It is not known how many of the Palestinian dead were combatants or civilians.[19] Because of army blockades ("closures") of Palestinian towns and the Israeli wall under construction, Palestinian labour in Israel proper has fallen to around 35,000 from 150,000 in 2000. Around 47 percent of 3.6 million Palestinians in the territories were considered below the World Bank's "poverty line" of $2 a day to live on in 2004, compared to 20 percent in 1999.[20] Israel's economy has also climbed back from the hits it took at the beginning from the Intifada (foreign investment climbed to a record $9.7 billion in 2005 from $5.8 billion the year before), and there is no more triumphalist tone in the Arab media about the physical and psychological blow to Israel caused by the uprising.[21] American commentators often suggest that the Palestinians' is a sick society, driven by the cult of death; but Arabs cite a wider context, of four decades of colonization of Palestinian land, expropriation of their water, suppression of freedoms, jailing of tens of thousands and systematic destruction of the social and material infrastructure.

Against this background, the cult of the suicide bomber grew as hundreds of bitter and desperate Palestinians, "nationalists" as much as they are "Islamists", joined in the death frenzy. It captured the imagination of the entire Arab world to the extent that it became very difficult for voices opposed to suicide attacks to get a hearing. Films like the 2002 hit *Friends or Business?* glorified the suicide bomber, and gave the false impression that most attacks were against Israeli military targets. Usually it is only Islamists who offer public justification of attacks on civilians inside Israel proper. Yousef al-Qaradawi, the Egyptian cleric who speaks to the Arab world weekly through his pulpit on al-Jazeera, has often argued that Israel is a "war society" where all its citizens are in one way or another playing a role in the persecution of Palestinians, who are fair game for the Israeli army, whether armed or unarmed, simply by existing on territory Israel wishes it could have entirely for itself. Whatever theorizing Islamists offer, the Arab public at large focuses on the individual who is desperate enough to give his life for the Palestinian cause against an enemy who considers his existence a threat. One often hears this view aired in the media. Ramadan Shalah, the general-secretary of Islamic Jihad, said after an attack in the Israeli town of Netanya in July 2005. "The Netanya bomber was 18 years old: Did I force him to do it? It was his choice. He wanted to martyr himself. You know what life has become worth today in Palestine. I condemn the killing of civilians in London and New York but not in Netanya because the victim is sitting on my land," he said.[22] Egyptian feminist Nawal al-Saadawi, the darling of the Western media for her critiques of Muslim fundamentalism and patriarchical Arab society, told BBC television that Palestinians felt they had nothing left to defend themselves with but their bodies.[23] Echoing the same view, celebrated Palestinian poet Sameeh al-Qasim said: "I'm not an expert in fatwas, and both sides have their justifications, but what concerns me is that Arabs – Palestinians – feel impelled to give their own life in this manner."[24] Public discourse in the Arab world compared the Palestinian struggle to that of Algerians of 1955–1962 against not only French control, but French *colons* living among them in a land they had come to consider their own. As Lebanese columnist Jihad al-Khazen bluntly put: "We, Arabs and Muslims, believe that Hamas, Islamic Jihad and others are national liberation movements, and that Ariel Sharon's government practices are full-scale terrorism."[25]

"Ethnic cleansing"

Intellectuals seeking to explain and understand the suicide tactic depict it as a product of the unique circumstances faced by Palestinians in an abnormal communal conflict – the last, desperate line of attack from a people dealing with an ideology that seeks to "ethnically cleanse" Palestine of everything non-Jewish. It is certainly not viewed as the unique product of Islam as a religion; rather, the oppressed are considered as having searched within their own religious-cultural tradition for a response to an existential threat which has reduced their society to its most precarious state since the hundred-year war with Zionism began. In other words, any religious tradition could produce a suicide bomber, given the right circumstances. Of course, the Palestinians were not the first. There have been other examples in modern history, from Japanese kamikaze pilots to the Tamil Tiger movement in Sri Lanka, which, though Hindu, was secular-nationalist in inspiration. It was in fact the Tamil Tigers who invented the "suicide belt".[26] Arabs admire the suicide option as the response of the politically or materially weak, yet culturally extremely strong, against an "overwhelming force", to use Pentagon parlance, that is intended to crush them. It is this very basic subversion of Israeli and American military power – obtained at vast expense – which inspires the Arab world in their admiration of the Palestinians.

How realistic is the Palestinian fear of extermination? Historical research has shown that the displacement of over 700,000 Palestinians from their homes during the 1947–1949 war in Palestine was largely engineered by Israeli forces and had essentially nothing to do with Arab governments telling them to run. Israel's "New Historians" used archive material available 30 years after the events in question to challenge the wisdom that the Palestinian refugee issue was not the unfortunate side-effect of Zionism's battle against Arab armies who asked Palestinians to leave to allow them to finish off the fledgling state. Zionist leaders planned to remove Palestinians to make their state viable, and, as further research is showing, continued to eschew peace in the 1950s and 1960s. Years before the war, David Ben-Gurion, Israel's hero-founder, wrote of expelling the Arabs in order to set up Israel and after the 1936 Palestinian revolt Britain's Peel Commission publicly advocated moving Palestinians en masse from coastal areas to make way for a Jewish state.[27] Yet, perhaps because it has been Israelis themselves undertaking this controversial rereading of history, the Arab world has been slow to publicize and discuss it. Perhaps the wound is too deep.

Today, Israeli politics knows numerous euphemisms for ethnic cleansing. The term "transfer" has been a feature of the Israeli political lexicon since Ben-Gurion's day. The English "transfer" was the favoured term of leading Moledet Party figure Rehavam Zeevi, who was assassinated by Palestinians in October 2001. Others used Hebrew phrases such as "voluntary transfer", Moledet's slogan in the 2001 Israeli elections, or "transfer by consent". Some on the Israeli Right began to talk openly of "transfer by war" in 2002, when the Likud Party government of Prime Minister Ariel Sharon (in office 2001–2005) included ministers who favoured this solution. An Israeli opinion poll in 2002 showed 46 percent of respondents backed "transferring" Palestinians out of the West Bank and Gaza Strip as an acceptable option to the Palestinian-Israeli conflict.[28] The idea of "transfer" retains respectability in intellectual circles, and even Benny Morris, the Israeli revisionist historian who began the movement of "post-Zionist" research into the darker side of Zionism's past with his *The Birth of Palestinian Refugee Problem, 1947–1949*, argues that "transfer" would be justified if Palestinians became a threat to Israel's Jewish majority, an argument he began to put forward vociferously in a number of interviews after the second Palestinian uprising erupted.[29] Here is one example. "There are circumstances in history that justify ethnic cleansing. I know that this term is completely negative in the discourse of the 20th century, but when the choice is between ethnic cleansing and genocide – the annihilation of your people – I prefer ethnic cleansing ... A Jewish state would not have come into being without the uprooting of 700,000 Palestinians. Therefore it was necessary to uproot them. There was no choice but to expel that population."[30] Morris went on: "From April 1948 [when the fighting entered a decisive, intense period], Ben-Gurion is projecting a message of transfer. There is no explicit order of his in writing, there is no orderly comprehensive policy, but there is an atmosphere of [population] transfer. The transfer idea is in the air. The entire leadership understands that this is the idea. The officer corps understands what is required of them. Under Ben-Gurion, a consensus of transfer is created ... Ben-Gurion was right. If he had not done what he did, a state would not have come into being. That has to be clear. It is impossible to evade it. Without the uprooting of the Palestinians, a Jewish state would not have arisen here." Due in no small part to Morris' research in the 1980s, this version of the Palestinian dispersal has become generally accepted by scholars.

The "Israeli Arabs" – the Palestinians who remained within the borders of what became Israel in 1948 – shared this fear no less after fighting broke out in the territories in September 2000. These Palestinians are often referred to as a "time bomb" in Israel because they have exploded demographically at a faster rate than the Jewish population. The remaining 150,000 Arabs left in what became Israel in 1948 are today pushing 1.5 million, representing at least one fifth of Israel's population. "Now we hear about a party who was only recently in government, Moledet, announcing its aim to gladly deport the Arabs. Benny Alon [then Moledet Party leader] says 'the universities should be closed in their faces, we make their lives so bad that they conclude that leaving is the best choice'. There are politicians in Likud too who say from time to time that if we don't behave as they wish, what happened to our brothers in 1948 will happen to us: deportation," wrote Salem Jubran, editor of the Israeli Arab weekly *Al Ahaly*.[31] "Incitement against Arabs is just one symptom of the general crisis in Israel. There are racist and anti-democratic forces which are against the peace movement in Israel and against the media in general."

Morris has attracted much attention, in the West and Arab world, because he expressed with such frankness opinions that many suspect the Israeli Right of holding. He has suggested that Palestinian fury against Israel is exaggerated in comparison to the responses of other wronged peoples in recent history, thus leaving the way open for putative pathological, psychological drives in Arab and Islamic culture that explain resistance to Israel, including suicide bombing. "The peoples of Africa were oppressed by the European powers no less than the Palestinians were oppressed by us, but nevertheless I don't see African terrorism in London, Paris or Brussels. The Germans killed far more of us than we killed Palestinians, but we aren't blowing up buses in Munich and Nuremberg. So there is something else here, something deeper, that has to do with Islam and Arab culture," he has said.[32] The Arab media has picked up on the such themes in American public debate. In an interview with *New York Times* columnist Thomas Friedman on al-Jazeera, presenter Hazem Mirazi asked: "You are accused of racism in presenting Arabs as having some inherent incapacity to be part of the modern world. How can Ahmed Zewail [Egyptian Nobel Prize in Chemistry winner] get the Nobel prize and Muslims in India do so well if Islamic culture is backward?" Friedman responded: "Maybe it's the regimes, maybe it's the culture that is resistant to these trends."[33] Friedman cited Dubai, Jordan, Qatar, Bahrain and Morocco as Arab localities that showed evidence of being consonant with modern society. In the Arab view, these opinions form part of a racist discourse that goes at least some way to explaining the abuses committed by American soldiers in Iraq, at Abu Ghraib prison and elsewhere (see Chapter 4). In the Arab world, the idea of a "clash of civilizations", advanced by Huntington in his book of the same name, springs from the same desire to demonize Arab culture. Huntington argued that, in the post-Cold War world, the main challenge to the predominance of liberal Western democracies would come from Islamic and Chinese cultures, which are seen as fundamentally averse to liberal democracy. "The survival of the West depends on Americans reaffirming their Western identity and Westerners accepting their civilization as unique, not universal, and uniting to renew and preserve it against challenges from non-Western societies," he wrote.[34]

Since the uprising of 2000, the Arab world has woken up to the Palestinian fear of mass expulsion. This is partly because some Arabs governments had an interest in making sure there was no new exodus of people. Arab leaders in countries bordering Israel and the occupied territories are particularly concerned, and Egypt's President Mubarak even raised the issue publicly. "Don't start thinking that you can expel the Palestinians out to Jordan or anywhere else. It will be the biggest danger for Israel if you did it," he said in an interview broadcast on Israeli television.[35] Egypt and Jordan, in particular, worried during the early period of the second Intifada that Israel's right-wing government under Ariel Sharon would try to escalate the conflict to a war situation, allowing Israel to create a refugee flow into either country, and thus leaving a Palestinian population small enough for Israel to handle with "citizen" status in a new greater Israel that would include the annexed territories. When Israel first began imposing economic blockades on the Palestinian territories, Jordan reacted by closing its own borders for fear that just such an exodus would be the result. Every time the Arabs entered into military confrontation with Israel, the Palestinians suffered a loss of territory and were forced to move – 78 percent of historical Palestine came under Zionist control in 1948, and the other 22 percent fell into Israeli hands in 1967. Thus, Jordan and Egypt have every interest in maintaining a semblance of civil relations with Israel, promoting dialogue between the parties, and if not bringing the Intifada to an end, at least denuding it of anything more than symbolic resistance to Israel's occupation.

For Arabs, Palestinians are engaged in a vicious battle for survival against an unscrupulous foe in the form of an Israeli Right which, despite divisions, is essentially inspired by Ariel Sharon, the man the Arabs called "the bulldozer" because of his policy of removing Palestinian communities to make way for the construction of Israeli settlements in their stead. Only modern media, global interconnectedness and Israel's image as a Western country that shares Western values on democracy and human rights, have prevented Sharon from following the path of great Middle Eastern destroyers of yore like the Assyrians or Babylonians, flattening towns, deporting populations and imposing new realities on the intransigent peoples of the Levant, or of Sharon's contemporaries such as Hafez al-Assad, whose Syrian troops crushed a rebellion in Hama in 1982. The American will to limit Israeli ambitions is in question for Arab commentators. "Sharon may be able to destroy whole Palestinian districts, rendering homeless thousands of families. He may even succeed in striking or deporting the Palestinian Authority [leaders]. But try as he might he will never restore calm or security to Tel Aviv's streets. The Intifada will go on," Egyptian columnist Ihsan Bakr says.[36] "The Palestinian people are never likely to surrender. They will use every weapon they have, modest though it may be, in their war against Sharon. Stones cannot defeat tanks, nor can small arms ever match American-made jet fighters. Still, the Palestinians will not give in." The Palestinian capacity to endure – *al-sumoud* – has been part of the Arab nationalist lore of resistance since the Nasserist era. The word *sumoud* is instantly recognizable for these political connotations to any Arab.

Arab attempts to influence America

The second Palestinian Intifada has been a salutary experience for the Arab world. It has forced Arabs to undertake a serious appraisal of the American views towards them and consider how to make themselves heard better in the United States. Two bodies of opinion have emerged on the central question of the nature and efficacy of violent resistance, the issue which Washington has made central to the conflict. Islamists and Arab nationalists say continued resistance to the Israelis, including suicide bombing, is the correct path and the only language Israel understands, while most governments and liberal opposition believe the direct challenge to Israel via taking up arms has not worked and the Arabs must concentrate their efforts on courting Washington and international opinion to force Israel to surrender the territories its seized in 1967. A number of intellectuals have publicly promoted dialogue with Israelis since the 1970s, including Egyptian Nobel Laureate Naguib Mahfouz, Egyptian actor Omar Sherif, Egyptian playwright Ali Salem and Syrian-Lebanese poet Adonis, not to mention prominent academics now based in the United States such as the Iraqi Kanan Makiya and the Lebanese Fouad Ajami. Most of these "normalizers", as they are dubbed, have suffered harsh treatment in the Arab world and are accused of using moderate attitudes towards Israel to gain an audience in the West.

Adonis was expelled from the Arab Writers Union in 1996 for meeting with Israeli intellectuals and Egyptian political scientist Sana Hasan was divorced by her high-ranking diplomat husband Tahseen Bashir as she conducted research for her book *Enemy in the Promised Land: An Egyptian Woman's Journey into Israel* in the 1970s. There was a minor controversy in Arab literary circles in 2002 when an Israeli publishing house sought publishing rights to translate Arabic novels into Hebrew, though in fact the publisher was a left-winger who wanted to educate the Israeli public about the Arab world.

Celebrated Saudi novelist Abdel-Rahman Munif summed up the dominant view when he wrote that not only was Israel the bridge to Washington for countries like Turkey and India, it was in many ways the arbiter of what was and was not worthy and acceptable in Arab culture for Western consumption. Arab writers who deal with the West find themselves having to conform to certain images and demands, he said. They might "make the visit [to Israel], offer an apology, or place Jewish characters in their work to show tolerance, good intentions and appease Jewish feelings", he wrote. "There are constant [Israeli] attempts to take the shortcomings of Arab culture and make them the defining features of this culture, thus encouraging both Arab and Western researchers to focus on these angles at the expense of others. Israel has an opinion on what should and shouldn't be studied in Arab culture."[37]

However, only a few writers have gone so far as to accept Zionism's original claim to at least part of Palestine as a state for the exclusive enjoyment of the world's Jews. Lebanese political writer Fouad Ajami has stood out in this regard, writing in his *The Dream Palace of the Arabs* that "the Zionist political enterprise has been vindicated".[38] Ajami also notes that some of the Egyptian "Pharaonic movement" intellectuals in the early decades of the twentieth century were sympathetic towards Zionism. Playwright Tewfik al-Hakim (1902–1966), as Ajami notes, once wrote: "Unlike the British and the Dutch who had colonized Southern Africa without having any historic links with that region, the Zionist who settled Palestine was returning to a homeland he had inhabited in the past."[39]

Controversy over the third Arab Human Development Report (AHDR) highlighted the difficulty in getting Arab opinions on America's penchant for Israel into the mainstream media. After heaping lavish praise on the first two such United Nations reports because of their stark portrayal of the need for political, economic, religious and educational reform throughout the Arab world, the Bush administration baulked at a draft version of the third – the first to come out after Iraq invasion – in which the authors, Arab intellectuals and reformers, said they saw no significant advances towards democracy in the region and linked this to the Israeli occupation of the Palestinian territories and the American occupation in Iraq. The United States was joined in this effort to hold back the report by the government of Egypt, which also did not like the criticisms of Arab reform (the Egyptian and other Arab governments had been no less keen on the first and second reports). The third report came out at least three months late in April 2005 with a disclaimer in the preface by the United Nations Development Programme's (UNDP) Administrator Mark Mallock Brown. "The very process of writing this AHDR has been a source of significant public and, unfortunately, highly politicised and often inaccurate speculation," he wrote.[40] "Some of the views expressed by the authors are not shared by UNDP or the UN ... [But] this report clearly reflects a very real anger and concern felt across the region," he added.

What did the report say? That the occupations gave Arab governments an excuse to postpone democratization, forced Arab reformers to divert some of their energies away from reform and strengthened extremist groups which advocate violence. The United States also undermined the international system by repeatedly using or threatening to use its United Nations Security Council veto, enabling Israel to build new Jewish settlements on occupied territory, confiscating land in the process and continue with its barrier in the West Bank, it said. In its analysis of the roots of authoritarianism in the Middle East, the writers cited the discovery of oil, the creation of Israel, the phenomenon of client states during the Cold War and the fragile and unnatural nature of most of the Arab states created during the decolonization period. The authors in effect challenge the current thinking in vogue in Washington, that solving the Israeli-Palestinian conflict should follow on from solving the problem of dysfunctional Arab states: "What has led Arab democratic institutions – where they exist – to become stripped of their original purpose to uphold freedom? The answers are not cultural – as some foreign analysts allege – but political, the authors argue, citing the decades-long imposition of 'emergency powers' by authorities across the region, the systematic suppression of independent courts and parliaments, and the 'double standard' of foreign powers which they say have accepted or even encouraged authoritarian rule in exchange for political stability and access to energy supplies."[41]

The attempt around the Arab world to effect American policy through a boycott of all things American showed the limits of what was possible in this regard. It was provoked by the administration's acquiescence in the massive Israeli military operations it began in 2002, and moves to prevent the UN Security Council condemning Israel for them (this was because the Arab group at the Council consistently refused to equate Palestinian suicide bombings with these large-scale Israeli military operations). Spread via the Internet, mosque sermons, fliers and mobile phone messages, the boycott gathered force against famed American consumer products. "Boycott America from Pepsi cans to Boeing," the website of popular cleric Yousef al-Qaradawi declared. Billboards in Damascus showed horrific scenes of Israeli troops razing the Jenin refugee camp, with the slogan "Boycott American products – Don't be an accomplice" in Arabic and English. Tabloid newspapers published lists of companies to be avoided and put out the idea such as that Pepsi, for example, is in fact an acronym for "pay every penny to save Israel". In response, a whole host of products and services are being touted on different Arab television channels as possessing "Arab authenticity" (*al-asala al-arabiyya*). Egypt's Americana ad agency, set up in the 1970s when all things American were the rage, now signs off its ads on television with the phrase "100 percent Arab". This rising anti-Americanism was also tied to the reports of treatment of Arabs and Muslims in the United States in the aftermath of September 11. Without government support, the boycott had little success in hurting the US economy. Total American exports to the Middle East amounted to $20 billion in 2000, just 2.5 percent of the US total. At the same time, Gulf Arab wealth in particular was massively invested in the West and the United States. There were some hits though: British supermarket chain Sainsbury had to close down newly opened mega-stores in Egypt after persistent rumours throughout 2001 that it was "pro-Israeli" affected sales badly, and sales of Proctor & Gamble's washing powder "Ariel" suffered because it carried the first name of Sharon. Opponents argued that many recognizable American brand names are actually franchises in the Arab world, and boycotting the product only threatens the jobs of local owners of the franchise and their employees.

Interestingly, one line of approach that no Arab constituency has so far followed, even at the level of intellectual debate, is to focus on finding support with elements outside the Anglo-Saxon core in the United States which defines state attitudes and directs public discourse on the Arab-Israeli conflict. The Arab world has yet to grasp the fact that Israel is specifically White America's fantasy: Why should Hispanic or black America automatically back Israel to the detriment of the Palestinians? Some 50 percent of America is defined by Huntington in his study as of "immigrant origin". They are expected to sign up to the political canon of interests and beliefs held by the Anglo-Saxon elite. Israel has succeeded in making itself a part of that canon, as the views of Ajami or *Newsweek International* editor Fareed Zakaria, respectively, of Arab and Indian Muslim origin, tend to demonstrate. Hispanic America in particular could have many reasons for thinking otherwise. The wave of Hispanic immigration from Mexico into the United States marks the return of the indigenous North American Indian population decimated by the European settlers, but speaking Spanish. Hispanic Americans have every cause to perceive a connection between white America's fear of "Mexica" and Israel's fear of "Isra-stine". Arabs have only to look south of the US border to find proof that it is possible: The Palestinian cause has long been popular in south and central America where there are significant Palestinian diaspora communities. Brazil hosted South American and Arab leaders in a 2005 summit to strengthen economic and political links between the two blocs. But typically, the initiative did not come from the Arab side, where regimes sent low-level delegations with orders to tread lightly for fear of a negative reaction in Washington.

The Arab world found in Palestinian leader Mahmoud Abbas, who succeeded Yasser Arafat as president of the Palestinian Authority in 2004, a civilian leader who could articulate a moderate line that American politicians and television audiences could appreciate (though he chooses to speak publicly in network-unfriendly Arabic). Bitter experience turned Abbas from a radical revolutionary into a sober politician. In 1983, he wrote that Zionism could only be stemmed through all-out assault. "The human element is forever the most difficult problem, one that America itself cannot solve satisfactorily in the required shape and size; it constitutes the Achilles heel of the Zionist project ... [Hence] All military operations should target population centers to inflict the greatest magnitude of losses on the enemy by striking its most precious possession," he said.[42] "The first and last duty of every Palestinian gun is to head toward the occupied land to expel its Zionists from the battlefield with all available, legitimate, and possible means and to target the human being, then the human being, then the human being." But Abbas told al-Arabiya in April 2005 that the idea that Arabs wanted to "throw the

Jews into the sea" had never been true, and he was welcomed with open arms by the White House as a statesman worthy of talking to. Having concluded that the two-state solution could soon be dead if the United States lets events continue to slip in that direction, Abbas announced that the era of the suicide bomber is almost finished. "I believe it is over," he said.[43] "We have started to deal with the culture of violence, we stopped the culture of violence and the Palestinian people have started looking at it as something that should be condemned and it should stop."

With Abbas, there was hope among some Arabs – tired governments and the democrats – that the Palestinians could now be taken seriously again by Washington, hopes destroyed by harsh reality when Palestinians suffering inside the occupied territories voted the Islamist group Hamas to power in 2006 legislative elections. Egyptian analyst Maamoun Fandy, one of the Arab liberal democrat lobby based in the United States, said Palestinians were politically "maturing". "I met the President [Abbas] and I heard from him and others that there is a fundamental shift that has taken place in the way the White House deals with the Palestinians under Abbas leadership compared to before. We now have a man of state in Abbas, and not a paramilitary leader. With Mahmoud Abbas the paramilitary adolescence has turned into the maturity of statesmanship," he wrote.[44] "I say to President Bush: Palestine could be the democratic example you are looking for the region and it might come quicker than it will in Iraq. If America had spent on Palestine a quarter of what it has spent in Iraq it would already have its model." There is a sense among intellectuals like Fandy that the Arab world has become trapped by its own rhetoric and that no one dare say honestly that it is time to stop fighting because it has not worked. During the second Intifada, one often heard angry comments from ordinary people on the street about the continuing violence because it was holding the region's economic fortunes to ransom. Together, the Intifada, September 11 and the war on Iraq scared tourists and business away from many countries. This was a particular blow to Egypt, with its 70 million-plus population and low per capita income, where the economy was not in a fit enough state to prevent a decline in the value of the local currency, rising prices and unemployment. Many commentators suspected that Egypt and some other Arab governments were secretly hoping for the collapse of the Hamas government, despite public rhetoric to the contrary about respecting the will of the Palestinian people in democratic elections.

Arab governments and appeasement of "Amerisrael"

What was interesting about the boycott was that it was a genuine grassroots attempt by Arab populations to circumvent the perceived ineffectiveness and even complicity of their governments in Palestinian suffering. If his government refused to challenge the United States, the man on the street would do it himself. Most Arab governments steered clear of the boycott calls, settling for downgrading or cutting ties with Israel – Egypt recalled its ambassador from Tel Aviv in November 2000, two months after the Intifada had erupted, but a new ambassador was back in March 2005 after much American pressure. Egypt's President publicly spoke out against an American boycott in December 2000. "We must examine the extent of the effect of boycotting American goods, for example, on our exports to the American market, and whether we should boycott spare parts, engines and planes, or be selective over products. The decision to boycott foreign commodities should be guided by the public interest and not romantic notions."[45]

In the view of intellectuals, this comment is typical of the stance of Arab regimes. The second Intifada – both more brutal and more visually present – engendered a new round of brow-beating about the state and fate of Arab-Islamic civilization. Intellectually, the Intifada threw the Arab world into another bout of almost obsessive depression about its inability to protect itself and maintain control of its own destiny. Egyptian novelist Sonallah Ibrahim said: "I've been very depressed and that affects what you produce. It's a feeling of extreme frustration and weakness before a very strange situation, in that there is a horrible crime being committed before you and the whole world and no one with the power dares to intervene to try to stop it. Arab governments participate in this crime in one way or another, by relying on the United States."[46] Some governments, however, blatantly abused the Palestinian cause for their own interest. Yemen's President Ali Abdullah Saleh said after the Intifada first erupted that he wished Yemen could have a direct border with Israel in order to join the fight – a comment Mubarak made amused passing reference to at an emergency Arab summit in Cairo October 2000. The TV cameras showed a guilty-looking Saleh smile with what could have been embarrassment. Yemen's high rhetoric about Palestine has served it well domestically against a backdrop of unprecedented cooperation with the United States to end the influence of radical Islamists and al-Qa'ida supporters. The CIA even killed an alleged al-Qa'ida operative in an air strike on Yemeni soil in November 2002. Two years earlier, al-Qa'ida supporters killed seventeen sailors and injured thirty-nine in a suicide blast using a small vessel that nuzzled up against the USS Cole while it was moored in Aden harbour.

Governments appear to have decided that the best way forward is to take the US administration at its word and work with it to bring about a solution to the conflict via neutralizing armed opposition to Israel and its occupation. Others argue that American and Israeli promises cannot be trusted, that resistance should continue and that Arab governments should unite in opposition to the US-Israeli alliance instead of being picked off one by one to join with it. Osama al-Baz, adviser to President Mubarak, told an Arab seminar on Israeli domestic and foreign policy in 2001 that Arabs should not despair of influencing American decision-makers, despite the access that Arabs believe they grant to well-organized pro-Israel lobbies in the United States. "However big the support for Israel of the Jewish communities in America is, America and Israel are not in the same boat. We have to differentiate between them. They don't always have the same opinions 100 percent." He went on: "Via joint interests and using the media well, European countries, companies and institutions – including Jewish institutions – can be persuaded that their real interests lie in responding to legitimate Arab rights and not sticking with Israel, right or wrong."[47]

But, by 2004, the Bush administration was openly talking about a Palestinian state as some kind of concession, a gift that would only come if its recipients worked hard to deserve it, and not as a natural right. Just days after Mubarak met with Bush in April 2004 to discuss the Gaza withdrawal plan, Bush said at a news conference in Washington that it was unrealistic to talk about Palestinian refugees returning and unrealistic to expect Israel to give back West Bank land where it had built settlements since 1967. Angry commentators on the satellite channels said Arab leaders were being humiliated; some suggested that the leaders had acceded to Bush's vision in a quid pro quo for softening his crusade for democracy and change in authoritarian Arab states. Egypt's main state-owned daily *al-Ahram* talked typically tough. "The new shift in the US policy on the Middle East peace process marks a new violation of international law and UN Security Council resolutions, and this will cause the cycle of violence to continue in the region. The US administration has offered unprecedented support to Israel, denying the right of the Palestinian refugees to return to their homeland and legitimizing the

Israeli settlements in the Palestinian territories," an editorial said.[48] It even added: "We are hopeful that the new shift in US policy will push the Arab countries to rally ranks and take a unified stance for guaranteeing the rights of the Palestinian people."

The public and the intelligentsia who are not privy to decision-making feel they have been led astray by a train of false promises, nudges and winks from their leaders that peace processes will end with justice for the Palestinians. For most, this means a return of all lands occupied in 1967 including East Jerusalem, minus the Jewish Quarter of the Old City and Wailing Wall, demands rejected by Israel's political establishment. Between 1993 and 1996, this system of silent understanding applied to the removal of the settlements, which Israel's Labour government denied would happen but which Arab leaders intimated was a dead cert, it is just that the Israelis could not admit it in public. With the renewed hope of an end to the conflict in 2005, when Mahmoud Abbas took the reins of the Palestinian leadership, this bond of hope between ruler and ruled seemed thinner than ever. Abbas has spoken of the Palestinian minimum for peace. "Peace, security and stability in the Middle East hinges on finding a just solution for a just cause based on international legitimacy, (which is) the right of our people to establish an independent state with Jerusalem as its capital and to find a just and agreed solution to the issue of refugees in line with [UN General Assembly] Resolution 194," he said in a speech broadcast to Palestinians to mark the 57th commemoration of their *nakba*, or the "catastrophe" of their dispossession in the 1948 war.[49] Palestinian officials said that despite Israeli statements about holding onto the West Bank, the Gaza pullout in September 2005 would create a dynamism for withdrawal that would spill over onto the rest of the territories in the new political playing field.

Arab governments did rally to the Palestinian leadership's defence when Yasser Arafat refused an American-mediated peace offer from Israel at Camp David in the summer of 2000. In fact, it was startling the way the writers in the state-controlled papers in Egypt, for instance, moved from ghostly silence on the talks to a sudden avalanche of writing on Arab and Muslim rights in East Jerusalem once they broke down. The same editorials were read out on countless state television programmes that discuss the daily press. Egypt and Saudi Arabia realized that, without this kind of orchestrated brouhaha over Jerusalem, they and Arafat would come across as the ones to blame for the failure of Camp David – which became the dominant theory in the United States in any case.

Time running out on two-state solution?

When Abbas met President Bush in May 2005, his message was that time is in fact running out before Israeli settlement and wall building make the two-state solution impossible to realize, and that while the Israeli Right appears to favour this denouement it will in fact lead to the end of the Israeli state in its current format as an entity exclusively for Jews. There are two contrary developments in process here: politically, the state of Israel is hardening its grip on the West Bank, East Jerusalem and Gaza Strip, but the Palestinians are an expanding demographic presence throughout that territory, as well as in Israeli itself. Israel left its Gaza settlements in September 2005, but its ultimate control over the thin, overpopulated coastal strip remains. Thus, without ethnic cleansing or a system of apartheid, Israel is set to become a mixed Arab-Jewish state. If Israel insists on maintaining its hold on areas of the West Bank – with the system of roads and army protection that involves dividing up the territory into Palestinian cantons – it is unlikely the Palestinians will accede to calling the remaining areas, which do not include East Jerusalem, a "Palestinian state". For Israeli Right-wingers and their supporters in America, the key to the current stage of the conflict lies in persuading the new Palestinian leadership to accept this version of a state. "Sharon is in the process of imposing a new relationship with the Palestinians negotiated directly with Washington that in his view will be sustainable for a generation, with or without Palestinian consent and cooperation," the Middle East Report has written about Israeli policy.[50] "Conscious as ever of domestic political calculations, and preoccupied himself with Iraq and his 'transformational' vision for the region, Bush seems almost certain to take the path of least resistance." With American acquiescence, Israel hopes to make the separation wall its eastern border with the Palestinians. The Israeli Left fears the Palestinians will not give their consent and that it will in fact lead to a third insurrection (most commentators in the Arab world suspect this is why Israel and its American ally are so keen for the Palestinian leadership to defang the armed the resistance). The Left argues that Zionism has generally overplayed its hand and overestimated the strength of its opponent – in pure military terms – and now it could fall victim to the overambition of its own dream. Winning the territory was one thing, but how to deal with the indigenous non-Jewish population has proved to be another question entirely.

There is an interesting comparison to be made to the period in history which saw the formation of Arab-Islamic civilization after the Arab conquests in the mid-seventh century AD. Islamic histories give the impression that the Middle East instantly became Arab and Muslim, and Western scholarship has until very recently accepted this version of events. In fact, most of the regions conquered by the Arabs were not ethnically or linguistically "Arab" at the moment of invasion, with the exception of the Arabian Peninsula. The Levant, including Palestine, and Iraq were ethnically similar to the Arabs of the peninsula and spoke a sister language of Arabic – various dialects of Aramaic. For the most part, they were at least nominally Christian. It took centuries for Iraq, the Levant, Egypt and North Africa to become fully Arabized and Islamized. In the first century of Arab control, "Islam" was the exclusive religion of the Arab tribes, similar to the manner in which Judaism was considered solely the religion of Jewish tribes. Islamic histories record incidents where the peasants actively sought to become "Arabs" through nominal membership of Arab tribes, thus allowing them to become Muslims and avoid special taxes on those who were not part of the ruling elite. The political transformation from the Umayyad to Abbasid caliphate represented a critical shift from Islam as an ethnic religion to Islam as a world religion. The Umayyads, based in Damascus, were defeated in 750 AD by the Abbasids, who moved the centre of the Arab-Muslim state to Iraq and their new city of Baghdad, where many nationalities, particularly Persian, mixed among the evolving Arabic-speaking population.

The Israeli state is also the product of a new religious-ethnic movement, Zionism, but it is a movement which retains an inherent resistance to accomodating its conquered peoples. Today there is no likelihood that the Palestinians will give up their Arabic language for Hebrew and lobby the elite running historical Palestine to allow them to become Jews. Israel does not want them to. Thus, as Palestinians obtain numerical parity with the Jews and threaten to outnumber them, the fundamental nature and structure of the Israeli state becomes increasingly untenable. Israel's wall through the West Bank, encircling and cutting off Palestinian communities, while attempting to bring Jewish settlements isolated in a hostile environment into the warm bosom of the Israeli state, perhaps speaks to this existential conundrum more than it does to the specific fear of the suicide bomber. Like China's Ming emperors, Israel builds a wall to keep out its barbarian hordes.

Palestinians are calling the security barrier "the apartheid wall". It is an interesting semantic usage that suggests that the psychological barrier towards demanding equal status in one state – whether it bears the name of "Israel" or otherwise – is in the process of being breached. Apartheid implies separation of that which naturally should go together. Palestinians of the occupied territories are not there yet but intellectuals are wondering it is merely a question of time. The Israeli Arabs, as the second Intifada has made clear, remain committed to the state they reside in; they have no wish to be joined to a Palestinian Authority state. Fatah leader Marwan Barghouthi brought the question up during his closing statement at his trial in Israel in 2003. "If an occupation does not end unilaterally or through negotiations then there is only one solution, one state for two people," he said in Hebrew. "The so-called security fence will not bring security. A fence of peace built by the two peoples together is what will bring them security. We have mixed up together the two peoples, masters and slaves, occupiers and subjects. Today three years have passed and I hope the Israelis have learned that the Palestinian people can not be brought to yield with force."[51] The Israeli Left, apart from a very small "post-Zionist" intellectual elite who favour the single-state option, fear such a future. Israeli peacenik Uri Avnery attacked Barghouthi for what he considered a threat and irresponsible scare tactic. "Marwan Barghouthi is not the only one who uses binationalism as a scarecrow. Lately, several Palestinian spokespersons have been waving this flag – not because they believe in it, but in order to frighten Israelis into accepting the two-states plan, which is the only realistic peace plan on the agenda," he wrote.[52] "It may seem that there are only two possibilities: One state in the whole country, which will necessarily be binational, or an Israeli state in a part of the country, inside the Green Line, next to a Palestinian state. But there is a third possibility: An Israeli state in all of the country, from which the Palestinian population will be expelled. Few Israelis speak of this openly, but a great many think about it." Avnery pointed out that, rather than Kosovo-type cleansing, Israelis pressure Palestinians to sell property with the argument that it is better to get money for it now before the authorities expropriate them for security reasons later. Many now wonder to what extent the United States, at least while Neo-Conservative thinking dominates policy-making, could allow itself to become complicitous in radical plans of the future the Israeli Right develops to ensure the de-Arabification of Palestine and survival of the Israeli state in its current configuration.

Chapter 4
The Iraq Project

Arab attitudes towards the 2003 war

The war on Iraq was not popular in the Arab world. Arab League Secretary General Amr Moussa warned it would "open the gates of hell", TV presenters rued the fall of Baghdad as the biggest disaster for Arabs since 1948 and the Arab media in its entirety was stunned to see that, five decades after the Western colonial enterprise was supposed to have been consigned to history, the foreigner could return with his armies to occupy a country that stands at the heart of the collective sense of Arab identity and shared Arab history and culture.[1] A minority of democracy advocates approved of Washington's plans, though only a few of them declared themselves in public. It became clear after the war that Iraq's Sunni Arabs, a minority strategically placed in the heart of the country who saw themselves as the traditional guarantors of Iraqi unity, were in tune with the attitudes of the wider Arab world. The majority Shi'ite Arabs and ethnic Kurdish minority – the two net gainers from the war – were not.

The Arab world shared the views of opponents of the war elsewhere in the world, with some of their own added in. The war was seen as an act of colonialism extraordinaire, which used false slogans of bringing democracy and removing a tyrant who was harbouring dangerous weapons in order to implement a grand plan to advance American geopolitical and economic interests. The war was also a favour to Israel, which formed part of that geopolitical interest, and it was Israel supporters who lobbied for and planned the war, the so-called Neo-Conservatives who had spent the best part of decade advocating the "picking off" one by one of radical opponents of Israel, namely Iraq, Syria, Lebanon's Hizbollah and the Palestinian resistance groups. Washington wanted to control Iraq's oil reserves – the second largest in the world – which could bring lucrative development contracts to American companies. The return of Iraqi oil to the world market would offer a lever against oil "kingpin" Saudi Arabia, which after September 11 had come to be seen as an enemy, not a friend. The "creative destruction" of a massive war would allow other contracts to American business in the rebuilding of a ruined land and consolidate America's position as the world's sole superpower. It would send a message to China and other potential rivals – Germany or Russia – that the United States intended to stay on top for generations to come, an argument put forward publicly and forcefully by Egyptian journalist Mohammed Hassanein Heikal in special television shows on al-Jazeera in the run-up to the war. An Iraq remodelled as a friendly democratic state would consolidate pro-Western regimes and currents in the Arab world, people who would be prepared to live in peace and normality with Israel and give up supporting the Palestinians in their resistance to an Israeli-imposed peace. The Bush administration's championing of human rights in Iraq was universally discarded as unconvincing, while there was little real consideration of whether Saddam's regime truly retained nuclear, chemical or biological weapons capability or not, or whether the stated fear of the Bush administration that such weapons could be passed on to radical Islamists was reasonable or not.

For the Arab world, the invasion was about America imposing its will on the region's unruly natives, who had proven unequal to the independence they had gained five decades ago, through a Pax Israelicana. In post-war Iraq, the debate as conducted on the satellite channels has centred on suspicions that the United States and its ally Israel want to pull Iraq out of the Arab nationalist fold into an Israeli–Jordanian–Turkish axis, mirroring the Baghdad Pact of 1950s. Amr Moussa said democracy could not be brought "on the back of tank" and Egypt's Hosni Mubarak warned the war would create "a hundred bin Ladens".[2] Central to this deep Arab resistance to the war was the long-held belief that a just solution to the Israeli-Palestinian conflict was the key prerequisite for ending the "dysfunction" in the region that sustained undemocratic military regimes and which now, post-September 11, was seen as a threat to American national security. No one liked Saddam Hussein. But as president, he was a symbol of Iraq – no matter to what lengths his propaganda had gone to exaggerate this fact – and, above all in the collective Arab view, he was *not the point*. The road to solving the region's problems passed through Jerusalem, not Baghdad. A war would aggravate anti-American sentiment and encourage radical Islam.

Regime fears over the war

Arab regimes had their own particular reasons for fearing the war. Some governments feared that if the United States was successful in Iraq, the idea of using military force to bring about change could be applied elsewhere. There was also a fear that oppressed populations would rise up either in anger at government failure to prevent the invasion or at the lack of democracy in their own countries. These theories, which were popular in the Western media at the time of the war, concerned essentially two countries, Egypt and Saudi Arabia. Egypt was the most ripe for a popular uprising and Saudi Arabia was most likely – or least unlikely – to face US military action (American concern with Syria only picked up pace after the war was over and the insurgency in Iraq began). There was a deep sense in the region that the administration's real targets after September 11 were Egypt and Saudi Arabia, the societies most seen as responsible for producing the attackers and probably, all told, the two most influential countries in the Arab world as a whole. One American think-tank report in fact advocated seizing Saudi oilfields and placing Jordan's Hashemite royal family back in charge of the holy cities of Mecca and Medina unless the Saudi royals took steps to end anti-Americanism and support for al-Qa'ida. The much-publicized presentation to the Pentagon's Defense Policy Board in July 2002 also referred to Iraq as the "tactical pivot", Saudi Arabia as the "strategic pivot" and Egypt as "the prize" if Washington was to win the Arab world to its side.[3]

Commentators close to the governments sought to calm the widespread fear that Iraq was just the beginning, arguing that Saddam's Iraq was so deviant even by Middle East standards that it could not be compared to its neighbours. Jamal Khashoggi, a prominent Saudi journalist, who later became media adviser to Turki al-Faisal, the Saudi ambassador in London and then Washington, told al-Arabiya: "The scene in Iraq couldn't be repeated anywhere again without a ruler like Saddam Hussein. The Iraqi situation is exceptional, we can't compare it with Iran or Egypt ... or a country like Saudi Arabia. This is an exceptional situation, a regime outside history and I hope Iraq returns and integrates with its brothers and neighbours."[4] The kingdom publicly opposed the war but it was an open secret that the air campaign was being conducted from the US air bases in Saudi Arabia. Ibrahim Nafie, then editor of the main Egyptian daily *al-Ahram*, did not even refer to the symbolic toppling of Saddam Hussein's statue in central Baghdad the day the city fell in his first editorial following. "Objective Arab media reporting of the unjust war against a people who are defenceless and besieged, and against an army equipped only with obsolete weaponry in Iraq, seems not to have gone well with the Americans. The reports of

Arab correspondents have exposed those in charge of running this war for what they really are – violaters of international peace," he wrote.[5] But Arab nationalist writers crowed in bitter amusement at the weakness of their leaders. Abdel-Bari Atwan, the Palestinian editor of the London-based newspaper *al-Quds al-Arabi*, wrote: "Saddam Hussein's statues will not be the only ones to go down. Other statues in other Arab capitals will follow soon. It has been demonstrated that military and security forces, however brutal, cannot protect a dictatorial regime, especially if its masters and protectors decide to change it. And we know that the British and American administrations have begun considering alternatives and mulling names in readiness for changing regimes in Egypt, Saudi Arabia, Syria and Iran."[6]

What Patrick Seale, the biographer of Syrian leader Hafez al-Assad, has described as "the Arab system" set up to defend independence in the post-colonial era was revealed for the mendacious failure it was.[7] It was for that reason that Arabs took to the streets in the protest during the war and that regimes feared their anger. The act of invading Iraq was not in itself seen as aiming to bring democracy to the Arab world. A political cartoon in Egypt's opposition *al-Wafd* newspaper showed Bush at his desk talking on the phone. "Hello, American forces command? I tell you what: don't kill all the Iraqis. Leave some alive because we are saying that we are freeing them from Saddam's rule."[8] Arab states were at pains to prove to their restive populations that they had done all they could to avert a war, but on the streets people accused their governments of political impotence and held almost daily protests, which at times turned violent. A last-minute Arab League summit held in Egypt even saw an argument between Libya's Colonel Gaddafi and Saudi Arabia's then-Crown Prince Abdullah over who was responsible for American military and political presence in the region. The row erupted when in a speech broadcast live on television Gaddafi criticized Saudi Arabia for hosting US forces since 1990, saying it had made an "alliance with the devil".[9] Abdullah, who became king in 2005, interrupted angrily, stabbing a finger at the smirking Libyan: "The kingdom of Saudi Arabia is not an agent of imperialism like you and others are. Who brought you to power? Don't speak or interfere in things which you have no luck or chance in."[10] Then he got up and walked out. The Arab leaders declined to adopt a last-minute proposal from the United Arab Emirates to call on Saddam Hussein to step down.

The regimes existing today have changed little since the years when the struggle against colonial control was very real. Mubarak is only the third leader of Egypt's republic since it was established in 1952; the Baath regimes in Syria and Iraq came to power in the 1960s, the decade in which both Hafez al-Assad and Saddam Hussein emerged as political players. The PLO under Yasser Arafat's leadership came to prominence in that same decade. Saudi Arabia, born in the crucible of the colonial era, the child of British then American imperial interests, remains Saudi Arabia, a tripartite of Saudi royal power, radical clerics and a US military guarantee-for-oil. The war transferred American political logic concerning central and south America to the Middle East; it was an unprovoked attack on an Arab country because America did not like its leader, just as previous American administrations had brought down regimes it had lost patience with in Grenada or Panama. Treating the Arab world in a similar fashion was a revolutionary shift in foreign policy and it indicated that the regimes and systems set up to maintain Arab independence after the Second World War had failed in their fundamental task of keeping the foreigner at bay. In the psychology of these regimes, true independence and their own survival had become completely fused as one.

Arab perception of "neo-colonialism"

Relations with Western countries are still viewed in the Arab world through the lens of Third World anti-colonial struggle, a struggle which has never reached a point of closure because of the state of Israel and the fundamental role the Arab-Israeli conflict has played in many Arab countries' relations with the West since independence. When the imperial powers left, the Arab world continued to observe massive intervention in its political affairs, from the CIA's plots against Nasser to propping up the Saudi regime to the war on Iraq.

So the template through which the Iraq experience has been viewed in the Arab world is decidedly historical, suffused with fear and anger. Late Palestinian-American intellectual Edward Said wrote in the *London Review of Books*: "This is the most reckless war in modern times. It is all about imperial arrogance unschooled in worldliness, unfettered either by competence or experience, undeterred by history or human complexity, unrepentant in its violence and the cruelty of its technology. What winning, or for that matter losing, such a war will ultimately entail is unthinkable. But pity the Iraqi civilians who must still suffer a great deal more before they are finally 'liberated'."[11] Some months later Hisham

Sharabi, a Palestinian academic at Georgetown University, wrote: "Resistance to the American occupation of Iraq will appear and inevitably crystallize and revolutionary explosions against the current paternalistic situation will erupt sooner or later. Although the situation in the Arab world in the foreseeable future will continue to deteriorate, something will inevitably happen in one of the three biggest, richest and strongest Arab countries, Egypt, Algeria and Iraq, or in all of them. Something that will turn the situation upside down and return the balance of forces between the Arab world and its colonial and settler enemies to their natural position."[12] In 2004, a title by US-based historian Rashid al-Khalidi (also a Palestinian), *Resurrecting Empire: Western Footprints and America's Perilous Path in the Middle East*, reflected the growing sentiment that the Iraq war and occupation were imperialism redux.[13]

There were indeed historical echoes in all this. Britain invaded Ottoman Iraq at the beginning of World War One and captured Baghdad in 1917. Facing a revolt in 1920 they brought in the Hashemite monarchy and promoted the Sunni minority as the ruling elite. The intent was to ensure a stable, friendly government because of British imperial interests in India and Iran, and growing Western interest in what oil reserves Iraq might have. When British forces under General Stanley Maude entered Baghdad in March 1917, they issued a declaration. "Since the days of Hulagu your city and your lands have been subject to the tyranny of strangers, your palaces have fallen into ruins, your gardens have sunk in desolation and your forefathers and yourselves have groaned in bondage," it said.[14]
"O people of Baghdad, remember that for 26 generations you have suffered under strange tyrants, who have endeavoured to set one Arab house against another in order that they might profit by your dissensions ... I am commanded to invite you, through your nobles and elders and representatives, to participate in the management of your own civil affairs in collaboration with the political representatives of Great Britain who accompany the British army, so that you may be united with your kinsmen in the north, east, south and west, in realizing the aspirations of your race." Maude's statement was an echo of Napoleon's words of welcome to Egyptians when he landed near Alexandria in the great French imperial mission of 1798. In his victory speech after the war, Bush also linked American national interest with the betterment of the country invaded. "In the images of celebrating Iraqis, we have also seen the ageless appeal of human freedom. Decades of lies and intimidation could not make the Iraqi people love their oppressors or desire their own

enslavement. Men and women in every culture need liberty like they need food, and water, and air. Everywhere that freedom arrives, humanity rejoices. And everywhere that freedom stirs, let tyrants fear," he said.[15] "The liberation of Iraq is a crucial advance in the campaign against terror. We have removed an ally of al-Qa'ida, and cut off a source of terrorist funding. And this much is certain: No terrorist network will gain weapons of mass destruction from the Iraqi regime, because that regime is no more." In 1958, the British-backed order collapsed in a violent coup in which the royal family and key supporters of the British-allied Hashemite regime such as Prime Minister Nouri Said were brutally murdered.

Arab governments fear the break-up of Iraq along sectarian and ethnic lines, whether by US intention or as an unintended consequences of the invasion of 2003. Their fear largely stems from the actions of Britain and France in the Levant after the First World War, when what could easily have been considered one single political and cultural entity was deliberately broken down into pieces for the sake of foreign interests. For avowed Arab nationalists, this wound is still deep, but in fact it informs the thinking of virtually all Arab political elites. "Syria is the only country in the Arab East or West that was broken up ... Over a hundred years ago the greater part of the Arabian peninsula united to become Saudi Arabia, at the beginning of the 1970s the Sheikhdoms of seven countries united as one country [the United Arab Emirates], and at the beginning of the 1990s Yemen united and held onto its unity," veteran Syrian foreign minister Farouk al-Shara, the representative of a nationalist regime, once said.[16] "Unfortunately, Syria was broken up by an English-French colonial conspiracy whose main aim was to pave the way for setting up a Jewish state in Palestine. And indeed, the Balfour Declaration came straight after the signing of the English-French Sykes-Picot agreement [which] divided Syria into four countries."

At every stage of the invasion and occupation, the Arab world has made comparisons between US policy in Iraq and Israeli policy towards the Palestinians. The Israeli attitude towards the ordinary Palestinian is mirrored in the US soldier's approach towards ordinary Iraqis – an inherent threat and an object of fear, even loathing. A senior US military official, Brigadier-General Janis Karpinski even revealed to the BBC she had come across an Israeli interrogator in a Baghdad detention centre.[17] Palestinian op-ed writer Abdel-Wahhab Badrakhan wrote in *al-Hayat*: "According to the confessions of Brigadier General Janis Karpinsky, Israelis participated as torture experts. There is no doubt that the

Americans, who planned for a long-term presence in Iraq, rely on Israel's services as a reserve force to tap into when necessary in the region."[18] Western media reports also had Israelis training Kurds in northeast Iraq, confirming a long-held suspicion in the Arab world about Kurdish contacts with Israel. The perception is widespread in the region that the new Iraqi authorities will be under pressure from the United States to normalize ties with Israel. Publicly, Iraqi officials have denied this will happen – establishing an oil pipeline from Mosul to the Israeli port of Haifa, for example – but they are generally not believed by the public at large. Al-Qa'ida in Iraq often says it has targeted hotels in Baghdad because it had information that Israeli Mossad agents were staying there. The major proponents of the Iraq war were, for sure, prominent lobbyists for right-wing Israeli interests in the United States (e.g. Paul Wolfowitz, Douglas Feith, Richard Perle) and invading Iraq had been in their sights since the mid-1990s as a magic wand for remodeling the region to Israel's benefit. Iraqi politician Mithal Alousi was ostracized after he attended a conference on democracy and terrorism in Tel Aviv in 2004. He was later the target of an assassination attempt that killed two of his sons.

When Saddam Hussein's statue was pulled down live on television screens across the region in April 2003, al-Jazeera's correspondent in Baghdad commented bitterly: "Now the future will have an American taste." There was almost no sympathy for those Iraqis – the Shi'ites and Kurds who suffered the most under Saddam Hussein's rule – who might prefer a new American reality to a continuation of the old order. The sight of Iraqis pulling down Saddam's statue with American help provoked widespread shock and disgust in the wider Arab world. One Egyptian commentator said: "This is just a continuation of the theatre that America and its propaganda organs are broadcasting. The Iraqis who fought and are still fighting in Basra, Nasiriya and Mosul are no different from the Iraqis in Baghdad. So God knows who brought these people here today, applauding the American flag being raised on this statue."[19]

Even in Saudi Arabia, where no tears were shed over the end of the hated Saddam Hussein and his secular Baath regime, people felt betrayed that the self-styled modern Saladin could not give the Americans a run for their money at the gates of Baghdad, the seat of the Abbasid caliphate established in 750 AD when Arab-Islamic civilization was at its height. "Although all my life I've wanted to see the end of Saddam's regime, I felt humiliation when I watched the US Marines site-seeing at Paradise Square in the heart of Baghdad, after they brought to the ground the biggest idol that Saddam had built for himself," wrote commentator Jaafar Abbas.[20] "Where was the battle of Stalingrad and the surprises they were preparing for the 'parasites', the 'bastards' and the 'mercenaries', as they called them?" he went on, referring to the colourful, fighting vocabulary of Iraqi Information Minister Mohamed Said al-Sahhaf. "Where was Baghdad in comparison to brave little Umm Qasr that defended its honour with dignity? What about all the millions that were spend on special forces to defend Saddam? Or was the people the only real enemy of the regime? What happened in Baghdad was a scandal and if other Arab capitals witness the same the shame will be alot worse ... Saddam has added to our list of defeats a defeat that is worse because it is infectious, in that it won't end at the gates of Baghdad."

Colonialism, for those at the receiving end of it, is in a profound sense all about derision of the other. One event in particular crystallized the instinctive feeling in the Arab world that was what the Iraq experiment amounted to – the looting of the Baghdad Museum while American troops stood idly by. Baghdad was plunged into a state of lawlessness in the immediate aftermath of the fall of the old regime. As the invading army streamed into the city on April 5, looters and well-organized thieves probably working in tandem with foreign collectors set to work, taking some 14,000 pieces, including the Lagash statue, a headless inscribed limestone statue of Eanatum, ruler of Lagash, dating to 2450 BC; large stone inscriptions from the Sumerian, Akkadian and Babylonian empires and the Nimrud lioness, an ivory sculpture of a lioness and Nubian from the city of Nimrud dating to around 800 BC. Over 5,000 pieces remain missing, but the question taxing many minds has been why no unit was given the specific mission of protecting the museum. That Iraq was one vast archaeological site was well known beforehand. Museums around the country were pillaged during the 1991 Gulf war and the Baghdad Museum had taken steps to protect and hide some items ahead of the 2003 invasion. Iraq was the home of one of the first world's first great civilizations, the Sumerians who lived in the south from around 5,000 years ago and invented cuneiform writing. They were followed by the Akkadians, Assyrians and Babylonians before the rise of super-Semitic Arab-Islamic civilization. Their empires were centred on famed cities such as Ur, Babel and Nineveh, and protecting them was considered by experts around the world as a global, and not merely an Iraqi national imperative.[21]

The robbery provoked an angry reaction around the Arab world and, in Iraq, the United States was inevitably blamed (had American troops opened fire on the looters, it may have played out just as badly in the Arab media). "America has not stopped its acts of pillage and murder. It has swept through the land and stolen the most valuable things Iraqis own – documents, manuscripts, heritage, oil and gold. It wasn't enough for America to take Iraq decades backwards, it has followed with organized theft," wrote one commentator in Egypt's *al-Wafd* newspaper.[22] "The biggest crime has been the challenge to moral customs and shunting aside Islamic laws. It has been humiliating and great since the American soldiers began feeling the bodies of Iraqi girls with the excuse of carrying out inspections. But that's not strange in this age of American whoredom!" The several weeks of looting of libraries and museums around the country were compared to the sacking of the city in 1258 by the Mongols. Already a land with over 2,500 years of recorded history when the Arab tribes arrived, Mesopotomia was a proud and learned civilization. The Arab-Islamic city of Baghdad reflected all of that, and many of the great achievements in learning of Arab-Islamic civilization were accomplished under the aegis of the Islamic state that had Baghdad, with its famed round city and its caliphs at its centre. The city's destruction is remembered bitterly to this day. Scholars of Islamic history believe the Mongol invasion stunned Iraq's development for decades if not centuries; it ruined the irrigation system as well as blowing a hole in cultural life. "Darkness fell upon the country after 1258," government guidebooks said in Saddam's time. "The people of Iraq have worked hard to rid themselves of the effect of centuries of stagnation."

Iraqis and the 2003 war

What Iraqis themselves thought of the invasion project and the United States plan for their country is a key and controversial issue that is easier to discuss in retrospect than it ever was at the time. The country is composed of generally three groups: the Arab Sunni Muslims, the Arab Shi'ite Muslims and the Kurdish Shi'ite Muslims. The Arab Sunnis form some 20 percent of the population, but are strategically located in the centre and west of the country, including Baghdad. The Arab Sunnis formed the nucleus of Saddam Hussein's regime and indeed since the Arab conquests of the seventh century AD and the rise of Baghdad in the mid-eighth century, the city and its environs – "Iraq" – have been almost uniformly Sunni-governed and Sunni in religious colour. The Arab

Shi'ites, however, are in the majority, forming some 60 percent of the population. They dominate the entirety of south Iraq up to Baghdad, barring a ring of Sunni towns to Baghdad's immediate south. Baghdad itself is a mixed city today. The Shi'ites have been largely shut out of politics in modern Iraq since the British decided to back the Sunnis as the back-bone of the state-in-making after the First World War. Britain brought in a Sunni royal family, the Hashemites from the Hejaz area of modern-day Saudi Arabia, with apparently impeccable religious credentials since they had been the guardians of the holy shrines in Mecca and Medina for 1,000 years and claimed direct descent from the Prophet Mohammad. The Kurds, a distinct ethnic group with their own Kurdish language, form some 20 percent of the population in the far north and northeast, where they border Kurdish populations in Turkey and Iran. Losers in the colonial carve-up of the Middle East after the First World War, the Kurds have retained only a half-hearted commitment to the Iraqi state, and they have been even more discouraged by the callous and brutal efforts of central government to ensure their loyalty.

Baathism and the once-strong Communist and Nasserist movements all sought to iron out these differences in the effort to create a modern state united by a common patriotic bond to the idea of Iraq. Briefly, Nasserism lost in 1958 when the Communist-leaning government brought to power by a military coup under General Abdel-Karim Qasim decided to stay out of the Egyptian-led Arab nationalist orbit. Two subsequent coups in 1963 and 1968 secured the country for the Baathist movement which in Iraq was more concerned with Arabism as a paradigm for the unity and identity of the Iraqi state, rather than as a force for merging Arab countries into one political entity. Baathism, the only one of the major ideologies of the time which really had the chance to put theory into practice, ultimately failed in this regard, though there remains a strong feeling among many secular Sunnis and some Shi'ites that the Baathist idea, even if twisted by the Saddam Hussein clan, was the most appropriate for their country.

In practice, the Kurds were often in rebellion and the persecuted Shi'ites increasingly turned to their religion as the source of solace and strength and the reference point for their sense of identity. They were further encouraged in this sentiment after the 1979 revolution in Iran, where many Shi'ite religious leaders sought refuge. The Baathist regime accused the Shi'ites of not being proper Arabs, through part Iranian origin – for the most part a patently ridiculous charge. Iran itself only became Shi'ite when the Safavid dynasty took power in the sixteenth century and made Shi'ism the state form of Islam to counter the challenge from the strong Sunni-based Ottoman empire, and the large Shi'ite presence in south Iraq simply offered Iran new vistas in the age-old Arab-Persian clash over the land of Mesopotamia, the seat of numerous Persian empires in the pre-Islamic era. Most Arab countries had backed Saddam's Iraq against Iran in the 1980–1988 Gulf war, but Syria backed Iran, since Iran was funding Hizbollah's battle against Israeli occupation in south Lebanon.

Though many educated Shi'ites will have opposed the idea of an American invasion and many educated Sunnis may have harboured some sense of relief in the final removal of Saddam ("if only" the West would live up to its human rights rhetoric, Arab democrats had been sighing years), it would be fair to say that the Sunnis opposed the war and the Shi'ites backed it, along with the Kurds. The politicians lobbying Washington for action over the years tended to be Shi'ites or Kurds, such as Ahmed Chalabi and Iyad Allawi and the Kurdish leaders Jalal Talabani and Massoud Barazani, though there were a number of Sunni ex-army officers also in conversation with US administrations. Shi'ite clerics and political Islamists such as Abdel-Aziz al-Hakim and Ibrahim al-Jaafari were meanwhile biding their time in Iran. Iraq's Sunni Arabs, like the rest of the Arab world, had a knee-jerk reaction against any foreign intervention. If the Americans wanted to "fix" the Arab world, they should start in Palestine, not in Iraq, they reasoned. Iraqi Sunnis – the core of the insurgency which was to emerge – shared the view of the rest of the Arab world that the Bush administration had come to play the classic colonial game of divide-and-rule. "The main trick of any colonial power in the world is divide-and-rule. We know it: they are trying to divide us," said Wamidh Nazmy, a politics professor at Baghdad University.[23] "The Americans would like to find leaders who believe in them, or at most who support them, when they can't. They can't have a genuine leader who will be accepted by the people and be pro-American at the same time." The Sunnis suspected that Washington did not really want capable Iraqis who would appeal to the broad base of Iraqis cutting across sectarian lines, because those are Iraqis who would not hold links with Washington close to heart and who may care more for the regional audience in the context of Arab nationalism.

Radical Sunni Islamists from around the Arab world have made common cause with Sunnis in Iraq, most notably under the al-Qa'ida aegis in a group led by the Jordanian Abu Musab al-Zarqawi (killed in 2006). In their view, the Shi'ites are not only "rejectionists" (*al-Rafida*) who follow a deviant version of Islam's true monotheistic message, they are also opportunists who were prepared to accept the occupation of their country for the sake of taking power; they were also prepared to allow another foreign power, Iran, unprecedented influence for political and ideological reasons. The broad anti-imperial aims of al-Qa'ida's ideology are shared by the Arab mainstream, both government and opposition. Jordan's King Abdullah went further than any other Arab leader by stating publicly his fears of a "Shi'ite crescent" running from Iran into south Lebanon before the democratic elections held in January 2005, the first to see Shi'ite political groups come to power.[24] Fissures later appeared between Arab governments and opposition groups over an American exit from Iraq – the governments fearing that Iraq would be vulnerable to even more Iranian influence if US forces left before fixing the political system to ensure the Sunnis more clout. By late 2005, when Arab governments showed their oppositon to a quick US withdrawal at a Cairo conference for reconciliation between the Iraqi factions, it was clear that a full-fledged civil war between Sunnis and Shi'ites was a real possibility. Nationalist and Islamist opposition groups around the region simply wanted the Americans out.

In an analysis of the political psychology of the region, Fouad Ajami, the pro-American Lebanese academic who has advocated comprehensive US-backed change around the region, has argued that Arab nationalism was and still is in essence a form of Sunni hegemony in disguise that implicitly marginalizes Shi'ites like himself – themes which exploded into the open in the sectarian violence of post-invasion Iraq. It was a fear that Shi'ites would take over the country that caused the United States to refrain from backing a Shi'ite uprising in the south in the aftermath of the 1991 Gulf war when Iraqi troops were left free to crush a rebellion that American propaganda had only weeks before encouraged. Politically aware Shi'ites have hardly forgotten, and say that their alliance with the United States now is of only a temporary and practical nature. One explained attitudes towards the United States and the Sunni accusation that the Shi'ites are "soft" on America. "People said in seances before the war that it was just bringing one Satan to get rid of another – the Americans to get rid of Saddam. The Shi'ites maybe hate the Americans more than the Sunnis. People still remember 1991 when they promised the Shi'ites, then let Saddam come in and throw them aside," he said.[25] "Sunnis wouldn't think twice about using the Americans to get influence. They want a disproportionate slice of the state, like Lebanon where the Christians are 20 percent but get 50 percent of parliament seats and the presidency. The Sunnis aren't fighting because of the Americans – they are just an excuse. They are fighting Shi'ites because the Americans came and took their power away and gave it to all the others."

Post-invasion Iraq, with Shi'ites in the ascendant, was a markedly different country to before. A secular Arab nationalist state (that had belatedly veered into the territory of Sunni political Islam during the 1990s) had become a Shi'ite Islamic state overnight. Shi'ite icononography and slogans were everywhere, the call to prayer on state television came in a Shi'ite format, Shi'ite clerics in religious attire were powerful figures in government, secular Shi'ite politicians as well as the clerics would seek audiences with the reclusive guru of Shi'ite Islam, Grand Ayatollah Ali al-Sistani, who Sunnis cursed for his Iranian upbringing. One word form Sistani could change the political course of an entire nation. It was the Najaf-based Sistani who laid down the principle for Shi'ites in general that they should work with the new US-formed order, and through democratic elections, rather than fight the Americans as occupiers. It was Sistani who called on Shi'ites to resist the temptation to engage in all-out revenge against the suicide bomb attacks of Sunni insurgents like al-Qa'ida in Iraq, who would kill dozens of civilians at a time in mosques, markets and bus stations with the stated aim of provoking civil war with the US-allied Shi'ite community. And it was Sistani who in August 2003 scuppered the plans of America's occupation administrator Paul Bremer to appoint members of a council to draft a new constitution, which would have delayed the process of elections and handing power to Iraqis. Sistani's prime concern has been unequivocally Shi'ite interests. Ahead of the parliamentary elections in December 2005, he instructed believers to do three things: turn out to vote, avoid voting for candidates who were not "religious" and not to vote for weak candidate lists so as not to split the Shi'ite vote.[26]

Sunnis suspected that the Shi'ite paramilitary group known as the Badr Brigades was behind sectarian murders of Sunnis which appeared to be in response to the wanton violence of al-Qa'ida and other groups, often targetting the families of men who had worked for the Baathist police or intelligence services. The Badr Brigades are the military wing of the Supreme Council for the Islamic Revolution (SCIRI), an Islamist dissident group led by Abdel-Aziz al-Hakim which was based in Tehran before the war. Sunnis accused the Badr group of working from within the Shi'ite-dominated Interior Ministry. The then interior minister Bayan Jabr Solagh became an object of suspicion in the wider Arab media. He was asked directly in an interview on al-Jazeera about accusations that he was not Arab at all but Iranian. "I'm proud of being an Arab," he responded, linking himself to the Zubeid tribe of Emara in south Iraq.[27] Sunnis complained that they were being shut out of government jobs, especially if they had Baath party connections. "We don't have any rights any more. They say in the National Assembly that we fought the Quran – and that's what they told me in the Ministry of Health too," one man said at a Sunni protest in favour of Saddam Hussein in August 2005.[28] Fighting the Quran meant Iraqis who fought Iran, with its system of clerical rule, in the 1980s war. Because of that, he said the ministry of health would no longer employ him. Such views would find sympathy around the Arab world.

Iraq on the eve of the US invasion

The political pulls on Iraqi heartstrings before the war were immense – a confused cacophany of Saddam's appeal to pride and history, America's cry for freedom and all the baggage of anger and ideology in the post-colonial Arab world, its kneejerk anti-Americanism because of Palestine. Saddam was a master at making great play of the past. Baghdad during Saddam's era was kitted out with a series of panoramas and statues harking back to the glories of early Mesopotamian civilizations, with which he likened himself to kings of Babel, Sumeria and Akkad. He appeared to be relishing his final showdown with America. In frequent appearances on television, he cast himself as a kind of semi-mythological figure from Iraq's rich history. He cast himself in a tragi-glorious narrative which placed him in a line of historical Mesopotamian rulers from the Sumerians to the Babylonians to the Assyrians whose enemies were as many as their ambition was boundless. In a televized speech to the nation on the anniversary of the beginning of the 1991 Gulf war, he called the Americans the "new Mongols" preparing to invade Baghdad like the forces of Hulagu Khan in 1258. But this time, he vowed, it would be different. Unlike the bloodbath that Baghdadis suffered then, the invaders would be routed on the city walls by a united and steadfast leadership, army and people (he failed to note that the Mongols ended up killing the Abbasid caliph and his two sons).

Saddam saw himself as a great arbiter of taste, but the arts he patronized were a prop to his authoritarian rule. Baghdad was a city of murals and statues glorifying Saddam, palaces and party and government buildings that mixed Soviet neo-classicism with ancient Mesopotamian architecture. Highways, airports, fine art schools – even mountains – were named after a leader who had personalized rule in his country to a degree that in the modern world was equalled only by Kim Jung II in North Korea. Such was Saddam's grip on the country and so legendary was his willingness to stop at nothing to stay in charge, that few dared open their mouth against him. Government minders accompanied journalists to most places they wanted to visit, but even in quick conversations grabbed out of earshot, it was clear that Iraqis had seen too much to risk an honest opinion.

After years of strident secularism, which had incidentally made Iraq in any respect one of the most advanced countries in the Arab world, in terms of education and infrastructure, the new realities of the 1990s had caused Saddam's regime to turn to religion. Saddam had introduced a "great faith campaign" to foster religion as a means of holding together Iraq's crumbling society under the United Nations sanctions system and to check the ability of Shi'ite Iran, Wahhabi Saudi Arabia or bin Laden's al-Qa'ida to make inroads with Iraqis. Thus the programme of constructing mega-mosques, setting up religious schools, Quranic radio stations and Islamic newspapers. When Washington became more threatening after the September 11 attacks, Hussein turned to the cult of the suicide bomber, the *istishhadi* who wants to die for his nation or his religion or both. In April 2002, when children dressed as suicide bombers featured prominently in a week of celebrations in cities throughout Iraq to mark the birthday of Saddam Hussein, celebrations that featured murals and replicas of the al-Aqsa mosque in East Jerusalem, and a street in central Baghdad was renamed after Yasser Arafat in honour of the Palestinian leader's defiant promise from the darkness of his besieged headquarters in Ramallah earlier that year that he was ready to die a martyr for the Palestinian cause. Special suicide squads known as *Fedayeen* were then set up in the months before the 2003 invasion.

Iraqis seemed remarkably calm on the outside at least for a people facing the prospect of their country becoming the testing ground for a new generation of high-tech American weaponry, on the one hand, and the scene of a Samson-like act of self-destruction from their own leader, on the other. After three decades of tyrannical government, war in the 1980s and sanctions in the 1990s, this striking *sang-froid* was perhaps understandable. There was more public interest in the love life of Iraq's most famous export in the Arab world, pop star Kazem al-Saher, to judge from the local press at the time. The Arab entertainment media outside

Iraq reported that Saher had taken a second wife in Paris, leaving his Iraqi first wife and mother of his two sons in the lurch. Sensing that the news could dent public morale at a critical time, Iraq's state-owned press urged Saher to make a statement. "We will reserve judgement on whether to believe it until Saher decides whether it is true, or that he will not take a second wife," one paper wrote.[29] Iraqis would readily express shock at the idea of their country being invaded by America, but could say little about the man whose many political blunders and dream of turning his police state into a regional superpower with a nuclear capability to match Israel had done so much to bring them to this dark denouement.

Among ordinary people, there was much denial about how bad the regime was. A local government employee in Mosul, when asked about the regime's gassing of Kurds in Halabja in 1988, answered: "It's only the foreigners that talk about Halabja, I've never ever heard a Kurd talking about it here. The Americans only started talking about it after 1991."[30] Mosul is one of the most ethnically mixed cities in Iraq, with various Christian churches making up around 40 percent of the area, in addition to Sunni Muslims, Kurds, Turcomans and Yezidis. In some ways, the government employee's comment was understandable: the brutality that Iraq's leader used to maintain his realm knew no ethnic or religious boundaries, though Sunni Arabs were generally favoured by his regime. A bishop of the Syrian Orthodox church in Mosul dutifully explained, in the presence of government minders, that he did not want a war and that the Bush administration was bringing the law of the jungle to the world, even if its stated goal was to "liberate" Iraqis. "What are they going to liberate us from? Ourselves?" he asked, rhetorically.[31] After a brief, deafening silence, he added, to no one in particular: "I can't imagine someone foreign coming to rule us."

The end of 'pan-Arab' Iraq?

After the war, Arab nationalism was out and Iraqi particularism was in. The only public slogans most Iraqis had known before April 2003 were the pan-Arab mantras of the ruling Baath Party, such as "one Arab nation with an eternal message". In central Baghdad, one of dozens smaller parties in existence was the United Nasserist Nationalist Party, where old-time Arab nationalists hung out in a dingy room on the fifth floor of a rundown block as if they had been sitting there since the 1960s, unaware that these were now distinctly un-Arab nationalist times. "Arab nationalists have been deliberately kept off the Governing Council, but we are reforming so that our presence will be felt. Our newspaper is about to start publishing and I imagine that we'll end up merging with other nationalist parties once the government sets out laws that organize political parties. At the moment it's chaos," spokesman Zeidan Khalaf said.[32] There was nothing passe about Arab nationalism, he affirmed, but it had been as abused by Baathism as any other political ideology. "The Arab nation has been targetted and is still being targetted since the battles of Yarmuk and Qadisiya [early battles of the 7th century Arab conquests] and since Islam spread to the east and the west, and today the Sykes-Picot Agreement has split it into statelets with manufactured borders in order to abort any unification project," a party statement of principles said.

The Baath party had numbered at least two million members, since it was the easiest way to get on in many walks of life, but many senior Baathists argue they and the party's ideology has been unfairly victimized in post-Saddam Iraq. This was a policy championed by the occupation authorities, which began a purge of Baathists from the bureaucracy, education system and judiciary, and continued by the now dominant Shi'ites. Some 35,000 Baathist public sector workers were put out of their jobs in May 2003 after a special Governing Council committee was charged with "de-Baathification", or "uprooting the Baath" (*ijtithath hizb al-ba'th*) from public life. These efforts were controversial. In some governorates, there were problems between locals and Baathists who were still in senior positions and in others there was resentment that the tag "Baathist" had demonized good people. In Baquba, in the Sunni heartland northeast of Baghdad, the governor reinstated hundreds of Baath party members from posts in the education sector in November 2003. "Sacking us in the first place was ridiculous. Uprooting the Baath is all about settling old scores," said Abdel-Jabbar Abdel-Sattar, a 53-year-old engineering teacher and former Baath branch leader who headed some 8,000 members in the area.[33] He had been a senior party member, and those any higher in the party structure had all fled or been arrested.

Abdel-Sattar argued that the ideals of the Baath itself were in no way problematic – a mix of socialism and Arab nationalism – it was rather regime practice that was wrong. "Our values were correct – we didn't teach people to be corrupt or destroy. The idea was one thing and the system was something else, just like the Soviet Union. After the system fell the Communist party remained and is represented in parliament today. It's the same in Georgia. This is not Germany and the Nazis," he said. But, in addition to a kind of mental block over the mass human rights abuse inflicted on the country by the party's leaders, Baathists were reluctant to admit that the leader they believed in had failed them so badly. Rather than the barbarity of the regime, they preferred to focus on the suffering engendered by foreign interference: "All Iraqis suffered from the war and the sanctions. In every house there was a martyr," Abdel-Sattar said, employing a phrase – "in every house a martyr" – that echoes around the Arab world. Egyptians use it in their narrative of years of conflict with Israel; Palestinians use it to describe their struggle against Israeli occupation; Algerians use it to describe how they sacrificed during the their seven-year battle for independence from France.

The attraction of the party, like Nasser's Arab Socialist Union, had always been that it presented a forum where all Iraqis could be one, crossing the sectarian divides. Baathists doubted that any party would have the same all-encompassing nationalist appeal of Baathism in a country like Iraq. They also argued that modern Iraq was a country built by them and which managed to resist the machinations of foreign powers, be it the CIA or Iran. "I joined the party in 1968 as a youth because it was the main nationalist party. We'll see if any other parties can be as nationalist as the Baath ... On every level it was the Baath that built this country over 35 years. It was the wars and the sanctions that prevented us completing the mission," said Abdel-Hafiz, a Baathist teacher from Baquba.[34] The Baath's strongest appeal was and is likely to remain this strident unifying and homogenizing nationalist discourse. Many commentators in the Arab world, and in the United States too, hoped that a secular Shi'ite such as Iyad Allawi could achieve something of that, and rescue the country from the religious factionalism it fell into.

In Arab-Islamic tradition, the Iraqis are depicted as infamously divisive people. The Prophet's daughter Zeinab is said to have declaimed them as *ahl al-shiqaq wal-nifaq*, "people of division and hypocrisy". The central passion play of Shi'ite Islam is the betrayal of the Prophet's grandson Hussein by the Arab tribes who had settled at Kufa, near Najaf. They had called on Hussein to leave Mecca and join them against the tyranny of the Umayyad caliphs in Damascus, only to leave him and his followers to be brutally cut down by the Umayyad forces at Kerbala in 680 AD. Iraqi writer Kanan Makiya called on Iraqis to come to terms with themselves and the fissures in their society in his *Republic of Fear*, citing an Iraqi proverb that says *id-daa illi beena minna wa feena*, "the malady we have is from us and within us".[35] The dictatorship had lasted because it understood and manipulated the fault lines and fears in Iraqi society, and because it formed some sort of vision for uniting a country of huge diversity, albeit through terror.

Iraqi particularism was an unwelcome development for the rest of the Arab world. It was viewed as a clear American device for delinking Iraq from the rest of the region, thus serving Israeli interests. Iraq's new political elite were heavily into the idea of "Iraq first". Their state television is very deliberately called *al-Iraqiya*, or "The Iraqi Channel" (in contrast to pan-Arab channels like *al-Arabiya*, whose name means "The Arab Channel"), and their was a brief backlash against Palestinian residents in the aftermath of Saddam's fall. Many were forced out of their homes by Iraqis angry at the privileges they had enjoyed under the Saddam's regime, which had been generous in providing jobs and homes to Arabs from around the Arab world. "Iraq first-ism" was the new paradigm championed by secular intellectuals in the immediate aftermath of the invasion, arguing that their country had suffered enough for the pan-Arab interests of the old regime. Many among the Sunnis who backed this thinking now have their reservations, as they see Shi'ite Islamist rule move the country into the Iranian orbit and the rift widen between Iraq and the Arab world. Fouad Ajami argued in his *The Dream House of the Arabs* that Arab nationalism and its obsessions with Israel had blinded Arab thinkers to the horrors inflicted on their peoples by regimes they had come too easily to accept.[36] His prime examples were Iraq, Egypt and Syria. Ajami and Makiya were loud supporters of the 2003 invasion of Iraq – advisers, even, to the US government – which was of course rejected among the vast majority of intellectuals the length and breadth of the Arab world. The war threw down the gauntlet to intellectuals and ruling elites alike: is it not time for individual rights to come before concepts of national interest and principles concerning Palestine, the wider Arab nation and the community of Islam? Should Arab countries not reject the grand concerns of Arab nationalism and focus on developing the individual nation-state and its citizens?

The Abu Ghraib scandal

The revelation that the US military abused Iraqi detainees at Abu Ghraib prison has encouraged the dominant image in the Arab world of the

United States as an arrogant neo-colonial power whose human rights rhetoric is little more than a cover for wider geopolitical aims. In that context, the abuse appeared to be fed by decades of denigration of Arab culture in Western public discourse, most notably in America where a specific reading of the Arab world and the Arabs is deliberately promoted by Israel and its powerful supporters. Islamic historian Bernard Lewis, for example, joined with Donald Rumsfeld and Paul Wolfowitz in a letter to then President Bill Clinton in February 1998 calling for the invasion of Iraq, a stunning example of Edward Said's vision of imperialist collusion between academia and politics. Lewis went on to become a favourite Middle East expert in the White House and the Pentagon. As Deputy Secretary of Defense, Paul Wolfowitz praised Lewis for teaching him "how to understand the complex and important history of the Middle East and use it to guide us where we will go next to build a better world for generations".[37] Lewis' post-September 11 blockbuster *What Went Wrong?* was said to be essential reading for many American soldiers in Iraq. In private briefings with US government officials, Lewis has argued that the Arabs will always be ruled by tyrants, so it is best to make sure they are friendly ones, and that Arab anger against America has nothing to do with its policies vis-à-vis the Israeli-Palestinian conflict. Therefore, the United States should not try to appease the Arabs by leaning on Israel.

The Arab reading of Abu Ghraib contrasted with that in the United Kingdom and America, where commentators often argued that there was no moral equivalence between decapitating random foreigners – the spate of beheadings in 2004 had only recently begun with the murder of Nicholas Berg – and torturing Iraqis for taking up arms against foreign occupation. British columnist David Aaronovitch came close to the Arab view when he said on BBC World that he suspected racism was behind Abu Ghraib. Abu Musab al-Zarqawi's al-Qa'ida group in Iraq made an explicit connection between American treatment of prisoners and their actions by dressing up Berg and others in red jumpsuits like those of Guantanamo detainees where al-Qa'ida suspects were held outside the jurisdiction of US law after the Afghanistan invasion of 2001.

Initially, the Arab satellite media did not seem to know how to react to the images, but with foreign news organizations splashing them all over television screens the major channels showed the material some hours later. Newspapers in Gulf countries like Saudi Arabia actually held off on printing the photos for a few days, possibly for fear they could bring people onto the streets in anger. Some opposition papers tried to provoke that very response. "The civilization of America releases dogs on prisoners to ravage their bodies, dozens of Iraqis died after trained dogs ravaged their sexual organs" online Egyptian Islamist paper *al-Shaab* said, carrying the infamous shot of an Iraqi dressed in an orange prisoner outfit quivering before a police dog.[38]. Though there was much symbolism in the image of a naked Arab male on a concrete floor – tethered to a female American soldier who looked down at him with arrogant disinterest – there was a deafening silence from Arab leaders, who left their foreign ministers to issue standard denuciations. Egyptian Foreign Minister Ahmed Maher said Washington should punish those found guilty and Saudi Foreign Minister Saud al-Faisal said it was "the result of the occupation".[39]

The great irony of Abu Ghraib was that most Arab governments allow treatment which is just as bad or worse of their own citizens. A talk show on al-Jazeera asked viewers the question: "Why is it that Arab regimes failed to condemn the pictures of abuse of Iraqi prisoners? Is the torture in Arab prisons not a hundred times worse than Abu Ghraib?" In the online and telephone poll, 86 percent of respondents said yes – Arab torture is worse.[40] In Lebanon's *Daily Star*, Iraqi rights activist Ibrahim al-Idrissi said the abuse in Iraqi prisons today was a "joke" compared to what went on under Saddam. He recounted one incident he witnessed himself when a woman was raped by 12 men then her unborn child cut from her stomach.[41] Human rights activist Yusri Fatyan wrote in Egypt's opposition paper *al-Arabi*: "Frankly, what happens in Egypt doesn't differ much from happens in Iraq's prisons."[42] Most commentators in fact blamed Arab governments for Abu Ghraib, since they had failed to prevent the invasion in the first place. "It's unfortunate that we don't hear one Arab leader say a brave word against this blatant American aggression against Iraq, Palestine and Syria. We haven't heard one Arab leader say that killing Palestinians or Iraqis with American weapons and Israeli hands is to kill all the Arabs and that punishing Syria is punishing against all Arabs," UK-based Palestinian commentator Abdel-Bari Atwan wrote in an article titled "American depravity and Arab obeisance".[43]

But the greatest damage was undoubtedly done to the American mission to create a new order in Iraq, one that would set the standard for a wider American-allied order across the despised "Arab world". "The whole world has realized that the so-called preachers of freedom have violated the simplest human rights at Abu Ghraib jail, which brings the American claims of defending human rights to an end," Egypt's state-owned *al-Gomhouriya* said.[44] Lebanese columnist Ghassan

Charbel wrote in the *al-Hayat*: "The neo-conservatives dealt with September 11 as a rare opportunity to launch a project that would have been impossible to carry out had the United States not been attacked on its own soil. But the Iraqi dream has collapsed now and the reasons are far deeper that the violations of Iraqi detainees. From Paul Bremer talking for the first time about withdrawal, to seeking the help of [United Nations envoy] Lakhdar Brahimi and drafting a new international resolution, it is clear that the Iraqi dream has been a costly adventure."[45]

Post-war reinvigoration of political Islam

The Iraq project has confirmed the status of political Islam as the radical ideology of choice in the Arab world today, reinvigorated the extreme elements of the Islamist movement when it was on the run in the aftermath of September 11 and maintained the predominance of the suicide bomber cult. The Iraqi resistance that emerged after the invasion has been dominated by Islamist groups and the Baathists of the insurgency are widely presumed to be operating in an Islamist guise, through groups with names like the "Islamic Army in Iraq", or others with nationalist overtones such as the "Revolution of 1920 Brigades". If the fall of Baghdad proved Arab nationalism had been reduced to nothing more effective than a warm sentiment, it was to propel political Islam to a new level of vitality and relevance. The most prominent Islamist group to emerge early in the resistance was the "Group for Tawheed and Jihad", a name which stamped ferocious Sunni Muslim themes on a guerrilla war that was clearly set to unleash its fury on the newly empowered Shi'ites. *Tawheed* means "to proclaim the oneness of God", and in the radical Sunni view – state ideology in Saudi Arabia – the Shi'ite heresy does not do this because of its veneration of the family of Ali as chosen ones with divine qualities (something akin to the Monophysite Christians, who believe Christ is entirely of a divine nature). *Jihad* in this context means "holy war", and, with its declaration, in Abu Musab al-Zarqawi's view all Muslims are obliged to join in. One year into the insurgency, the group announced it had Osama bin Laden's blessing to change its name to the "al-Qa'ida Organisation for Jihad in the Land of the Two Rivers [Iraq]". Zarqawi was a Jordanian who had adopted the Wahhabi-influenced Sunni ideology of al-Qa'ida while spending time with bin Laden's people in Afghanistan in the 1990s.

Both the American government and its Iraqi ally sought to play up the foreign element in Zarqawi's group in an effort to discredit it as an indigenous resistance movement. Evidence from the lists of al-Qa'ida in Iraq fighters who lost their lives in the fighting posted by the group itself on Islamist websites suggests it has gathered hundreds if not thousands of recruits from Arab countries, including Saudis, Algerians, Yemenis, Syrians, Jordanians, Egyptians and Moroccans. But a significant number of suicide bombers and other activists operating under the group's aegis have undoubtedly been Iraqis, otherwise it would not be able to function. Iraqis protest that their country never knew the phenomenon of the suicide bomber before, though in fact this is true for most Arab societies.

Government-allied clerics in Saudi Arabia called on young men to stay out of the Iraqi quagmire, but many headed there because of the government's post-September 11 crackdown on activities which could be associated with Osama bin Laden and his supporters. After two decades of supporting jihad in Afghanistan, Chechnya and elsewhere, Saudi Arabia was suddenly not the capital of Salafi activism that it once was. "In the Saudi street, people are not happy with the mass operation against former mujahideen, who were encouraged by the Saudi government. Without American pressure, our own government would not be as harsh against their own people," preacher Mohsen al-Awajy said.[46] "Most youth think the only safe road is to go to Iraq. They are trapped between the international campaign against terrorism and this campaign at home. The only save haven for them is to go Iraq. We are hearing stories of families who get mobile phone messages from their sons saying they're going to Iraq." The Iraq war had hardly finished when the jihadists turned on Saudi Arabia itself. Three residential compounds in Riyadh were attacked in suicide bomb operations that killed twenty-six people. It was the beginning of a campaign of violence that continued throughout 2004, as al-Qa'ida waged an open campaign to bring down the Saudi royal family because of their alliance with the United States, which the insurgents regarded as having no purpose for the ruling Saudis other than to preserve their hold on power.

The extent to which al-Qa'ida activists penetrated other countries was unclear – Yemen had made large efforts to root them out before the war, and Kuwait saw clashes with Islamists termed "militants" by the media, but it was not impossible that the police had deliberately coaxed them into confrontation in order to rid the state of a potential threat. Al-Qa'ida has become a trademark that radicals opposed to foreign influence and their governments for tolerating it can plug into wherever they are in the Arab world. In Egypt, where the government had succeeded in smashing radical Islam after a revolt that lasted five years in the mid-1990s, Islamic violence returned in 2004 and 2005 with a series of attacks against tourist targets in Cairo and the Sinai, killing Egyptians, Israelis and Europeans. Competing claims for these attacks often surfaced on Islamic websites and, though they were often not taken seriously by the authorities or political observers, they were interesting for the fact that they tapped into the language of the al-Qa'ida revolt against all things Western. The same was the case regarding other Islamist attacks around the world, whether it be in Madrid, London or Istanbul: the al-Qa'ida brand had successfully established an entire framework of thought and practice for Arabs and Muslims to follow.

The Islamist spread into cyberspace since 2003 has been striking. Dozens of Islamist websites promote the al-Qa'ida agenda and seek to win new converts. For example, the Iraqi "branch" posted a statement on one site in April 2005, which advised readers how to spread the message. "There are hundreds if not thousands of forums around the world and forums in all Islamic countries, and you can take part by posting the statements and videos from al-Qa'ida on them – we shouldn't just sit and read the statements or watch the films," it said. "There are Iraqis who were suspicious of our dear Sheikh, Abu Musab al-Zarqawi, but who now lean towards his thinking," it said, because they had come across its propaganda and its propagandists in a host of Internet chatrooms.[47] "There are thousands of brothers you can mobilize for al-Qa'ida by making hardly any effort at all." In 2004, the Islamist insurgents in Iraq moved into new territory with the shock tactic of beheading Iraqis and foreigners who they concluded were helping the foreign troops or foreign-backed authorities in any way, and making videos of the decapitations available on the internet and sending copies to media outlets like al-Jazeera.

Designed to have maximum impact on governments helping the United States in any way, often the victims would simply be nationals of a particular foreign country where the public would clamour for action to ensure their release. The Philippines government decided to pull its small military contingent in order to save the life of a Filipino hostage Angelo de la Cruz who was threatened with death by the Islamic Army in Iraq in July 2004. Two Americans, Eugene Armstrong and Jack Hensley, and a Briton, Kenneth Bigley, were not so lucky when they fell into the hands of

Zarqawi's people in September that year. Each one was murdered in stomach-churning videos put on the Internet after their governments refused to meet deadlines issued for the release of Iraqi women prisoners. Bigley's final murder was the most drawn out, as the group released several video broadcasts, crouched in a cage and dressed in an orange jumpsuit, in which he pleaded for Britain's Prime Minister Tony Blair to meet his captors demands. Bigley's brother Paul told al-Jazeera: "This war is illegal and it must stop. The United Nations declared this war illegal. There are no weapons of mass destruction, which were taken as a foundation for this war. Therefore, this war must stop."[48] The hostages killed (around fifty by mid-2005) included Egyptians, Italians, Nepalese, Japanese, Turks, Pakistanis, Bulgarians, Macedonians, Americans, Brits, Lebanese, Sudanese and Jordanians. Often they were merely truck drivers making deliveries to wherever their employers sent them in Iraq. The insurgency largely dumped the beheading strategy in 2005, realizing it was risking support in Iraq and the Arab world. "The groups are increasingly mindful of their image, aware of public opinion and believe more than ever that they will be victorious," the International Crisis Group (ICG) wrote in February 2006.[49] The brutality of the occupation forces, as ICG noted, was propaganda enough for the insurgents.

Some Iraqi Shi'ites were fighting their own war against the Americans. The followers of young cleric Moqtada al-Sadr (known as the Mahdi Army) had a number of major armed confrontations with the American forces in the holy city of Najaf, stand-offs which boosted Sadr's nationalist credentials in the jockeying for power and influence among Shi'ite clerics and politicians. This gave Sadr a certain appeal to Sunni Arabs, who have much respect for him. More similar in political outlook to Lebanon's Hizbollah, which is admired around the Arab world for fighting the Israeli occupation of twenty-two years in Lebanon and withstanding the Israeli army during the summer war of 2006 in Lebanon, the Sadr movement thrives on a reputation for action and sacrifice and of Iraq's Shi'ite forces is perhaps the most in tune with the Arab nationalist spirit of the rest of the Sunni-dominated Arab world. Sadr's tone is also different from Sistani and the constellation of Shi'ite leaders close to him, consistently placing an end to the foreign occupation as the country's main priority. It was not until the December 2005 elections that his people openly aligned themselves with the ruling Shi'ite coalition.

In the new Iraq, even the communists have gone religious. The Communist Party is officially banned in Egypt and few anywhere else in the

Arab world would publicly adopt the title "communist" today because of its implication in the popular imagination of "atheist". In Iraq, they have survived and are accorded an important place in the narrative of the emergence of the modern nation state. Thus, a communist was given charge of a ministry in the governing council and subsequent interim government which were formed under the American occupation. But they had to contend with the Islamic architecture of the emerging state. Iraqis in general were still lax in their observance of religious occasions, at least in Baghdad where eating or smoking in public during the fasting month of Ramadan was acceptable behaviour. But, there was no mistaking that for more and more Sunnis and Shia alike, their religious background has become their prime identity marker and source of pride and respect. "We are a country where the absolute majority are Muslims and we cannot ignore the fact that Islam could be in many ways important for us," the minister, Mufid alJazairy, said in November 2003.[50] "We have no reason to think that things are going to change just because they are religious parties and we are communist party, unless extremist groups and personalities try to move in and influence that. I hope there's no reason for fear."

In Egypt, the Muslim Brotherhood emerged stronger from the Iraq war. The group maintained its carefully preserved image as Egypt's decades-long, patient-to-perfection government-in-waiting and its new leader Mohammed Mehdi Akef pursued a markedly different line from his predecessor Maamoun al-Hodeiby in actively engaging the Arabic media, promoting the Brotherhood's campaign to be recognized as a legal political party in Egypt and making sure that its opinion on every major political issue in regional politics was out there in the public arena. The group felt strong enough to continually challenge the authorities throughout 2005 by holding more and more street demonstrations, with only a perfunctory word to the interior ministry in advance, and, benefitting from the American pressure that forced the Egyptian government to ensure the fairest elections in its history, it made striking gains in parliamentary polls later that year (though the authorities still resorted to foul play, such as closing off polling stations so that Brotherhood supporters could not enter to cast their vote). Though democrats also felt stronger to challenge the authorities with protests, there was no escaping political commentators in the Arab world that the Islamists were the strongest.

The Brotherhood and the other moderate Islamist movements round the region are old-hands at playing the long waiting game, as they bide their time before the day comes when they are in charge, but feeding on the anger of the Iraq war, there has been a tone of feverous anticipation of late. The Arab nationalists, in contrast, can only squak at "the fall of another citadel of Arab endurance", to quote Egyptian editor Mustafa Bakry ruing Syria's ejection from Lebanon, but Islamists sound convinced that now their time is soon to come.[51] Rachid al-Ghanouchi, leader of the banned Tunisian party al-Nahda, said from his London exile: "It's true that the Islamic nation might look in bad shape, ruled by the worst regimes of the era who practice the worst forms repression, but the fact is there would not be this international mobilization against Islam and it reawakening were it not for the growing spirit of resistance throughout our nation ... Don't listen to those who are cowed by today's balance of power [with the West], those who think our endurance, resistance and refusal to sell out is 'suicide'. Don't listen to those who think we cannot mobilize resistance so that we change the balance of power and get back our rights and our land. There is no question that our attitude towards Islam is the reason why we still have an *umma* [Islamic nation] with a history of great civilization and renaissance behind it. Islam is the world's fastest-growing religion today."[52] Egyptian Islamist intellectual Mohammed Emara wrote that "Secularism is not the solution, it's the crisis that reasoned Europeans and Westerners are complaining about for having drunk from its poisoned cup. Shame on the secularists in our country for continuing to proclaim the coming of 'Western modernism', even after its own inventors turned it into the nothingness and disintegration of 'post-modernism'. They call for secularism when it has been proven bankrupt in its own societies. We need to look East and get over the temptations of the West."[53]

The war in Iraq became a lightning rod for Arabs disillusioned with their own governments over a whole range of social, economic and political troubles. The invasion and occupation of Iraq captured the imagination of millions as a sign of the disregard with which the United States viewed Arabs and Muslims, their culture, their history and their passions. Event after event, incident after incident only strengthened the theory that America was out to rubbish all that was Arab and Muslim, from the looting of Baghdad Museum while American troops stood by, to the torture and sexual abuse of Iraqi prisoners at Abu Ghraib. Iraq became a rallying call for Islamists throughout the region and while the majority could not head to the land itself to fight the "New Crusaders", they were confirmed in their belief that, as the Brotherhood slogan has it, "Islam is the solution".

Alienating Iraqis in the "new Iraq"

There has been much debate in the West, and to a lesser extent in the Arab world, about whether the United States could have done things differently and thus ensured a more positive response to what they were doing from Iraqis and the Arab world in general. Two factors commonly cited are the decisions by the early occupation administration to ban the Baath party and uproot former Baathists from public life and administration, and to disband the Iraqi army including its officer corps, without maintaining salaries and pensions, which was regarded as one of the most professional in the region and not necessarily ideologically beholden to the old regime. A third factor was the heavy-handed manner in which the American military dealt with ordinary Iraqis in everyday situations. A huge number of those who died during and after the war were innocent victims, and it has been a controversial issue, cutting to the central question of whether the war was justified or not. As the Americans became increasingly nervous in the face of the insurgency, Iraqis could be shot dead if they approached checkpoints too fast or failed to steer clear of patrols. Some were killed in air attacks on wedding parties that the military believed to be rebel gatherings. Iraq Body Count, an American-British non-profit group, estimated 25,000 civilians were killed in the first two years after the war began, figures they compiled from media reports. More than 2,000 American troops died by the end of 2005 and more than 13,000 were wounded. British medical journal *The Lancet* estimated in a report published in October 2004 that since the invasion in March 2003 at least 100,000 Iraqi civilians had died.[54] The figure was extrapolated from a study of nearly 1,000 households from around the country in September 2004 and mortalities in the fifteen months before the invasion and first eighteen months after (and strongly rejected by the British government). The Geneva-based Graduate Institute of International Studies gave a figure of 39,000 in July 2005 by trying to pinpoint cause of deaths gathered in the Lancet study.[55] By mid-2005, more than fifty reporters and media workers died since the invasion, making it the most dangerous place in the world for the media to work.

In the publicity war in the Arab world, the United States seemed to dig itself into a bigger hole with every major offensive to remove the insurgents from major cities such as Falluja, Tel Afar, Haditha, Samarra or Ramadi. The publicity was invariably bad around the Arab world, as al-Jazeera and al-Arabiya reported the events from the other side. It was during the Falluja campaign in April 2004 that Washington allegedly considered bombing al-Jazeera's headquarters in Qatar, which is in fact a US ally and home to the US Central Command that masterminded the invasion. Al-Jazeera, which was listed as one of the world's five most influential brands in 2004 alongside Apple's iPod, Google, Ikea and Starbucks, made major play of the revelations when they surfaced in November 2005, scoring another blow to America's standing in the region.[56]

It was largely the civilian suffering that sealed the rejection of the Iraqi enterprise in the Arab world, though given the historical backdrop it is doubtful whether there was anything Washington could have done to win the hearts and minds of Arabs in invading Iraq. Virtually every policy has been construed as a mistake, from the decision to disband the Iraqi army to de-Baathification, from the appointment of Jay Garner as the first American administrator (a retired general who had become a defense contractor backed by the Neo-Conservatives and admirer of Israel's handling of the Intifada) to delaying the first parliamentary elections until January 2005. The fundamental disaffection for the whole Iraq project has been so strong from the outset that it is hard not to conclude that whatever the Americans had done it would have been construed a mistake among Iraqi Sunni Arabs and the wider Arab world, and that the insurgency was an inevitability come what may. America started on an uneven playing field, because of its support for undemocratic regimes and its behaviour throughout the long and painful tragedy of the Israeli-Palestinian conflict. The Arab media was primed to pick up every nuance of similarity between American operations in Iraq and Israeli actions in the occupied territories. The army used tactics reminiscent of the Israelis to face the insurgency and in the process alienated the Sunni population in central and west Iraq even further. The army employed translators who were invariably from minority Assyrian Christian, Turkmen or Kurdish communities, a coopting of certain natives which smacked of colonial divide-and-rule.

In an operation in to pick up fifteen men including Saddam's right-hand man Ezzat Ibrahim al-Douri, 1,000 men stormed into the same town of Huweija and its surrounding villages at dawn one day in December 2003.[57] Guided by GPS devices and information gleaned from informers who often had ulterior motives, they homed in on their list of houses, breaking down doors and stomping across living room carpets in muddy shoes, in many cases only to be directed to a house further down the street. Old men were dragged from their homes and forced to kneel in filthy streets with yellow bags over their heads. "I've got breathing problems," one, Adel Saleh, protested. "They all say that," the soldier guarding him said with a smile. "He has Fedayeen tattoos on his arm. He's on our list." With his stubble and grubby pyjamas, it was difficult to say if he fitted the Fedayeen profile or not. "He's a good man. He's an Arab, I'm a Kurd, but we're friends," a concerned neighbour said, as the man's wife looked on with a small child in her arms. Others were less lucky, depending on the mood of the commanding officer. Whole families were forced to sit outside on the freezing ground as their fathers were bound up with a bag on the head, sometimes after door-breakers (or "breachers", in military parlance) had forced their way into their homes. Units in other parts of town rounded people randomly off the streets in the vicinity of "target houses" if they were judged to "look like a bad guy", in soldier parlance.

Major Doug Vincent was the head of the military public affairs office in Kirkuk and charged with winning hearts and minds on these operations, or "giving lollipops to kids", as he put it. "We're very sorry", he would tell the Iraqis in earnest, and hand them fliers in English and Arabic saying: "The coalition forces apologize for any inconvenience you have experienced during the recent operations in your neighbourhood. These operations were conducted with the local authorities to ensure your security and a more safe and free Iraq for all Iraqis." The fliers went on: "We are committed to providing this community and country a safe and stable environment in which to raise your children and practise your religion without fear of oppression. Coalition forces will leave this country when, and only when, this condition is met." The town itself, situated in the north near Kirkuk, was strewn with anti-United States and pro-Saddam grafitti in Arabic such as "Saddam is the pride of the Arabs", "Death to the collaborators," and "Don't be armour for the Americans." At the central square, soldiers found that a monument bearing a mural of Saddam had been cleaned so that Saddam's chipmunk like face was fully visible again. A tank was brought in to smash it up. Townsfolk gathered in large crowds and stood in silence around the cordoned off center of the town – now a "secure zone" – but erupted in anger when questioned by journalists. "Frankly, I prefer Saddam. Now the streets are filthy, the electricity goes out and crime has become a big problem," fumed one, reflecting the nation-wide disgust at the collapse of law and order. Zooming through the streets in his humvee, Vincent waved at the bewildered residents shouting *"assalamu aleikom"*, peace be upon you. The Iraqis would stare back in silence.

Children ran after the jeeps shouting insults in Arabic such as "you infidel dogs", but the translators would say nothing. Iraqi children offered an interesting window onto the void of communication between the liberator and the liberated. They were fascinated by the American military and their toys. They would gather around the soldiers asking them questions in rudimentary English. "Mister," they would begin every staccato sentence, and the Americans, threatened by their boldness, would answer sarcastically in words the precocious children did not understand. "Mister, pen?! Mister, money?!" they persisted.

In an effort to break the back of the insurgents and frightened people from helping them, the Americans were employing massive firepower in the early days of the occupation. In one instance at Baquba northeast of Baghdad in November 2003, two F-15s flew from Qatar to drop four 500-pound bombs on farmhouses and other sites where insurgents whose roadside bombs were regularly taking American lives were throught to be hiding out. "We had taken action on these targets before, but this is to demonstrate one more time that we have significant firepower and we can use it at our discretion," admitted the ground commander, Lieutenant Colonel Mark Young. In October 2003, the military had pulled up an orchard of date palms near Tikrit – another echo of Palestine for the Arab world. In one instance, in Huweija, the army brought in a bulldozer to take down the front wall surrounding a villa owned by an elderly couple whose son was suspected of making bombs. They threatened to destroy the entire house, but the wanted man's mother offered information at the last minute on where her son might be. The liberating troops did not appear to have much affection or understanding of the oppressed people in question. The relationship was an antagonistic one from the beginning. When the Abu Ghraib scandal hit the media in 2004, it merely confirmed what the Arab world had thought all along.

Chapter 5
Peace with Egypt

Israel, the gateway to Washington

The question of Egypt's relationship with the United States has been at the centre of political life since the 1950s, when the United States took over Britain's role as Anglophone imperial power in the Middle East peninsula after the Second World War. The United States looked favourably on Egypt's military coup of 1952, but it was the US decision in 1956 to refuse funding for the Nasser's Aswan High Dam project that marked the beginning of Egypt's troubled post-colonial relations with the West, propelling Egypt into the Soviet bloc. After the 1967 defeat against Israel, there was much rancour in Egypt that the Soviet Union had provided second-rate military equipment and suspicion that it had behaved dishonestly and not fully backed the Arab side. When he came to power in 1970, Anwar Sadat turned away from the Soviets and plotted a policy of rapprochement with the United States through peace with Israel, in return for which he expected generous financial assistance and a chance for Egypt's economy to catch up with the West. In 1977, Sadat made his famous trip to Jerusalem, leading to the Camp David talks in 1978 and the peace treaty that was finally signed in 1979. Since then the United States has been the constant if invisible player in Egyptian domestic politics, deeply influencing government policy and the course of relations between the government and the Islamist and secular opposition.

Aid for Egypt has been the key element to the special relationship between the two countries since then. Until the mid-1990s, this regular cash injection comprised of around $1.3 billion annually in military aid and $815 million in economic aid, making a total of around $40 billion received since 1979.[1] The amounts have gradually lowered since the mid-1990s to less than two billion dollars a year. The aid programme offers incentives for Egypt to buy the bulk of its annual wheat imports from the United States – a valued prize for US farmers since Egypt is one of the world's biggest wheat importers. Egypt also won the write-off of $25 billion of foreign debt for its participation in the 1991 Gulf war, and won some extra financial aid to fill a $2.5 billion funding hole and cushion the after-effects on its economy – principally tourism – from the September 11 attacks, though this was tied to advancing its IMF-backed privatization programme, liberalizing its exchange rate mechanism and easing the flow of foreign direct investment, all issues the government had dragged its feet on since the US alliance of 1979. The relationship with Israel is often termed by observers as a "cold peace", and, mindful of Sadat's fate, gunned down by Islamist radicals who considered him a traitor to his religion and culture, Mubarak has personally kept his distance from Israel. He has visited only once for the funeral of Yitzhak Rabin in 1995. Ordinary Egyptians who during the 1990s sought work there or married Israeli women, whether Jews or Arabs, risked harrassment by the Egyptian intelligence and security apparatus. The authorities wanted only the minimum of relations with Israel in order to maintain its lucrative alliance with America.

Critics have seen in the peace a form of bribery, dependency and neutralization of Egypt's regional role – abandoning the dignified independence that Nasser ambitiously set as the objective for Egypt and the Arab region in the decolonization period. Crucially, the peace was unpopular at a basic, street level as well as among the intelligentsia, and this marked a fundamental shift from the Nasserist period when, whatever the many criticisms levelled about the death of parliamentary democracy and human rights abuse, the system did reflect the passions of the masses – to the extent that even intellectuals who suffered in Nasser's prisons admit admiration for him and conclude that he understood the mood of the times better than they.[2] For most of the period since 1979, most Egyptians would be hard put to find a link between peace with Israel and any significant, discernable improvements in the economy emanating from their government's move into the American-Israeli orbit. In the 1990s, the government media often cited the improved telephone network or the Cairo metro system as gifts of the Mubarak era, comments which merely strengthened the belief that net gains had been relatively slight. The outbreak of a violent struggle between the authorities and Islamic fundamentalism in the 1990s was in fact a clear sign of the political and economic failure of the authoritarian military republic inherited and maintained by Mubarak.

An entire political system was built around the central policy of protecting the pro-Western regime and keeping out elements which could threaten it. Egypt's current multi-party democracy is the child of Sadat's rapprochement with the West of the 1970s. After Islamists assassinated

Sadat in October 1981, emergency laws were introduced which remain in place to this day. Sadat willed three political parties into existence in 1976, all led by military officer friends: the left-wing Labour Party, the right-wing Liberal Party and the centrist Egypt Party. This last was intended to be the main "party of state", but when it joined with the other parties in denouncing his idea of unilateral peace with Israel, Sadat told parliament he would create yet another party, the National Democratic Party (NDP), which he headed himself. President Mubarak assumed its leadership in 1981, and the government has maintained strict control of who is licenced to operate freely as a political party ever since. One of the oddities of the era is that the Egypt Party survived. The man who became its head, Gamal Rabie, spent years fighting Sadat's "merger" of the party with the NDP. His office – in the same downtown Cairo building housing film director Yousef Chahine – is immaculate, as if nothing had changed since 1977. "We're all just empty bodies, just a decoration for the system of the ruling party," Rabie once lamented.[3] "Real parties come from the people, not the will of the ruler." Sadat created multiparty politics to absorb the popular anger that he knew would attend his very personal peace with Israel, which was nothing less than an earthquake for Egypt and Arab politics.

Sadat also prepared the ground for the peace enterprise by cracking down on secular opponents – Arab nationalists, Nasserists and leftists – and freeing Islamists and allowing them free rein after the oppression of the Nasser years. Famed televangelist Sheikh Sharawi, who played a kind of Rasputin role to Sadat's Czar in the 1970s, is said to have prayed in thanks to God on hearing news of Nasser's defeat to Israel in 1967 when he was working in Saudi Arabia. Though Sadat styled himself "the believer president" (*al-ra'is al-mu'min*), in another attempt to cushion himself from anger at his radical policies, Sadat was to come to regret his actions. He found that the Islamists no less than the nationalists were leading virulent anti-Israel protests in the turbulent period between his Jerusalem trip and the subsequent long-drawn out negotiations with the Israelis under American tutelage.

Eventually, of course, the Islamists killed him. Compared to what followed in the Mubarak era – a gradual return to Nasser-style suspicion of all things Islamist – the Sadat era is now recognized by Islamists as a mini golden era. Sadat was "merciful", Montasser Zayat, a lawyer who was part of the Gamaa Islamiya ("the Islamic Group") and close to Osama bin Laden's right-hand man Ayman al-Zawahiri. Police were under orders not to torture detainees, but "we don't regret his assassination because he would have ravaged the Islamic groups and he had refused to implement Sharia law as he had promised".[4]

In September 1981, Sadat took the last gamble of his life when he ordered the mass arrest of 1,536 opposition figures, carried out in the early hours of 3 September. Those thrown together included politicians, religious figures and writers from across the spectrum of Egyptian political life and society. Feminist Nawal al-Sa'dawi later wrote of how she wracked her brain in prison over why this range of characters had found themselves rubbing shoulders with each other in prison. She concluded that they had nothing in common but their opposition to Egypt's peace treaty with Israel. The president planned to release the detainees on 26 April 1982, the day when Israeli forces were scheduled to complete their withdrawal from the Sinai peninsula.[5] His thinking was that at that point these troublemakers, who constituted the totality of the country's intelligentsia, would realize that his policy had been wise.

Furious debate rages to this day about Egypt's peace with Israel, for many reasons. The central player in the Arab-Israeli dispute, the Palestinians, have still not achieved freedom and independence and that fact continues to have serious consequences for the political, economic and social health and stability of the Arab world as a whole; the more so for countries directly bordering Israel and the occupied territories, less so for those as distant as North Africa or the Gulf. Its defenders argue that if Egypt had not cut a deal for the return of Sinai at that time, it is quite possible the peninsula would still be in Israeli hands today. Handing the territory over was controversial enough for Israel – Israel had settlements in Sinai and a budding tourism industry – and Jewish right-wingers had their religious justifications for regarding Sinai as ancient Israelite territory.[6] Although Sadat seems to have misread Israel's political psychology at the time and the thinking of the right-wing Likud Party that had come to power under Menachim Begin – Sadat genuinely thought Israel was interested in land-for-peace with not only Egypt but also the other Arab parties including the Palestinians – the "breathing space" given to Egypt by ending the state of war with Israel was worth any price, his supporters argue. Unfortunately, high military expenditure continued in Egypt. The exact figures are to this day kept out of the published annual budget, and most of America's aid has in fact been military. The "militarization" of Egypt's politics and economy continued after Sadat. Power remains in the hands of a narrow band of security and intelligence men hovering around the military president, who has moved ever closer to the rising class of "crony capitalists" patronized by Sadat.[7]

Egyptian commentators have not only criticized Sadat's policy of peace with Israel in general, but specifically the manner in which it was carried off. Was too much given away for too little? What role did the US administration have in the negotiations at Camp David of 5–18 September 1978? Almost all of the major players in those talks have committed their version of events to writings, including US President Jimmy Carter in in his biography, Egyptian Foreign Minister Ibrahim Kamel, who resigned at the time, his number two Boutros Boutros-Ghali, Israeli foreign minister Moshe Dayan and Israeli defence minister Ezer Weizmann. Egyptian political analyst Wahid Abdel-Meguid published a study of the talks based on all the testimonies available which amounted to a damning indictment of Sadat. In *Camp David 20 Years On*, Abdel-Meguid concluded that Egyptian negotiators were "incapable of taking advantage of the fact that for the first and last time, the United States took a balanced position", and Israel learned a lesson from that experience.[8]

All the accounts show it was largely because of Carter that Begin agreed to scrub settlements in Sinai. On West Bank settlements, Carter wanted a written guarantee that all activity would be frozen until some form of Palestinian self-rule was established and then negotiations could go from there. Carter sent word to Arab capitals on 17 September that Israel had agreed to a settlement freeze, but Begin's written guarantee the next day was only for three months. Carter felt cheated, while Sadat gave public backing for Begin's position on 19 September. The whole episode showed "negotiating illiteracy" on the part of Egypt, Abdel-Meguid says. Because of chaos in their ranks – Kamel had resigned by then in protest at the loss of the West Bank and Jerusalem – the Egyptians had failed to support Carter in his challenge to the Israelis.

"It was the same story on Jerusalem," Abdel-Meguid writes. The Egyptians complained that the Americans were set on "fluid, floating formulations on freedom of movement and religious worship", in Kamel's words. But in fact Carter and Dayan had several angry exchanges over Carter's demand that the Israelis make a formal agreement to the principle of withdrawal from East Jerusalem. Begin threatened to walk out on the conference if pushed on the point, as Weizmann revealed in his 1984 memoirs. Dayan wrote in 1985: "I told the Americans in one of our sharp discussions that if the Security Council refuses to accept Jerusalem as our capital, then they will have to rewrite the Torah and sever some of our beliefs and rituals from our hopes and ambitions."[9] Having come with no clear strategy, the Egyptian team had fallen into bickering about how to proceed. Sadat was concerned with a withdrawal from Sinai, the foreign ministry was more interested in ending the Israeli occupation in the West Bank, while some individuals were focused on Jerusalem. "There were no clear principles and rules for communication between the president and his advisors, or among the advisors themselves," Abdel-Meguid says.[10] Among the Israelis, entirely the opposite was the case. There was a vigorous public debate at the time and for years after on the performance of their politicians. It is exactly because such scrutiny was and still is absent in Egyptian political culture, says Abdel-Meguid, that the Arabs lost the peace in 1978 and have continued losing ever since. This, he says, was the consequence of the emasculation of political life effected by the military regime that took power in 1952.

In his 2003 publication *Amrikanli*, celebrated novelist Sonallah Ibrahim suggests that Egypt and the Arab world are dependencies of an American empire along the lines of the Ottoman empire, when Egypt and most Arab countries languished for three centuries under foreign, though Muslim, control. Where before there was *osmanli* – Ottoman, or Ottoman-like – there is now *amrikanli* (American, or American-like), a pun on a three-word phrase in Arabic (*amri kan li*) meaning "I used to have control over my affairs." Noting the fashion of the conquered to adopt the manners and customs of their rulers, as Arab historian Ibn Khaldoun explained in his famous treatise, Ibrahim's protagonist remembers certain traits about Sadat, traits that suggest someone out of touch with his own people. He notes "his love for elegant clothes, audiences with kings and bons vivants, appearing before the cameras smoking his pipe and stroking a large dog, just like the British aristocrats, and the fascination of both he and his wife with the American dream and its stars such as ... Elizabeth Taylor".[11]

Sadat effected a major political realignment of the most populous and military strong country in the Arab world, hitching its future to the United States. In return for an annual dollar injection which made Egypt the second biggest recipient of US aid after Israel itself, Egypt had withdrawn its army from the military equation between the Arabs and Israel before the wider and more fundamental conflict was solved. At the same time, Israel under Likud rule set itself on a new course of settlement in the territories it seized in 1967. The trauma of pulling itself out of the Sinai had been enough to frighten Israel's political class against the thought of giving up any more territory, and the land that remained was of far more significance to the Jewish state, religiously or strategically, than the Sinai peninsula, which was the easiest of its conquests to hand back.

Political Islam after Camp David

Protection of its US alliance became the number one priority of Egypt's ruling establishment. The political party system was a mechanism for keeping the opposition in check, but was to prove incapable of dealing with the threat to the authorities from political Islam, the most implacable opponents of Egypt's new American orientation. The government restricted the right to form political parties, and used the emergency laws to stop the official and unofficial parties from organizing, cohesing and proselytizing. There also existed an informal ban on discussing the details of the peace treaty and the demilitarized status of the Sinai, which many people considered an affront to national sovereignty. Adel Hussein, the late editor of the Islamist paper *al-Shaab*, found himself in detention for a month after he made an issue of this in provocative articles in 1995. Popular Defence Minister Abdel-Halim Abu Ghazala was removed from government in 1989 partly, political observers contend, because of concerns that he favoured surreptitious rearmament in the peninsula.

But on university campuses and in poor districts around the country the radical Islamist groups, the Gamaa Islamiya and Islamic Jihad, were quietly regaining strength, making use of the one organizing ground that the authorities could not control: the mosque. The Muslim Brotherhood meanwhile moved towards the political mainstream, taking the decision in 1984 to join the political process through an electoral alliance with the Wafd party which allowed it to obviate an official ban on the group. The Brotherhood also focused its energies on the professional syndicates, making up for being shut out of mainstream party politics by turning the syndicates into something akin to normal political parties. The doctors, lawyers, engineers and teaching syndicates became Muslim Brotherhood strongholds in the late 1980s, as the group took control of their boards through elections that were more fair than those to parliament. These organizations were henceforth run as political institutions for a kind of government-in-waiting, or alternative government, carrying out charity, social and political work whose efficiency and relative transparency was a source of embarrassment to the authorities. The Brotherhood was able to run its own "state within a state" and provide a plausible alternative to the existing state system. The engineers' syndicate, which it took control of in 1987, for example, comprised 200,000 members and controlled $5 million in assets. The group also organized help for students in study costs, including accomodation, food, transport and textbooks.

The Brotherhood-run syndicates were a comprehensive political, religious and social package: they organized cheap hajj trips to Mecca, fund-raising for Bosnian Muslims and assistance for victims of the 1992 Cairo earthquake, and they helped with housing, transport and other living costs. A visit to their immaculately clean offices offered a stark contrast to the bureaucratic and physical decay of any number of government ministries. Where the Brotherhood inspired people, the state turned them off. The official left was at the same time coopted through the regime playing on the secular-Islamist divide. New arms of the culture ministry and their literary magazines, such as the Higher Council for Culture and the monthly *Ibdaa*, were stuffed full of coopted leftists in the late 1980s. The Tagammu (Socialist Rally) party, the leftist grouping that used to be Sadat's biggest headache, became the opposition party closest to the government, defying an opposition boycott of the 1990s parliamentary elections. In 1995, its secretary-general Rifaat al-Said was nominated by Mubarak to the upper parliamentary chamber, the Shura Council. For much of the left, the Islamist groups were a far greater menace to society than the US-allied regime, and their hope was that corruption and lack of democracy would be the noose with which they could finally hang the government in the late 1980s.

But events conspired to confound those hopes. Alongside the moderate Islamist movement, there was a growing radical movement to the right of the Muslim Brothers. During the 1990–1991 Gulf crisis, when Arab governments had to find religious scholars to legitimize for the public at large their participation in a US-led war against Iraq, the scene was set for a confrontation between political Islam and the Egyptian government. The radical groups, with their ideologies rejecting Western political models and cultural values and demonizing Arab governments who promoted them, were becoming increasingly emboldened throughout the country by their semi-independent communities where they create their idea of an original Islamic Utopia such as that which Islamic tradition says existed at the time of the Prophet. Some had taken to attacking foreign tourists, who they regarded as spreading Western immorality in society. In 1992, the government was embarrassed by news reports that showed the strength of the extremist groups, who were running their own "Islamic republic" in the teaming Cairo slum district of Imbaba.[12] Those reports prompted a massive police operation to uproot the fundamentalists from the area, a shock-and-awe strategy that rights groups in Egypt and abroad said involved random arrests of thousands of people and brutality in detention. It was after this that the radical groups launched their open warfare against the state, staging several assassination attempts on government ministers and Mubarak himself (there were some dozen attempts on his life, the most prominent being in Ethiopia in 1995) and targetting more Western tourists in a prolonged guerrilla campaign against symbols of the state that was largely concentrated in southern Egypt – all of which ended with a bang in 1997 when fifty-eight foreign tourists were massacred at a Pharaonic temple site in the tourist centre of Luxor. After that the Gamaa Islamiya as a fighting force was no more. The Islamic Jihad group under Ayman al-Zawahiri, meanwhile, had given up on Egypt, throwing its lot in with bin Laden in Afghanistan.

Throughout this period an army of some 20,000 political detainees grew in Egypt's prisons, though the exact figure has never truly been established (New York-based Human Rights Watch said the number was still 15,000 in 2006). In the late 1990s, when the government was sure that the storm of Islamic violence had passed, it began releasing large batches of prisoners in periodic "amnesties" to mark Muslim religious festivals. Rights groups suspected that many had been arrested simply on suspicion of having links with extremist groups, often for praying at mosques known for their militancy, and those tried and convicted numbered only a few hundred. The interior ministry built five new prisons in the space of those same five years and the stories of systematic abuse they suffered there is legion among human rights groups. In 1992, the government began referring captured Islamists to military courts which routinely condemned them to death; Mubarak turned to the military justice system after a civilian judge acquitted defendants because their confessions had been obtained through torture. Abdel-Harith Medani, an Islamist lawyer from Imbaba, became a poster child for the rights movement when he died in police custody after being arrested while jogging by the Nile in 1994. A massive lawyers syndicate–organized protest in central Cairo, which police broke up by force, was seen as a watershed in the war against the government, after which the scales began to tip the state's way. There was no significant groundswell of international pressure against the government over Medani's death, the break-up of the protest or the detention for most of the year of Montasser Zayat, the Gamaa's unofficial spokesman.

In 1995, the government launched a major crackdown against the Muslim Brotherhood. It argued publicly that the Brotherhood was directing the violence from behind the scenes, but was convinced at a deeper level that as long as the group remained strong the problem of radical Islam would forever threaten the stability of the republic. In a series of high profile trials, Brotherhood syndicate leaders such as Essam al-Erian, Abdel-Moneim Abul-Fotouh and Mokhtar Noh were sentenced to up to five years in prison for membership of a banned group that sought to "overthrow the system of government" (*qalb nizam il-hukm*).

The regime's decision to come down on the Brotherhood had been something of a surprise. Mubarak cited them in a positive light in one interview in 1994 discussing the violence in which he defended the religion from the actions of the insurgents saying that Egypt had its own moderate Islamists who were peaceful.[13] Mubarak's apparent willingness to tolerate political Islam in the 1980s had led to the Brotherhood endorsing his 1988 presidential nomination, and its leader Hamed al-Nasr was known to have had relatively civil relations with Mubarak, who paid lip service to the idea of implementing Islamic Sharia law over the long term.[14] Yasser Arafat even headed to the Brotherhood's offices in downtown Cairo in 1994 during one visit to seek their influence with the Palestinian group Hamas, which was partly an outgrowth of a branch of the Brotherhood in Palestine. Throughout this period, many observers including prominent pro-democracy activist Saadeddin Ibrahim argued that the government should bring moderate Islamists into the political system to neutralize the danger from those who were more radical, but the conventional argument against them in government circles was that the Islamists were "distributing roles", that the moderate Brothers hoped to take power on the back of the violence of their more radical ideological bedfellows – after all, they all raised the slogan "Islam is the solution" (*al-islam huwa al-hall*). Ironically, one factor which may have played a role in turning the government against the group was suspicion that the United States was making tentative moves towards a dialogue with it, fearful of where the violence in the country was leading. In an interview with US magazine *The New Yorker*, published in January 1995, Mubarak accused the Brotherhood of being "terrorists" and lashed out at them over contacts with the US government. "You think you can correct the mistake that you made in Iran, where you had no contact with the Ayatollah Khomeini and his fanatic groups before they seized power. But I assure you, these groups will never take over this country; and they will never be on good terms with the United States," he said.[15]

It was argued at the time in the editorials of senior state scribes such as Ibrahim Nafie, then editor of the main daily *al-Ahram*, that political Islam, like Fascism in Germany, sought to take advantage of democracy in order to instal a dictatorial theocratic system not unlike Iran's where no one would have the right to vote again. The government also periodically stated, and continues to argue, that allowing an Islamist party will lead Egypt's Coptic Christian minority to demand the same right for a Christian political party, thereby destroying the sectarian harmony that has been Egypt's idyllic self-image since the nationalist struggle against the British. The argument was flawed in that the secular-national system was already neither free nor democratic, and in fact Iran had a parliamentary system arguably freer than Egypt's, but, Western governments, including the United States, generally accepted the government's line. A multitude of opposition voices inside the country arguing otherwise were essentially ignored. "The state doesn't understand that freedom of political competition is enough to end terrorism and to expose the actual size of the religious current in Egypt," leftist politician and writer Salah Issa said.[16] "The Muslim Brotherhood once had a million members in the 1940s and 2000 regional units, but they never succeeded in parliamentary elections. People realized that they are religious not political people. In Sadat's time there was a preacher from Mahalla [town north of Cairo], a Sufi who'd grown the long beard and so on, who was elected to parliament. But what did he do? When the call to prayer came he'd demand the session be adjourned. He wasn't elected the next time. People sent him there to represent them, not to continue his job as a mosque preacher."

Courts placed the lawyers syndicate, or bar association, under sequestration in 1996 after government-backed allegations of financial mispractice by its Brotherhood-dominated board. The intended message appeared to be that working with the Brotherhood at any level higher than the syndicates was unlikely ever to work, since a coalition of political groups under their domination had failed to work together. Lawyer Mohammed Asfour, who once served as temporary syndicate president, disagreed. "Not at all, disputes are normal in any institution – but it's an issue for the syndicate itself to solve. If anyone has transgressed, there are mechanisms for them to be prosecuted," he said.[17] The government was determined to marginalize, destroy and ignore the Islamist movement while many recommended engaging with it in order for a democratic, pluralistic system to develop.

The Brotherhood's response to the state's blows was to roll over and take the punches. While the syndicate middle-generation railed – "There is a struggle between two trends. One which wants to impose Western, Zionist domination and another [the Brotherhood] which wants to restore this nation's dignity and unity," doctors' syndicate figure Abdel-Fattah told a news conference after the January 1995 detentions – the group's leadership was dominated by older men of the generation that suffered under Nasser and freed from prison by Sadat, and the group's Free Mason-like structure demanded blind obedience from the rank-and-file.[18] Although some prominent younger members on the group's governing council favoured challenging the government during the elections of late 1995 through pro-democracy protests, the leaders felt that this would only risk their long-term waiting strategy.[19] There was no reason why the government would feel obliged to listen to the language of protest – an implicit call for third parties to sit up and get involved – and it could even tempt a crackdown more similar to that of the 1960s.

The result was a partial split in the movement and a fillip to develop its ideas. A group of "third generation" Brothers – professionals who had not been hauled up in the military trials – hoped to set up a political party called al-Wasat, the Centre, led by Abul-Alaa Madi, Essam Sultan and a Christian intellectual named Rafiq Habib who was convinced that Egypt's problems could not be solved without a historic reconciliation between secular nationalism and political Islam. "The reality is there exists a very powerful Islamist movement in Egypt and we must take this force and establish peaceful and moderate channels for it to express itself," Habib said at the time.[20] "The opposition in general in its present shape is meant to be nothing more than decor. What we aim to do is to reactivate political life in Egypt, which at present is more like political death." Though the government refused to licence the group, fearing it was a front for the Brotherhood, it marked a further stage in the modernization of political Islam in preparation for its eventual entry into mainstream political life. Madi said at the time: "We think that we have put to rest two accusations that are always levelled at Islamists. One is 'monopolizing the truth'. We are happy with the idea that there are many faces to the truth, and we don't make claims to it, on any issue. The second is using generalizations and vague slogans. On specific issues we came up with answers. In the Wasat party program we went into the 'minefield' issues – the arts, tourism, the West, the peace process."[21] But if the government feared that projects like al-Wasat could attract the attention of foreign powers like the United States, out of interest in helping Egypt's ossified political system find a way forward, they had little to fear since it appeared that neither the Clinton nor the Bush administration was interested in shaking the status quo.

Secure in its US alliance, the government did nothing to develop its thinking and approach vis-à-vis political Islam during this period. Mubarak backed the Algerian military's decision to abort elections in 1992 that looked likely to bring Algeria's equivalent of the Brotherhood, the Islamic Salvation Front (known by its French acronym FIS) and never tired of telling Washington how dangerous the Islamist movement, in its entirety, was for Western interests. Egyptian, Arab and foreign rights groups said the emergency laws were merely a prop to maintaining totalitarian rule, and when asked about the issue in an interview with al-Arabiya in April 2005, Mubarak even joked: "You want to get rid of emergency laws when that's what the whole world is now bringing in?! And we have complete violence (in Egypt)!"[22] Western governments not only acquiesced in the arguments offered by countries like Egypt, they followed in their footsteps – Arab governments, so often attacked by Western media and occasionally by Western governments over their closed political systems, were vindicated after September 11 when those Western countries took measures to clip civil rights in the name of the "war on terror". The Islamists harbour a deep grudge over how they have suffered. Prominent Muslim Brother Mohammed Abdel-Qaddous has written bitterly of a colleague who was tortured at a state security detention centre in 1981 – tortured by a former high-ranking officer who now regularly appears in the pan-Arab media as a security expert. "The number one suspect in his murder is still alive and I see him sometimes on television talking as a terrorism expert," he wrote.[23] "When the sun of freedom shines in my country this terrorism expert and his likes will be the first to face trial, and, if God wills, the tyrants will be punished in this world before the next."

The violence of the 1990s: a state-provoked war?

In his celebrated novel about the decay of revolutionary Egypt *The Yacoubian Building (Emarat Ya'qubian)*, Alaa al-Aswani depicts a member of an extremist Islamist group arguing at a dawn meeting with a mosque imam that the Islamist revolutionaries should respond to the government's campaign of random detentions and abuse in custody. This is the period immediately before the 1991 Gulf war when Arab governments including Egypt took the unpopular move of backing the American-led military intervention to remove Iraqi troops from Kuwait. But the Sheikh tells the protagonist that since the regime has "allied with the Americans and Zionists to liberate Kuwait", the last thing to do is invite trouble: "I think you've realized by now, my son, that the security forces are provoking us so that we respond and give them an excuse to completely crackdown on the Islamists ... If I attacked Egypt's taking part in the coalition they would close the mosque down tomorrow, but I need my mosque so that when the war comes I can rally the youth. My son, it's not wise to give them the chance. Let them kill our Muslim brothers in Iraq under the leadership of the infidels and Zionists and you'll see yourself what we'll do then, God willing."[24]

This passage above reflects the suspicion among many political observers that the slide into violence in the early 1990s was not entirely the doing of zealots bent on warring the secular state: did the regime, with its eye firmly fixed on the American alliance, want to "smoke them out"? Islamists and their sympathizers argue that the authorities, determined to ward off all challenges to the American-backed post-1979 order, intentionally provoked the radical movement into an all-out war during the 1990s because they feared their growing strength. The radical groups were also invigorated by the success of the Islamic resistance against the Soviet Union in Afghanistan. Many of these "Afghan Arabs" returned to their countries thirsting for more action and determined to change their world one way or another. Zayat says a *modus vivendi* between the government and the main radical Islamist group the Gamaa Islamiya broke down with the murder of Gamaa spokesman Alaa Mohieddin in August 1990. Though the state press blamed the murder on Gamaa infighting, Zayat says it was a police provocation which met its response with the Gamaa's assassination of parliament speaker Rifaat Mahgoub. Many believe this attack was carried out by Zawahiri's Jihad group and aimed at the interior minister. But either way it was certainly the beginning of a spiral of tit-for-tat attacks that led to the full-blown war of the mid-90s. "Before the killing of Alaa there was relative calm ... Then the seas of violence and blood exploded, and it became established policy to strike them in the heart," Zayat said, describing a proactive campaign to eliminate the radicals.[25] Rights activist Hisham Kassem agrees this was the beginning of a new state policy of *tasfiyya gasadiyya* – "physical liquidation" because the Islamist groups were getting out of hand.[26]

There had been trouble between the state and Islamist groups throughout the 1980s, but it was sporadic and the groups involved tended to be extremist splinters of the "mainstream extremism" of Gamaa Islamiya and Islamic Jihad. Former interior minister Hassan Abu Basha was the target of failed assassination attempt in 1987 (Islamists accused him of having tortured them personally). Zayat has detailed various mediation efforts between 1990 and 1993.[27] In the first, Gamaa Islamiya spiritual leader Omar Abdel-Rahman wanted freedom for radical preachers to take to pulpits around the country and a lifting of Abdel-Rahman's house arrest in return for the Gamaa ending all form of violence against the state. In the end, Abdel-Rahman was allowed to leave the country (and went on to play a role in the 1993 plot to destroy the World Trade Centre twin towers). Freedom of the country for the mass Islamist movement was again on the cards three years later, according to Zayat. A committee had been formed negotiating between Gamaa Islamiya leaders in prison and the Interior Ministry, including a number of popular preachers and Islamist intellectual figures. But the interior minister of the time, Abdel-Halim Moussa, was sacked and the mediation was off. There is a comparison to be drawn with the secret deal which Algerian president Chadli Benjadid is suspected to have carved out with the FIS, allowing Islamists to come together as a political party in 1988 ahead of free elections. The agreement is thought to have been scuppered by Abbasi Medani's miscalculation in pushing for a general strike in the summer of 1991 prior to parliamentary elections aborted by the military leadership in January 1992 when it became clear the FIS would win. In Algeria, the military at the last minute said no; in Egypt the government also said no, but before things ever got to the stage of free elections and an imminent victory for the Islamist movement.

Egypt already had a huge network of Islamists making their influence felt socially and politically in the form of the Brotherhood. But if the Gamaa Islamiya, and perhaps even Jihad, the group behind Sadat's death, had made a peace with the state that transcended the sporadically violent and uneasy relationship of the 1980s, then together Islamists would have formed a huge pressure group in Egypt, straining the state's American alliance to breaking point. Zayat says the first five years under Mubarak were relatively calm – when Mubarak had promised not to stay in office more than two terms and the opposition including the Brotherhood gained sizeable representation in parliamentary elections – but then "maybe the West protested at the development of the Islamist movement ... maybe the Islamist movement working freely and growing represents a danger in the end to the governing circles".[28] American journalist Judith Miller of the *New York Times*, for one, was goading the government to crack down on the mass Islamist movement. In her *God Has Ninety-Nine Names*, she writes of numerous meetings with President Mubarak during which they discussed the problem of how to de-Islamize the country and strengthen civil society. "Some perhaps feared that if they created democracy the Islamic groups would find quite a bit of support and would turn against them (the state)," Zayat says.[29] If the government made peace with the Islamist movement, this accomodation could jeopardize the Western financial backing that for the regime had become an end in itself.

Beyond its victory at the level of force and diplomacy – the "security solution" at home and charm offensive abroad – the government and its supporters have tried domestically to muster a challenge to the powerful discourse created by both Islamists and nationalists, primarily through the media. The state media's huge machine presents both Sadat and Mubarak as the heros of the 1973 war against Israel, a theme that Mubarak lent on heavily as late as 2005 when he launched his bid to stay on as president for a fifth term. Among many of the regime's secular opponents, on the other hand, Nasser's memory has been airbrushed, tinted and expanded to gargantuan proportions as an ideal against which Egypt and other American-allied Arab regimes can be judged. In a dummy run for the Iraq war five years later, opposition papers taunted the government when Iraq was bombed in 1998. "Gamal Abdel-Nasser travels to Baghdad and meets with Saddam Hussein: Abdel-Nasser says an missile attack on Baghdad is an aggression against Cairo," one paper said in a front-page headline that used in content and presentation took readers back to the days when Egypt, in their view, was a force to be reckoned with politically, a country which commanded respect and which would step in to stop foreign meddling in Arab countries.[30]

One of the most powerful responses the state managed to mobilize came in the form of cinema. In a string of films written by government-allied secular scenarist Wahid Hamed, popular comedy actor Adel Imam targetted the Islamist movement head-on, ridiculing them as backward and counterproductive for the continuing nationalist struggle while at the same time acknowledging the corruption and inefficiency of the state. It was a powerful propaganda that the authorities did everything to encourage – even government ministers would turn up for the premieres of Imam's films. The 1998 film *Risala Ila al-Wali* (*Message to the Ruler*) encapsulated a secular-nationalist message that it was still the fumbling, rickety Arab nationalist regimes like Egypt's that were capable of protecting any country's independence from foreign predations, be they Israeli or American. Imam played an Ottoman knight sent to Cairo to help repel the British forces invading the northern coastline in 1807. But he finds himself walking into the present day. In the movie's climax, the knight finally arrives at the court of nineteenth century ruler Mohammed Ali in the Cairo citadel, where he delivers a speech before what he does not realize is no more than a hall of wax dummies of tourists to imagine former times. In anger, he chops off Mohammed Ali's head. Political Islam, the film wants to tell us, is bent on recreating a past that cannot be recreated. Not only that – there is need to go back there in any case: Imam's love interest, the actress Yousra, consoles him in the following dialogue (which was met with an eerie, embarrassed silence in many cinema halls):

"Today we don't have a *Wali* [ruler], he's called the 'president', and he's Egyptian."

"Really? And who chose him?"

"We chose him."

"That's amazing. And what's he like?"

"He's a national hero. He led the airforce in the war against Israel."

"Did he win?"

"Oh yes, he won."

The war in Iraq – a new political ballgame

With the Iraq war of 2003, the Islamist and other opposition that the government had done so much to marginalize were back, and the American response to these movements lies, once again, at the heart of Egypt politics today. The irony was that it was almost entirely because of a fundamental shift in the relations of the sole superpower with the Arab world that this was possible, a shift that even more than the 1991 Kuwait war had exposed the powerlessness of Arab governments to solve regional issues themselves without foreign interference. Incensed by the war and benefiting from American pressure on the government to encourage open politics, eight of the officially recognized parties, including the liberal

Wafd Party, the leftist Tagammu and the Arab nationalist Nasserist Party, formed an alliance in September 2004 to press for political and constitutional reform. Though they conspicuously left out the Brotherhood, the interior ministry still prevented the group holding rallies anywhere in the country. In November 2004, a small group of people demonstrated in Cairo's central square with placards saying "Enough!" (*Kifaya!*) and carrying images of an ace of spades with Mubarak's head at one end and his son Gamal's at the other. Although they were drowned in a huge security presence of thousands, these protestors had crossed a red line in Egyptian politics – a public protest against Mubarak, his son's conspicuous role in Mubarak's ruling NDP and what were taken in the country as preparations for him to eventually step into his father's shoes.

Ayman Nour, a member of parliament who broke away from the liberal Wafd party, attempted to set up a new political group (the Tomorrow Party, or *al-Ghad* Party) and held rallies calling for constitutional reform ahead of presidential elections in 2005. Since he came to office, Mubarak had habitually been reelected in a yes-or-no plebiscite after two-thirds of parliament, controlled by the NDP, approved his sole candidacy for the vote. After the Iraq war, it was no longer feasible for this system to continue. The United States weighed in with pressure for change when President Bush spoke directly of Egypt in his State of the Union address: "To promote peace and stability in the broader Middle East, the United States will work with our friends in the region to fight the common threat of terror, while we encourage a higher standard of freedom. The great and proud nation of Egypt, which showed the way toward peace in the Middle East, can now show the way toward democracy in the Middle East". Nour was arrested in early 2005 on charges of having falsified signatures required to prove that his party had enough members to gain a licence to operate, and a court jailed him for five years in December 2005 once the election season was over. A reformist secular politician, Nour became a *cause celebre* in the United States, such that when he was released from detention in June 2005 he found the NDP running an orchestrated campaign against him portraying him as a US agent. In one interview, Nour was asked by an opposition paper about accusations in the state press that he had committed the great sin of discussing the domestic political scene with the American ambassador. "I'm surprised to hear these accusations from people who meet more Americans than Egyptians. I don't make pilgrimage to the Whitehouse every year and I don't receive any aid," he replied.[31] Like the Brotherhood a decade before, the "new opposition" was accused of being soft on the United States, or relying on it for support. Employing a familiar argument, the government also wanted to let Washington know that its haste for reform could finally bring the Islamist bogey to power – the argument long used to justify maintaining the status quo. Intelligence chief Omar Suleiman was reported to have carried with him to Washington in early 2005 "25 points" concerning what the Brotherhood was all about – a list of distasteful facts and figures and opinions from the group's past and present, designed to shock.[32]

Mubarak still took the country by surprise when he announced a constitutional amendment allowing multi-candidate elections to the presidency, but while the move was a serious shift in Egypt's political topography, brought on by American pressure, few believed that the government was about to voluntarily cede power. The restrictions on the proposed legislation made it difficult for any serious contenders to run. The amendment was approved by a referendum in May 2005 that was preceded by weeks of protests, mainly led by the Brotherhood. Bush told Mubarak in a telephone conversation in May: "Now is the time to show the world that his great country can set an example for others … People ought to be allowed to vote without being intimidated, people ought to be allowed to be on TV, and if the government owns the TV, they need to allow the opposition on TV, people ought to be allowed to carry signs and express their pleasure or displeasure. People ought to have every vote count".[33] Soon state television began airing twenty-second TV commercials for the al-Ghad party that it had delayed showing for weeks despite receiving its fees for them.

The question of US interference was the issue around which the furious toeing and froeing between the government and opposition turned throughout 2005. The government said the opposition was backed by America, the opposition said the government had failed to maintain Egypt's independence by giving Washington reasons to interfere. With US acquiescence in the status quota, the government had given the most minimum of space to what it sometimes termed its "responsible" opposition (as opposed to the "irresponsible" Islamists), such as the secular-liberal Wafd party or Tagammu party. Inviting them into government, even in a token capacity, was never seriously considered throughout the 1980s or the 1990s when Islamist violence broke out. Turkey's model where the military stood back and did its best to promote secular parties while shutting out Islamists was never entertained. Back in 1997, when the government was secure in Western backing because of its role in the Israeli-Palestinian peace process and check on Islamist militancy, Nour once said bleakly of his parliamentary experience: "As an educated citizen, I should have the right to play a role in the future of the nation. But you have to fight to perform this duty. This is the real tragedy ... The government doesn't make deputies feel their participation is serious".[34]

The protests of May 2005 electrified the Arab world for a period – for the first time the Brotherhood looked to be flexing its muscles against the government, which looked worried. Prime Minister Ahmed Nazif was despatched to Washington for discussions with the government's reform plans at the top of the agenda. Adel Imam, the star of anti-Islamist films, took a swipe at the Islamists, telling the pan-Arab TV media in May 2005: "The protests in my films are patriotic, but the protests we are witnessing right now are not".[35] Under its new leader, Mohammed Mehdi Akef, a 75-year-old elected in January 2004, the Brotherhood had clearly made a decision to make a fundamental break with policy in the years since Mubarak came to power and join with other opposition groups in taking to the streets in peaceful protests demanding democratic reforms and the end of Mubarak's rule. It did so after Washington finally changed the rules of the game, suggesting it had abandoned the traditional US preference for repressive secular governments in the Middle East over the Islamist alternatives. As one newspaper said: "The peace is over and the fight is on between the government and the Brothers".[36] Even if Washington palpably stepped back from its promotion of reforms lest Islamists benefited, the Brotherhood had been coaxed out of its shell and taken its overt activism to a new level.

Ultimately, the Bush administration chose to limit its pressure on the government during 2005's "year of protests", precisely because of fears over how successful the Islamist movement might prove to be and what consequences that could have for relations between Egypt and the West. Although the parliamentary elections of November and December 2005 were more free than ever before, the state employed all the familiar tactics against the Brotherhood. What was striking was that they did so in earnest after the Brotherhood surprised observers by doing so well in the first of the three rounds of voting. The group won eighty-eight seats, nearly a fifth of the total and its strongest showing ever in parliamentary elections. More significantly, it was way ahead of the officially recognized secular opposition parties who only managed nine seats. The result was also despite significant efforts by the authorities in the second and third round of voting to make sure the Islamists' victory did not go any further. Hundreds of Brotherhood campaign workers were arrested, workers in state companies were bussed in to polling stations with incentives to vote NDP, and police blocked off entire polling stations to stop Brotherhood supporters entering them to cast their votes. Twelve people were killed in election violence, and rights groups witnessed abuse by police and NDP supporters of election monitors and candidates and their supporters. The Brotherhood chose not to challenge Mubarak in the presidential vote of September 2005, when Ayman Nour managed to poll 7.9 percent of the vote, ahead of the Wafd party leader's 2.9 percent, confirming Nour as the leader of the secular corner in Egyptian politics. Mubarak won with 88.6 percent, which was much as was expected. Saadeddin Ibrahim wrote: "This is far from a level playing field. Mubarak still commands disproportionate assets: name recognition, a virtual monopoly on state-controlled electronic media and some 85 percent of the print media".[37]

But, throughout the election experience of 2005, the US administration was notably muted in its criticisms of the violence and vote rigging. After the Brotherhood protests of May, observers noted a subtle shift in the administration's attitude towards democratic reform in Egypt – it did not have to be so drastic as to let the Brotherhood form a serious challenge to the government. Voters facing riot police closing off polling stations in November and December came to the clear conclusion that the United States was the power behind the government. When the final results came in, the administration said the process was "flawed" but was happy at the limited gains of the opposition. "(The election) represents a broadening of the representation of opposition and independent candidates in the Egyptian parliament and we think that's going to have a substantial impact on political life in Egypt," State Department deputy spokesman Adam Ereli said.[38] In March 2006, Mubarak was able to tell newspaper editors that Secretary of State Condoleezza Rice had been won over to Egypt's way of thinking on this democracy business. "She was very polite as she was listening to Egyptian opinions and points of view. She didn't bring up difficult issues or ask to change anything or to intervene in political reform, as some people say," Mubarak said, citing a meeting with Rice some days before.[39] "She was convinced by the way that political reform and the implementation of democracy is being done in Egypt ... She said that democracy in the Arab countries needed a generation." Following the parliamentary vote, the government delayed local council elections scheduled for April 2006 by two years, making it difficult for independent candidates – who would include the Brotherhood, since it is banned as a political party – from fielding a presidential nominee in the next vote in 2010. The complicated rules require candidates to obtain the support of a certain number of local council members, and the 2005 election showing suggested that the NDP would have trouble preventing a Brotherhood whitewash of the decrepit and corrupt councils, which the NDP solidly control. It was also back to business as usual concerning public protests: when demonstrators staged peaceful protests in May 2006 against disciplinary hearings for two judges who had blown the whistle on some of the election abuses, they were beaten and clubbed by an army of police and security forces who apparently had a new mandate to stamp out dissent.

Alongside the old dirty tricks, the NDP found modern ways to run its election campaign. The NDP had gone to considerable lengths to Americanize the face if not the substance of politics in 2005. Mimicking the slogans and style of Britain's revamped Labour Party of the late 1990s and the Democrats under Clinton when he came to power in 1993, the NDP acted as if it was a real party in a real political game. At campaign rallies during the presidential vote, Mubarak would turn up dressed casually in the manner of his son Gamal, seen as one of the gurus behind the new image, in front of cheering crowds of young people dressed in white "Mubarak 2005" baseball caps and T-shirts. He would have photogenic tea breaks with carefully selected farmers in rural areas, before going on to deliver well-crafted speeches filled with promises that address the real concerns of the people. The media coordinator of the campaign was Mohammed Kamal, a former professor of political science at Cairo University who received his doctorate from Johns Hopkins' School for Advanced International Studies in Washington, DC, on the topic of US politics. The Mubarak campaign also hired a professional advertising company to produce their campaign commercials and a polling expert whose staff of 100 pollsters met with people to fine-tune the campaign's message. Mubarak's speeches, which are now written by campaign staff rather than the office of the presidency, have a much more compassionate tone than previously. Where he once exhorted citizens to "export or die", he now talked about young people who could not find work. "I feel their pain and the lost dreams of each one of them", he told one rally, echoing Clinton's famous 1992 line: "I feel your pain".[40]

Egypt's changing position in the Arab world

Camp David and the sudden movement of Egypt into the US-Israeli axis caused an immediate rupture in Egypt's relations with other Arab countries. Egypt was ejected from the Arab League, whose headquarters moved from Cairo to Baghdad until a reconciliation was effected in 1988. Egyptian diplomacy worked hard during the 1980s to regain its central role in Arab politics. Iraq helped in return for Mubarak's support during the 1980–1988 Iran-Iraq war, but ultimately Egypt was back because, ironically, the peace treaty established Egypt's centrality and importance in the Arab world – it was the sole country with a direct line to both Washington and Tel Aviv. This was despite the setbacks for Palestinians as a direct result of the treaty. Israel was free to set about its settlement plan for the occupied territories and free to invade southern Lebanon in 1978 and Beirut in 1982, with no threat of an Egyptian military response. The Sinai was to be returned to Egypt in stages, so that the last part of the peninsula to be handed over, Taba, was not in Egyptian hands until 1989. Palestinian hopes to end the occupation meanwhile went nowhere, as Israel and the Palestinian Liberation Organization (PLO) fought in Lebanon and Palestinian residents of the occupied territories were offered a local-council autonomy plan rejected derisively as the "Swiss cheese" option.

It was against this background of increased regional violence as well as entrenched Israeli control that the Palestinians "of the inside", as they were often termed to set them apart from the Palestinian diaspora, decided to take matters into their own hands with the first Intifada launched in 1987. It was the Intifada that was to fundamentally change the balance of power with Israel and give Palestinians for the first time at least a semblance of a role in their own fate after years of haggling among Arab, Israeli and Western politicians. The Intifada exposed Israel to the world and to its own public as an occupying power, and suggested that maintaining the occupation was going to be costly in both political and financial terms. It was essentially these reasons that propelled Yitzhak Rabin into the Oslo accords in 1993, taking the historic Arab-Israeli conflict to a new level where the possibility of an end was finally in sight. There are usually two interpretations of PLO leader Yasser Arafat's role in the Intifada. One is that after the disaster of expulsion in 1982 from Beirut to Tunisia – a relative backwater in Arab politics – it offered him a chance to reinvent himself and continue the struggle on a new front. The conflict between the Palestinians in exile led by Arafat and those in the occupied territories challenging Israeli control on a daily basis has been well-documented. This grass-roots fight for independence was a clear challenge to the nationalist movement Arafat had led and developed since the 1960s. But, and here the second view of Arafat's role comes into play, he managed to turn that challenge to his advantage because Palestinians living under occupation were prepared to acknowledge his leadership role when it came to their future. At the political level, the Palestinian question was still very much a unified struggle where the cause of those still living in Palestine under occupation and the cause of those who had been left on the outside after the war of 1948 were still conceptualized as one and the same thing.

Interestingly, for the Israeli leadership these two sides of the Palestinian situation offered different possibilities: Rabin wanted Arafat, the leader of the exiles, to return to lead the occupied who remained on the inside. But in doing so, the Israeli political establishment was not conceding any points on the claims of those exiles Arafat represented, nor was it acknowledging explicit independence rights for those on the inside who Arafat was being asked to lead. On the contrary, one key Arab view of the failure of the Oslo years – from 1993 to 2000 when the second Intifada broke out – is that it resulted from an Israeli desire to make Arafat their policeman in territories they were not ready politically or psychologically to give up. The rights abuses of Palestinian police against Palestinians during this period are often invoked to back up this argument. Arab liberals only saw the creation of another Arab dictatorship in the manner of Egypt. Egypt's government became Arafat's closest partner and advisor during the Oslo enterprise – despite Arafat's long-held principle of not finding himself reliant on any of the Arab parties and maintaining independence, for the sake of Palestinians' own interests. Both regimes were dictatorial in character because they had to defend a status quo vis-à-vis Israel that was not to their people's liking and both Israel and the United States expected them to take measures to keep their people in line until peace talks produced the hoped-for resolution.

For Egypt, Oslo was a triumph and vindication of its own separate peace with Israel in 1979. Egypt argued that it had pioneered the principle of "land-for-peace" which other Arab countries should and could emulate. Jordan did so in 1994. By the same token, the unravelling of Oslo was troublesome for Cairo. In the initial welling of anger against Israel when the peace talks ran into the ground in the summer of 2000 and the Intifada began, the government had no choice but to back the massive demonstrations and encourage its print and television media to vent the frustrations of the political class and the street. The government's strategy in this was to ride the wave of resentment, take charge of it and channel it, all the better to ultimately lead it to a safe harbour. Protests in repressed political systems like Egypt's where the people have a long list of other grievances they could start protesting about could also easily get out of control. In October 2000, Mubarak called for an emergency Arab summit, expressed disgust at the shooting to death of Palestinian boy Mohammed al-Durra and withdrew Egypt's ambassador from Tel Aviv. But he was clear when asked directly on state television that there was no interest for Egypt in getting into another war with Israel.

At the time, the government faced considerable pressure from the United States that it was not doing enough to make sure the Palestinians under Arafat's leadership agreed to end the conflict at Camp David in 2000. Editorials and commentaries by senior columnists openly said that this was the least Washington had the right to expect from Egypt in return for two decades of US aid and support, to which the indignant response was that Egypt had done America more of a favour than it realized in backing America's military entry into the Gulf region during the 1990–1991 Gulf crisis. The Egyptian and Saudi leaders agreed in a meeting before the Intifada broke out to back Arafat on his refusal to concede Israeli sovereignty over East Jerusalem, or, crucially, to agree to a deferral of the issue, thus allowing a basic agreement to emerge from the summit on the other issues. *New York Times* columnist Thomas Friedman wrote, in a mock letter from President Clinton: "Hosni, I have to tell you how disappointed I and all my foreign policy aides were with your behavior during the Camp David summit ... More and more people are asking me: What exactly are we getting out of our relationship with Egypt – to mention $30 billion in aid to Egypt since 1978? ... Ever since Camp David, we in the US have judged Egypt on only one yardstick – how nice you were to Israel. And as long as you were not totally hostile, we made excuses for you and turned a blind eye to your regime's corruption and lack of democracy".[41] In response, Ibrahim Saada, editor of Egypt's state-owned *Akhbar al-Youm*, confirmed Friedman's point on Jerusalem, saying "no Arab party supports an agreement in which this issue is not yet solved", and added: "Your humiliating tone on the subject of aid forces me to mention Egyptian help during the Gulf war ... If it wasn't for Egypt, the Gulf crisis would not have been solved ... If it was not for Egypt and other allied Arab troops, the United States would not be able to land one soldier on the Arabian peninsula".[42]

The "Egypt first-ism" instituted by the state over twenty-five years ago has finally filtered down to some of today's democracy movement, sick of the long history of manipulation of the Israeli-Arab conflict by their leaders in order to maintain an inequitable and stifling status quo. "For the first time since 1977 Egyptians go to the streets over a domestic issue. Since then Egyptians have only protested over Palestine and Iraq. But now they go and demonstrate again over reform which is domestic," says political analyst Emad Gad.[43] The Brotherhood, on the other hand, remains wedded to populist rhetoric that places wider regional issues of dispute with the United States at the forefront of their political agenda. For example, it wants to put Camp David peace with Israel to a vote.

Egypt's position in Arab-Islamic culture and its relationship with the West has been a controversial issue over the last century. Egypt's intellectual class before the 1952 revolution drew inspiration from Europe and its ideas of freedom and democracy. Ever since the reign of Mohammad Ali in the early decades of the nineteenth century, like Ataturk's Turkey, Egypt has tried to "catch up" with Europe as an industrial secularist polity. The government as well as the intelligentsia had been reticently Arabist and sympathetic to the Zionists (who had chapters in Egypt in the 1920s and 1930s) for fear that the Palestinian nationalist movement would provoke anti-Jewish feelings in Egypt and ruin Egypt's complex social fabric. Some intellectuals, as Fouad Ajami has pointed out in his *The Dream Palace of the Arabs*, were openly favorable to Zionism and their aim of establishing a Jewish national homeland in Palestine.

Arab nationalism was a developing ideology during this period. As Europeans succeeded in spreading their political and economic and technology control over the world, the Arabs and the Turks, held together under the aegis of the Ottoman Empire, began to foster mutual resentment about whose fault this was. The "Young Turk" movement wanted to jettison the non-Turkish bits of the empire, and many Arabs wanted to ditch the Turks and take control of their own affairs. But for the Arabs there was no concensus on what type and size of political body they should form. Initially there were calls for an Arab caliphate with Islam and Arabic language as the unifying force. By the 1930s, Levantine intellectuals had refined the idea to an ethnically defined Arab nation. Many of them did not consider the Maghreb as part of the project, nor Egypt. But Egypt, strategically positioned and populous, was a great prize. And the efforts of the Muslim Brotherhood to popularize the

Palestinian cause against Zionism (backing the 1936 Palestinian uprising and staging huge demonstrations in Cairo) had helped swing Egypt towards Arabism, against the instincts of the liberal Wafd party elite that hoped it alone would be able to steer the country to complete independence from Britain.

By 1952, the Arab nationalist movement had taken a maximalist course and expanded to include all those countries the Arabs had first conquered in the Islamic conquests 1,300 years ago, when Islam first spread and the Arabic language took root. Under Nasser, pan-Arabism – *al-'uruba* or *al-qawmiyya al-'arabiyya* – became a living creed practiced by millions of people. Although in popular parlance the word "Arab" usually referred to Bedouin tribes, in 1958, the Egyptian regime acted on its nationalist ideology when it joined the United Arab Republic with Syria, effacing the name of a 5,000-year-old polity from the map. Arab had also been a term used as an insult by foreigners rather than as a term of pride by those it referred to. As such, Egyptian sociologist Leila Ahmed has said, Nasser was responsible for an ingenious transformation of "arab" to "Arab", just as Americans of African descent had taken "black" and made it "Black".

While Arab nationalism has failed to achieve its stated political goals, Arabism has been an astounding success on a cultural level, and Egypt has played a pivotal role in this regard through its immense cultural output over the last fifty decades in terms of film, literature, theatre, television, radio, dance and sport. The Cairence dialect has become a new *lingua franca* for the Arab world, in addition to classical Arabic. While political Islam has transplanted Arab nationalism as today's political project of choice, what Iraqi political scientist Adeed Dawisha calls simply "Arabism" carries on regardless.

Egypt's self-ejection from the political and military front against Israel was, then, a major psychological jolt for the Arab world. While it meant that the Nasserist political project was dead, the authoritarian apparatus and mentality of the Nasserist period remained in place while Egypt continued its cultural domination of the region. The result has been resentment and anger from just about every political group. Secularists and liberals who consider the application of Western political, economic and social models as of paramount importance see Egypt as a backward influence on the Arab world, while Islamists and Arab nationalists want Egypt back in the radical camp leading a new renaissance of independent action among Arab and Islamic countries in the face of an arrogant and exploitative West led by the United States. Fouad Ajami thinks Egypt is in danger of "falling yet again through the trap door of its history of disappointment", while Mohammed Hassanein Heikal says its time to stop believing the psychological warfare that aims to keep Egypt down and to realize that it is possible to stand up to the West.44

The future of the US alliance

1952 was meant to be the revenge of the wounded civilization, when Egyptians would not only take control of their own affairs and direct their economy and their politics for the benefit of the country's own sons but at the same time also lead all the peoples of the Arabic-speaking cultural bloc from foreign interference, from Algeria to Palestine. The last decade has seen a vigorous debate over why the great project veered off-track, not only in Egypt but all over the Arab world. In Egypt, the debate crystallized around the fiftieth anniversary of the July Revolution in 2002, an anniversary that allowed some reflection on the state of the nation. Egyptian economist Galal Amin asked poignantly in his book of the same title, "whatever happened to the Egyptians?" In 1952, Egypt could feed itself, had a vibrant parliament, an urban middle class, an economy that could produce – a sense of hope. Five decades later, the arrival in the age of progress is always just around the corner and the sense of foreign interference in its affairs is uncomfortably real. "The complete renaissance which Egypt is entering now and the secure society we live in would not have been possible without the previous efforts," President Mubarak said in a speech praising the revolution at a military academy parade in 2002. Egypt's leaders have been talking about the "complete renaissance" for decades. On the fiftieth anniversary day, boats floated up and down the Nile with massive posters of all four post-revolution presidents amid huge fireworks. But the efforts to drum up a carnival atmosphere could not have come at a worse time. Tourists were not coming, investors were not investing, the economy was not producing enough jobs to match population growth and the ossified US-backed political system creaked on. The government seemed unsure over whether to continue dismantling the Nasserist state that guaranteed jobs for life; democracy and free-market economics were, and still are, seen as weakness.

How much to blame the foreigners for this state of affairs remains a salient undercurrent of public discourse in Egypt. The military leadership gave up on the grand scheme for regional leadership because the Western powers, namely the United States, Britain and France, had done their utmost to destroy Arab nationalism. They were aided by those in the Arab world who never believed the project would or should work. Decay and corruption ate away at Egyptian society. In July 2005, al-Jazeera ran a documentary where some who saw the worst of the Nasserist state at first hand recounted the experience and revisited some of its prisons.[45] They detailed how 38,000 people were rounded up after Nasser announced he had discovered a new Brotherhood plot to overthrow him, and of those 38,000, fifty-seven were put on trial. They recounted daily deaths from being run over by cars and trucks, heads smashed against brick walls until death, maulings by specially trained dogs and the blatant seeking of false confessions to fulfil their quota and the scenario sought by the politicians, and this overseen by a security officer who to this day appears on discussion programmes as an expert on securities issues related to al-Qa'ida. Nasser's Egypt was surrounded by enemies; the United States and Saudi Arabia were backing the Islamists in order to bring down Nasser. But the result of the abuse suffered by Islamists in those years was the emergence of a virulent Islamic extremism that damned modern secular Arab society, leaders and peoples, as *kuffar*, unbelievers. In the 1970s, they called themselves names like Islamic Jihad and the Islamic Group; today they call themselves al-Qa'ida.

America, as Egyptian commentator Emad Gad says, has been the "absent but present" element in Egyptian politics for nearly three decades.[46] The new opposition, the old opposition and the regime are all trading accusations over who is playing America's game. The ruling NDP, which presides over a political and economic system fed on millions of US dollars in handouts, as well as significant European Union, Japanese and other aid, accuses Ayman Nour, the head of the al-Ghad party of being a "US agent" and a "rat" (words on posters near his party's offices in Cairo). As already seen, Nour accuses the regime of making annual "pilgrimage" to Washington. The regime suspects the Brotherhood is preparing for a critical dialogue with the US administration, while the Brotherhood makes elaborate public displays of anti-Americanism to reassure its rank-and-file and Arab public opinion in general. The Islamist movement is extremely reluctant to reformulate its carefully constructed anti-American intellectual edifice. Says a Brotherhood student leader from Zaqaziq in north Egypt: "We are building a global Islamic project. There will be diverging interests – we consider the Palestinian issue as number one. Israel is America's baby in the Middle East, they have ignored the rights of others and the Jewish state is an occupation. We can't deal with the United States because we can't trust it ... The government has already given all its concessions away. The US government – not the people – are the Egyptian people's number one enemy ... We tell the government 'we are your muscles, you don't need to let America interfere'".[47]

If the government says the opposition benefits from American pressure and blatant interference, the opposition says it was the government's stupidity to fail the nation to the extent that it allowed foreigners a look in, from its virtual one-party-state political system to its ineffectiveness in Arab politics. "We would have preferred that the regime makes peace with the people so that reform springs from an Egyptian desire," Brotherhood leader Mohammed Mehdi Akef said.[48] While editorialists in the pro-government papers say of the reformers, old and new: "Their treacherous call to 'saving' Egypt is misplaced. Nor will the noble Egyptian people be terrorized by such a debased campaign. The stances of these conspirators in the past shows their disgraceful identity and the hatred and envy entrenched in their hearts. Everybody should understand that Egypt is a strong nation with firm institutions ... I am sure that the Egyptians will turn a deaf ear to anyone who has sold himself cheap and meekly knelt to receive hand-outs from anyone".[49]

Receiving foreign money and support has been the insult of choice for the last two decades in Egypt. It was the petard on which Egyptian academic and rights activist Saadeddin Ibrahim was hung during his 2000–2003 detention and trial on charges of receiving European money to monitor elections and thus "defame Egypt's reputation". It was also used successfully in the 1990s to ruin the reputation of Egypt's budding rights movement and the justification for considerable state interference and restrictions codified in a 1999 law regulating NGOs. As Ibrahim has said: "Look at Egypt: they get $4 billion a year, $2 billion from the United States and another $2 billion from Europe and Japan. This creates a rentier state where there is no accountability for the state to its people since it is supported from abroad".[50] The Bush administration said in 2005 that its annual non-military aid handout to Egypt would now go not only to the government but would also include six NGOs.

Even if the regime gradually loosens its grip on the country and allows new forces to come into play and new players on the scene, the United

States is set to remain the great mover behind the scenes. As the moderate Islamist movement begins its march into mainstream political life, key questions will be what kind of relationship it develops with the US administration, which officially backs the government's ban on the Brotherhood and how American attitudes develop towards a revamped NDP, with Gamal Mubarak leading the party and/or the government.

In return for any eventual place in political life as a licenced party, the Brotherhood will find itself under pressure to move in the direction of the Islamist movement in Turkey. Under Necmettin Erbakan, the Welfare Party came to government but was chased out of the power by the military, and a more moderate version, Tayyip Erdogan's Justice and Social Development Party followed in its wake. The Brotherhood already has a younger clone in the form of the Wasat party and an attempted break-away movement under Khaled Zafarani, a well-known Islamist from Alexandria. Any of these three groups could emerge as Egypt's leading moderate Islamist force in the coming political order, or others may emerge.

Chapter 6
The House of Saud

The formation of Saudi Arabia

Saudi Arabia was chaperoned into existence by Britain and survived through the backing of the United States after British imperial power waned. The piecing together of the Saudi state in the 1920s was largely conditioned by the extent to which Britain had little imperial interest in the desert hinterland where the Bedouin Saudi family was left to sought to carve out a polity in the Arabian peninsula. Saudi Arabia won United Nations recognition in 1932, and might even have incorporated Yemen in 1934 were it not for British and Italian interference. British influence lingered on further in the coastal areas of the peninsula in order to ensure smooth passage through the Red Sea, Arabian Sea, Indian Ocean and Persian Gulf for imperial trade between Britain and India and the Far East. Britain did not formally leave the Gulf until 1971, when the United Arab Emirates came into being. While the "mandates" awarded to Britain and France after World War One allowed British oil interests to entrench themselves in Iraq, no one imagined that Saudi Arabia was also sitting on one of the world's largest oil reserves. However, the fact that the kingdom is the result of an indigenous campaign of unification, and not the direct handiwork of the foreign powers, is the source of great pride for Saudi Arabia.

With Britain more focussed on Iraq, the United States was able to establish a foothold in Saudi Arabia in what was to become one of the most solid, long-lasting and influential alliances in the modern Middle East. Through its company Aramco (Arabian American Oil Company), which was gradually nationalized throughout the 1970s and 1980s, the US government helped set up much of the state infrastructure that oil development required in the nascent Saudi state. For most Saudis, development was synonymous with the American oil company, which was based on the Persian Gulf in Dhahran. During the early years after oil concession was granted in 1933, Saudi Arabia was a huge but precarious country, paranoid about Britain's support for the Hashemite royal family in Jordan and Iraq (until 1958), countries which both had large tribal populations with origins in Saudi Arabia, and happy to develop political and military links with the United States. It was through Aramco that Saudi Arabia acquired its "first wave of Saudi administrators, technocrats, civil servants and oil millionaires, but also the first political prisoners, dissidents, exiles and opposition literary figures", anthropologist Madawi Al-Rasheed writes.[1] Egyptians, Palestinians, Indians and local Bedouin tribes and sedentary Shi'ites mixed and shared ideas, problems and political ideologies, helped by the spread of radio, creating new disturbing realities for the second Saudi king, Saud bin Abdel-Aziz (1953–1964).

Government in the Saudi dynastic possessions was minimal, partly because of its expense, and the law was the province of the class of religious scholars, or *ulema*. Modelled as a classic Sunni "Islamic state", the Saudi family assured the support of the clerics by allowing them free rein to rule society through the imposition of Islamic Sharia law: clerics, in Islamic theory, are in fact judges and legal experts and the courts remain the realm of the Islamic jurists today. Only commercial law is codified in Saudi Arabia. The founder, Abdel-Aziz (d.1953), cemented the unity of his vast realm through an inordinate number of marriages with the women of Arabian nobility, regional clans and families (the exact number of marriages is not known).

Preservation of their shaky realm in the face of a multitude of foreign and domestic pressures was the main concern of the Saudi rulers from the beginning, and their survival is one of the surprises and enigmas of modern Middle East politics. To piece the country together into a whole, the Saudis employed Bedouin warriors, known as the Ikhwan ("Brotherhood", no connection to the Egyptian political movement of similar name), from the central Najd area who were settled in special sedentary camps, called *hujar* (sing. *hijra*), where they were indoctrinated by preachers of the puritanical Najdi school of Sunni Islam that has come to be known as Wahhabism. One of the recurring problems throughout history with nomadic armies who have been united into a formidable fighting force is what to do with them when the job is done. The Arab armies faced this issue during the Islamic conquests of the seventh century, as did the Mongols several centuries later. In the case of the Saudi enterprise in the twentieth century, there was only limited room for maneuver. Greater European powers imposed restrictions on where the Bedouins could go. Having taken the Eastern Province in 1913, the province of Ha'il bordering Jordan and Iraq in 1921 and Hejaz area on the west coast in 1925, there was no possibility of getting Yemen or Kuwait because Britain would not allow it. Neither was there any scope for a zealous raiding campaign on the Shi'ite cities of Iraq, as the Saudi-Wahhabi armies had done a century before. They caused enough violence seizing the Hejaz cities – in Taif, in 1924, the Bedouin army killed hundreds who their clerics told them were *kawafir*, or "little infidels".

The result was a rebellion against the Saudis in 1927–1929; the Bedouin felt their allies had betrayed the Wahhabi cause by quitting the puritanical campaign of military expansion for Islam. The rebellion was repeated in 1979 when a group of tribesmen who were descendants of the original Ikhwan occupied the Grand Mosque in Mecca for two weeks, again denouncing the Saudi state for failing to live up to its Islamic ideals – an event that spurred the Saudi government into promoting Islamic values even more during King Fahd's reign (1982–2005) in a bid to pull the rug from under the feet of those in the Wahhabi clerical establishment who might think of replacing or even usurping them. Tension between a certain set of uncompromising Islamic ideals and the reality of modern state-building has been at the heart of the Saudi state since its inception.

The Saudis were particularly concerned about Hejazi separatism in their country's first two decades of independence. This area on the Red Sea includes the port cities of Jeddah and Yanbu and the hinterland holy cities of Mecca and Medina, as well as the mountain resort of Taif. In their conquest of the area in the 1920s, the Saudis had ousted the Hashemite family, who had ruled Mecca for 1,000 years. After allowing their demise, Britain installed Hejazi Hashemites as monarchs in Jordan and Iraq. They were violently deposed in Iraq in 1958, but govern Jordan to this day.

In the 1950s, the Saudi royal family also became concerned about the popularity of the anti-imperialism and pan-Arabism championed by Egypt, which spread among Shi'ites and other Saudis who worked with Aramco on the east coast. In 1956, Nasser received a rapturous reception on the streets of Dhahran, the oil town, and Riyadh, the capital of Saudi Arabia in the country's Najdi heartland – an event which so alarmed the royals that King Saud infamously hatched a plot to assassinate him.[2] The Shi'ites rose up against Saudi rule in 1980 after the Iranian revolution, complaining about treatment as second-class citizens in the Wahhabi state. Wahhabi zealots registered violent protest against modern innovations at numerous stages – King Faisal was assassinated in 1975 by a nephew apparently angry over the introduction of television. After the 1991 Gulf war, a number of Wahhabi clerics were jailed over calls for reform and criticism of the presence of American forces. Then, after the invasion of Iraq in 2003, the royals faced a revolt from Islamists under the al-Qa'ida banner, angry specifically about the kingdom's political alliance with the United States.

Saudi Arabia is based on a number of contradictions. "It's almost like four countries and that's why people are wary of change, because it could all deconstruct," says Saudi anthropologist Saad al-Sowayan, referring to the four regions of the Najd, the Hejaz, Asir bordering Yemen in the south and the Eastern Province, with its native Shi'ite population.[3] "The wealth is somehow expected to make it a melting pot, like America, but it's based on one product, oil, which is concentrated in one region, the east. In the Eastern region people could say 'it's ours and we're going away'. The Hejaz could easily say 'we want to be alone', and the rest will be left with poor resources." The country was modelled on two previous attempts by the Saudi family to set up a Najdi state. In the mid-eighteenth century, a cleric named Mohammed ibn Abdel-Wahhab offered his services to the Saudi family to establish a puritanical realm, which the Saudi family did by firing the Bedouin tribes up into a zealous fighting force. Abdel-Wahhab was a pious man from an isolated desert town near modern-day Riyadh who thought that the urban ways of Muslims in the peninsula – venerating holy men through visiting their graves, or celebrating the birth of the Prophet and other figures from early Islam – were a heretical divergence from the original monotheistic message of Islam and its call for worship of the one true God, and represented a return to the pre-Islamic ways of the Arabs. For some of his followers, even using rosary prayer beads was against the monotheistic spirit of Islam. In their view, the Bedouins in the central plains where he came from did not have any religion at all.

The first aim of the alliance in 1744 between the "Al Saud" family and Abdel-Wahhab and his followers was to unite the Bedouins of this central Najd area. The Saudi-Wahhabi Bedouin alliance went on to invade the cities in the west – then under Ottoman Turkish control – and stormed north into Iraq where they sacked the tomb of the Prophet's grandson Hussein in Kerbala in 1801. This first Saudi state (1744–1818) collapsed when Mohammed Ali expanded his Egyptian empire into the peninsula, but then Al Saud plotted its return. They came and went again in the mid-nineteenth century (1824–1891) but were back in 1902 for a third time, seizing Riyadh and gradually adding territories until by 1932, after following the same tactic of unleashing Bedouin zealots against urban Muslims considered unworthy of their religion, they had united most of the peninsula, bar the mountainous southern regions of the Yemen and Oman and the coastal states of the Gulf, which were all propped up by Britain.

An inadequate distribution of resources and absolute control maintained by the ever-expanding Saudi family has created a strange-shaped polity. The wealth that was to follow the oil price hike of the 1970s allowed the ruling family a spendthrift lifestyle that clashed with their Islamic ideals as much as their close political alliance with the United States. They allowed foreign troops on their soil during the 1990–1991 Gulf crisis and then on a long-term basis. The country was inordinately wealthy and claimed Islamic leadership through its housing of Islam's two holiest shrines in Mecca and Medina, yet its sovereignty was skewered by the absolute monarchy's ultimate need to turn to foreigners to protect themselves. Sharp disparities of wealth have emerged in recent years, not only in the mountainous provinces on the border with Yemen but also in districts of the capital Riyadh itself due to rural and provincial migration. In 2002, Crown Prince Abdullah had made a surprise trip to a poor neighbourhood of Riyadh, toured the streets and asked people how they were living. A few months later, the government declared it was putting together a national stategy to combat poverty. The country had known for a decade that it had structural problems because the days of unlimited oil wealth could not continue forever as the population grew and prices fell, and the Crown Prince had said so bluntly and publicly in 1998. But still the bald statement that there were poor Saudis came as a shock to many people inside the land of fabled wealth.

American protection for Saudi Arabia

The most controversial contradiction in the modern Saudi state has been its reliance on foreign arms. Thousands of US troops stationed there since since the 1991 Gulf War only left in August 2003, after the demise of Saddam Hussein had made their presence obsolete. But military advisers remain and in any case the troops have not really gone from the peninsula, they simply relocated to neighbouring Qatar and Bahrain whose population and political constituencies were by and large too small and disinterested to question their rulers' decision to host a mass American military presence. This presence in Saudi Arabia was among the first grievances aired by bin Laden to justify attacks against the United States.

Few Saudis really felt the Americans' presence in their daily lives, since they kept well out of the way at an airbase outside Riyadh from where they manned the so-called "no-fly zone" over southern Iraq during the 1990s and from where part of the 2003 Iraq invasion was coordinated. The idea that the Saudi royals are propped up by America is widespread in the Arab world and is a salient feature of opposition to their rule within the kingdom and elsewhere. In the Internet age, it has even become a source of humour. The government stages an annual cultural festival called the Janadiriya, a celebration of Bedouin values where tribesmen including the top Saudi royals and the king himself join in sword dances and other demonstrations of valour from the days when the tribes fought each other for control of oasis and territory. A satirical website asked in February 2006 ran a caption alongside a picture of King Abdullah, son of the kingdom's founder who really did fight in the old manner, "if you're such a heroic swordsman then why did you ask the Marines and other women to protect you from Saddam?"[4]

When asked, Saudis seemed mystified at their country's need to hire a foreign army for protection rather than do it themselves. With unemployment such a problem, a standing army of substance could have some real purpose. "Having the Americans here causes a lot of trouble, because our soldiers end up just relying on them. The Saudi royal family would rather pay the Americans to protect them," a young Shi'ite from Dammam said.[5] "They don't want to lose Saudi lives, or they cannot depend on Saudi soldiers? It doesn't make sense. Sometimes they say that they simply depend on God." The general flavour of Saudi Arabia is not militaristic at all – the state intends to give the impression of a depoliticized Islamic paradise – and a large native army may have seemed an unworldly, un-Islamic thing to have. Yet this phenomenon is a recurring feature of Islamic history. Two hundred years into the Islamic era the Abbasid caliphs, always struggling to find legitimacy for their tyrannical rule, appeared to fear turning to their own people to defend their realm and so imported Turkish slave soldiers from Central Asia. The Abbasid caliph, who ran one of the most powerful polities on the planet, hired foreigners to defend himself. Why? The answer perhaps lay at the point where rosy ideology and harsh reality collide. The caliphs according to their own self-legitimizing theory were guardians of the God's chosen society: putting some of their own Muslims at arms, at least domestically, would imply that their subjects might have reason to challenge them. They could not trust their own people because too few in fact recognized their right to rule. Thus, they and what Islamic scholars theorized as the Dar al-Islam ("the realm of Islam") could only be defended by hired outsiders, held as slaves, infidels with no interest but collecting their paycheck and ensuring a living.[6] (There are perhaps similarities in the phenomenon of hiring an army of over six million foreigners to carry out the menial and other jobs required in running a modern state that Saudis find distasteful.)

The Turkish soldiers went on to convert to Islam and take control of the Abbasid state from within. They established the Mameluke state in Egypt, and Turkish tribes went on to establish the Ottoman Empire. No one was expecting anything similar from the Americans during the 1990s (though the native Emiratis are extremely jumpy about their minority status among the hired foreigners in the UAE). When Saddam Hussein's Arab nationalist army stormed into Kuwait, the House of Saud, which also styles itself as the protector of a model Islamic society, discovered it could not protect itself. Nearly half a million American troops were sent to the Gulf to drive the Iraqi army out of Kuwait and make sure they did not cross what the then-president George Bush called a "line in the sand" into Saudi Arabia, America's strategic oil-supply partner. After the war, the United States military maintained a basic force of 20,000 men and formalities such as a ninety-day notice for US warships to enter the ports of Jeddah and Dammam were waived. There were over 3,000 military personnel based in Dhahran alone, in addition to 35,000 American civilians in Saudi Arabia. This was one reason why, Arab opposition figures always noted, Washington always had little to say about Saudi's human rights record during the period.

In June 1996, suicide bombers struck a complex housing American air force and army personnel at Khobar near the Persian Gulf, killing nineteen Americans; in November, a bomb strike killed five Americans at the Saudi Arabia National Guard. Apparently embarrassed by their need to host the American military, the Saudi authorities had grown notably terse with the Americans, reports said, delaying landing clearance to American aircraft and arguing over fuel arrangements and weapons storage.[7] "The Gulf War produced results similar to Nasser's revolution in a way – it made the regime's reliance upon a foreign power absolutely obvious to everyone. The concentrated presence of Americans on the streets caused a religious reaction against them, socially and politically," Egyptian opposition figure Abdel-Halim Qandil said after the Khobar bombings in 1996.[8] "After the Gulf War the American presence has been massive and provoked ill-feeling. The American military reminds Arabs in general of occupation and colonialism, whereas the state should be the one making its decisions," Egyptian intellectual Rafiq Habib said.[9]

Turning to foreigners to prop up the kingdom already had a precedent in the short history of the Saudi polity. Fearing a depletion of US oil reserves after the First World War, Washington demanded that colonial powers Britain and France allow an open door policy towards oil in the region, and US oil interests became participants in Iraqi oil and then acquired concessions in the Arabian peninsula in the 1930s. British involvement in Saudi political affairs continued unchallenged, however, until 1943 when President Roosevelt formally declared Saudi Arabia as of vital interest to the security of America, opening the door to US aid to the kingdom which at that time had few of the trappings of a modern state. In 1951, the United States signed a low-key defence agreement with Saudi Arabia. Nasser in Egypt virulently opposed US efforts to make itself the region's protector against an imagined Soviet threat. In Nasser's view, there was no such threat, and the Arab region was capable of pulling together to defend its own interests without American, British or French meddling. Days after the Yalta conference in 1945, when Winston Churchill and Joseph Stalin laid down the lines for post-war Europe, President Roosevelt met King Abdel-Aziz on a US ship on the Suez canal. The Eisenhower Doctrine of 1957 stated that US military and economic assistance would be available to any state in the Middle East which requested it and was threatened by communism. Egypt's Czech arms deal and Soviet help in building the Aswan dam helped identify radical Arab nationalism with international communism in US minds. Egypt's backing for Yemeni republicans, while Saudi Arabia backed the monarchy, confirmed US suspicions that Saudis and not Egyptians were their kind of Arabs. Three Saudi pilots flew to Cairo in protest over Saudi Arabia's position against Egypt at this time[10] and in fact British pilots, far more dependable that Saudis who might harbour Arab nationalist sentiments, were flying British fighter jets sold to the royals in the mid-1960s.[11] As Egypt drew closer to the Soviets, the Saudis drew closer to the Americans. After the 1967 war, Israel, Iran and Saudi Arabia were clearly established as the United States' three main allies in the Middle East. After 1979, Egypt replaced Iran.

The discovery of oil in Saudi Arabia changed life in this new country beyond all proportion and in a more radical manner than perhaps life in the peninsula had ever changed before. In the classic trilogy *Mudun al-Malh (Cities of Salt)*, by late Saudi novelist Abdel-Rahman Munif, the men of a lost valley wonder why these foreigners, Americans, have appeared in the area, claiming they look for water. "What could they really want? What is there in this waterless desert other than hunger, sand and clouds of dust? ... And they ask sly questions, like 'have any foreigners been here, have you heard about any English or French who've come here, did they stay long?' ... They said more of them would come, and they said 'wait and be patient, every one of you will become rich!'"[12] The Bedouin even mistake the Americans' early morning exercises for a strange form of prayer. Like his Mooran, Riyadh was transformed from a dusty desert town into an expanding city of foreigners and the accoutrements of modern, foreign culture. For his frank, unflattering depiction of how Saudi rulers developed the country in alliance with America Munif remained without Saudi nationality for some four decades, until he died an exile in Damascus in 2004.

Saudi Arabia did not have a council of ministers until 1953 and only some twenty-seven state schools and twenty-two private schools, and much of the state budget, meagre as it was, went on buttressing the extensive royal lineage in order to consolidate Saudi rule and the territorial integrity of the fragile state. It was Aramco itself which was left to build much of the country's infrastructure, including roads, pipelines, ports, airports, schools, hospitals and even the railway. The company's bosses ran the operation from the secluded "American camp", a little piece of America in the main oil town of Dhahran on the east coast, and thousands of Saudis from around the country would dream of finding lucrative work with the foreigners. The influx of Americans was constantly justified by Abdel-Aziz himself through a famous Quranic verse: "O Unbelievers, I do not worship what you worship, nor do you worship what I worship. I shall never worship what you worship and you shall never worship what I worship. You have your religion and I have mine."[13] But it was an injuction that applied equally to other Arabs and the seditious ideas they harboured, such as Arab nationalism and communism – ideologies that filtered into the kingdom through the Aramco camp in the Eastern Province and through radio.

Aramco features heavily in novelist Turki al-Hamad's tale of Saudi-US relations, *Sharq al-Wadi (East of the Valley)*. In this examination of the culture clash between Saudis and Americans, the main character Jaber finds work in Aramco, discovers Arab nationalism and then has an affair with the wife of an American manager before winning an appointment in

Austin, Texas. "She said: 'Shave your beard and I'll shave myself down there.' That got him angry, so he said, screwing his eyes up and holding back the urge to hit her: 'You compare my beard to your pubic hair? You vulgar whore!' Then Ethel got angry at being described as a whore and threw him out of the house, saying: 'You wretched worker, you filthy Arab'."[14] Fitting into American life, he shaves off his beard and moustache as his American lover had been imploring him to do in Saudi Arabia; he "completely Americanizes", Hamad writes. Now Ethel wishes he would keep his Arab looks. "She wished he wouldn't shave since with a beard it reminded her of Clark Gable and Errol Flynn, who he was nicer than anyway with his brown skin. When he managed to watch their films, since he didn't know who Clark Gable or Errol Flynn were, it made him feel good that she compared them." Hamad's novels are all banned in Saudi, like those of Munif.

Under King Faisal (1964–1975), Saudi Arabia found its stride within the sphere of regional politics, advancing a pan-Islamic ideology that stood as a credible alternative to Egypt's radical Arab nationalism, which remained a threat to the rule of the Saudi royals themselves. A major plot was uncovered to assassinate Faisal in 1969. With the death of Nasser in 1970, Saudi Arabia was able to emerge as a major regional player, with political influence to match its oil wealth and it could offer large sums of money to the newly established Palestinian Liberation Organization as well as other Islamic causes in Africa and Asia. Eventually, Saudi Arabia and Egypt were to become close allies, as Egypt followed Saudi Arabia into the American orbit in the 1970s. Sadat's expulsion of Soviet military advisors in 1972 paved the way. Islamic groups thrived in both countries, in one through the tolerance of the state (Egypt) and in the other in alliance with the ruling family (Saudi Arabia). Saudi Arabia's use of the "oil weapon" in 1973 to back the Arab side in the Egyptian-Syrian October war with Israel did wonders for the country's image in the Arab and Islamic world but in fact little harmed the strengthening relationship with the United States. As Al-Rasheed writes: "The rhetoric of confrontation over the oil crisis and the Arab-Israeli conflict masked a partnership that had been developing behind the scenes."[15] Prior to the 1990–1991 Gulf crisis, Saudi Arabia had sought American help to protect its vulnerable status. The kingdom bought billions of dollars of US goods, including numerous arms contracts, placed billions in US government securities and other investments, and built three military cities near its Iraqi, Jordanian and Yemeni borders.

But despite its uniquely close ties with the United States, despite its wealth and despite its standing in the Islamic world, Saudi Arabia had a negligable impact on US policy towards Israel.

Crisis in the kingdom after 9/11

Saudi-American relations were thrown into crisis by the September 11 attacks. It was in fact the worst crisis in the kingdom's surprisingly long lifetime, since it cut to the very heart of the survival of the state: its oil rent relationship with Washington. The United States wondered whether one of its best friends – so good that it had done next to nothing to influence American policy in the Arab-Israeli conflict – had been acting against it all along. Fifteen of the attackers were Saudi nationals, working for an anti-American Islamist network headed by another Saudi. But worse was the suspicion that money from all levels of Saudi society had found its way into al-Qa'ida's coffers, financing its plan to drive the United States out of the Middle East. For the Saudi state, it was a dreadful denouement that even risked its nightmare scenario of an American intervention in the Eastern Province to secure the oilfields – the idea of overthrowing the Saudis or occupying the oilfields was famously bandied around Washington when King Faisal withheld oil in 1973. In this view, the Shi'ites were transformed overnight from a potential fifth column for Iran into a potential fifth column for the United States. Moves to ease the persecuted status of Shi'ites did indeed follow, to head off any American championing of them as a human rights cause. For ordinary Saudis, 9/11 marked a new era of suspicion in the West and the United States, in particular, simply for being the holder of a passport marked "Saudi Arabia" – in fact, this may have signalled the beginnings of a shared sense of "Saudi" identity among the country's disparate populations for the first time in its modern history.[16] Only since the early years of the twenty-first century had the Saudi education system begun to encourage pupils to have pride in a Saudi identity, where previously all that mattered was being a Sunni Muslim in the Wahhabi state.

A corollary to this crisis came two years later. One month after the fall of Baghdad, on the night of 12 May 2003, nine men, three each in three separate vehicles, drove into three foreign residential compounds named after the Arab cities of long lost Andalucia (Qurtuba, Ishbiliya and Ghurnata, Cordoba, Seville and Grenada) and blew themselves up, taking

26 people with them, a mixture of foreigners and Saudi nationals. The attacks shocked ordinary Saudis and shook the authorities. There had been attacks by radical Islamists in the country before, notably against US troops at Khobar in 1996, but never on this scale in the capital itself, never against civilians and never in a manner that would so wantonly kill Saudis too. For the government, it was a further sign of the need to tackle the obscurantism of its own Wahhabi religious establishment, though interestingly some key royals blamed Egypt's political Islam movement for having radicalized its own Wahhabis during the 1970s when many Muslim Brotherhood figures taught in Saudi Arabia. The al-Qa'ida campaign against the Saudi royal family was a sign of the crisis of legitimacy and identity that a country that appeared to have it all and want for nothing had fallen into. It also presented risks and advantages vis-à-vis its alliance with the United States. If Saudi Arabia could not meet the al-Qa'ida challenge, it faced the possibility, yet again, of American intervention. If it was seen to vigorously fight them, with American help, it could regain American favour.

This latter was what in fact happened. Fighting al-Qa'ida has led to a marked improvement in Riyadh's relations with Washington. Saudi Arabia was aided by the debacle of America's involvement in Iraq, which helped send world oil prices to new highs and warned of the danger of the direct military tampering with the map of the Middle East. Interior Minister Prince Nayef had opposed such intimate American intervention in the country's affairs – perhaps a kneejerk reaction to the country's massive reliance on this outside power – but a mixture of American pressure and the shock of a domestic war against the Saudi royals acted to change that. By 2005, the US media was praising Saudi security chief (and Prince Nayef's son) Mohammed bin Nayef and the Saudi intelligence war on al-Qa'ida in general as one of the world's best anti-terror operations.[17] After 9/11, Saudi Arabia also opened up to the international media and took tentative steps towards expanding political participation in the kingdom – both moves strengthened the country's image and relations with the outside world, and helped dissuade any foreign parties from ideas of dismantling the Saudi state or replacing it. The authorities talked publicly of their opposition to the American invasion, while quietly facilitating the air war from the airbases the Americans had been using in the kingdom for the last decade.

A decade before, young zealous Saudis like Mansour al-Nogaidan were attacking small-scale targets in a crusade against immorality. As an idealistic twenty-one-year old, full of ultra-pious Wahhabi outrage,

Nogaidan took part in a firebomb attack on a Riyadh video store. "We were young and we were angry. Prominent clerics supported us, so after serving over a year of a 16-year sentence we were pardoned by King Fahd," he says.[18] "The situation is much more serious today and the big difference is that religious anger is being directed against the state itself and foreigners here. It's easy for young people to get into militant groups which think the state is subservient to America. They think that we must get rid of this ruling system in order to strike the Americans. They think these are all illegitimate Arab regimes." While these ideas were not new in the Arab world, first emerging in Egypt in the 1960s, they were new to Saudi Arabia, where the strict Islamic codes at home and lavish funding for Islamic causes abroad had kept radical youth from turning on the House of Saud. Mohammed al-Mas'ari, an Islamist dissident based in London, argued the same: young Saudi radicals had finally focussed on their own country, despite a sweeping domestic implementation of Islamic Sharia law found nowhere else in the world, because the regime, so allied with Washington, did not practice what it preached at the level of foreign policy. "The main reason there was no militant action in Saudi in the last ten years was ideological – it would have involved Muslims getting killed. Now people are getting over this," he said.[19] In February 2006, the movement staged its first direct attack on a major oil installation, the giant plant at Abqaiq in the Eastern Province which processes two-thirds of Saudi Arabia's daily oil output. Afterwards, they issued a statement, using the al-Qa'ida brand name, which declared: "We restate our determination to crush the Crusader forces and the tyrants, and to stop the theft of the wealth of Muslims which the tyrants have allowed their Crusader masters easy access to."[20] They said they were acting on a call by bin Laden in a message broadcast months before to attack the kingdom's oil interests.

The idea of warring the Saudi royals stemmed from the first Gulf war. In a story that has become legion, bin Laden offered to defend the kingdom's oil fields against a possible Iraqi invasion after Saddam Hussein's forces took Kuwait in 1990.[21] But the royals rejected the offer, and made a false vow that the US troops would only be there until the end of the war. The episode confirmed to bin Laden that Saudi Arabia was hopelessly wedded to its Western alliance at the expense of Arab and Muslim causes. His declaration with Ayman al-Zawahiri of a "World Islamic Front for Jihad against Jews and Crusaders" in February 1998 accused the United States of seeking to "destroy Iraq and fragment states of the region like Iraq, Saudi Arabia, Egypt and Sudan into paper mini-states, and through their disunity and weakness guarantee Israel's survival and the continuation of the brutal Crusader occupation of the Arabian peninsula".[22]

The idea that "Saudi was next" was popular in the Arab media at the onset of the Iraq invasion in 2003. On Saudi television, preachers pronounced that Saudi was the real target of the war on Iraq and columnists in papers close to the state argued back nervously that the fears were exaggerated, while being careful to avoid mentioning the kingdom by name. "There have been fears that this war will not end at Iraq and will include other countries in the region, according to an American strategy these people see to redraw the regional map," the daily *al-Watan* said in an editorial.[23] "We do not think this analysis is correct, since redrawing the region's map cannot be done through military circumstances alone." Reports were rife in the Arab media that some sort of debate was going on inside the beltway prior to the Iraq war in 2003. Think-tank reports said the real target in the war on terrorism was Saudi Arabia and Egypt and the US government appeared to have leaked these musings of its political advisers deliberately. The Rand Corporation told the Pentagon in a presentation that "Iraq is the tactical pivot; Saudi Arabia the strategic pivot, Egypt the prize."[24] An Internet symposium some months later, featuring pro-Israeli analysts and academics Daniel Pipes, Laurent Murawiec (a former Rand analyst) and Daniel Brumberg of Georgetown University, raised similar questions.[25] "Al-Qa'ida wishes to reign supreme in Saudi Arabia once it brings about its collapse, even if such a collapse means a total break up of the kingdom and the installation of a radical Islamic government on only a portion of its land. Chaos is al-Qa'ida's weapon," *al-Hayat*'s New York bureau chief Raghida Dergham wrote at the time.[26] "But a clique of American and Israeli extremists is aslo working to bring about the collapse and break-up of Saudi Arabia. Control of the oil-rich eastern region is one of their goals. Another goal consists of dividing the Arab region in general to remove any threat or challenge it poses to Israel. Al-Qa'ida and this radical American-Israeli clique agree on the desire to sever the American-Saudi relationship, even if for entirely different reasons."

America and the Saudi reform movement

Saudi Arabia's reform movement has had nothing near the American support which that of Egypt has won since the Iraq invasion in 2003.

Opposition groups were largely ignored, just as they were in Egypt, throughout the 1990s. The first Gulf crisis, like the second one, provoked peaceful dissent in the kingdom. Influential clerics in Saudi Arabia, as in Egypt, challenged the legitimacy of the alliance with the United States against Iraq, though religious scholars in the pay of the state argued that their governments' choices were justified. Against the support for the war from Saudi's highest official religious authority, Sheikh Abdel-Aziz bin Baz, independent but hardline Wahhabi scholars said the real enemy was the West, upon whom the kingdom was becoming so dependent, and not Iraq.

In an effort to release tensions, King Fahd set up a consultative body, the Shura Council, in 1992 to advise on and propose laws but dozens of people were arrested, including well-known clerics such as Safar al-Hawali and Salman al-Awdeh, for their direct criticism of the Saudi political system, corruption and alliance with America. Most were released after a few years at most, after promising to refrain from attacking the royals themselves, though one, Said bin Zuair, remained incarcerated until 2003 and was rearrested a year later after making comments to al-Jazeera that put Osama bin Laden in a positive light (making Zuair a poster child of the new Islamist movement that began fighting the state after the 2003 Iraq war, a *cause celebre* on Islamist websites).

After the 2003 war, liberal democrats in alliance with some moderate Islamists have led calls for democratic reform. But sharp divides have emerged among the liberal-Islamist group and the cleric reformers. One crucial difference has been the role of Saudi Arabia's special morality police, the "authority for forbidding undesirable practices and encouraging accepted behaviour" (its official title), known colloquially as the *Mutawwa'*, which patrols the streets and shopping malls to make sure women wear their cloaks and veils properly, that men in women's company are relatives and that shops close during the call to prayer. They also have wide powers to follow up on alcohol and drugs use and detain individuals. The cleric reformers want the religious establishment to be free to speak its mind, the liberal democrats want their powers further curtailed.

The US position on the second wave of protest and dissent in Saudi Arabia has been lukewarm at best. After years of dealing lightly with human rights abuse in its annual rights reports, the State Department began paying Saudi Arabia some attention after September 11. Given the underlying reasons that brought the two together in alliance in the first place – oil rents – it was only a matter of time before things returned to normal. To ward off the pressures again, municipal elections were held in late 2004 and early 2005, but women were barred from voting, only half the seats were chosen by vote and Islamists, better organized and free to operate, won control of most of the councils. A number of petitions to Crown Prince Abdullah (king since August 2005) by academics and writers called for parliamentary elections, women's rights, an end to discrimination of minorities such as the Shia, good governance and better distribution of resources around the vast country.

Three of the petitioners were jailed for terms of six to nine years in May 2005 for inciting people at a critical time in Saudi Arabia's history when "its enemies are lurking and looking for excuses to intervene in the name of reform", a reference to the United States.[27] They were arrested in March 2004, after the petitions had been made and publicized. One was criticized by the judges for blaming the al-Qa'ida campaign in Saudi Arabia on its Wahhabi school of Islam. Washington spoke out about the trial. "In Saudi Arabia, brave citizens are demanding accountable government," Secretary of State Condoleezza Rice said in Egypt before visiting Riyadh in June 2004. "Three individuals in particular are currently imprisoned for peacefully petitioning their government – and this should not be a crime in any country."[28] But she made no such statements from inside Saudi Arabia itself and there is no record of what she told its leaders when she met them in private. Wrote one Saudi liberal: "The centrality of 'price-at-the-pump' issues has created a simple logic: a Saudi-American agenda that has oil at its center is one that reduces democracy, religious freedom and respect for human rights to what they had always been: footnotes."[29] The men were pardoned after King Abdullah ascended the throne in August 2005.

Fearing the advances of the liberals, the cleric reformers mounted a counter-campaign with the interior ministry's support. In 2003, Hussein Shobokshi found his TV show on Saudi-owned al-Arabiya had been stopped, his weekly columns in Arabic and English-language Saudi papers had been withdrawn and Islamists had spread rumours that he claimed to the foreign media that Crown Prince Abdallah supported his reformist views. He was one of around one hundred writers whose articles were banned after the war, according to pro-democracy dissidents based in Washington who had been counting. "They rubbish your reputation and slander you, and it's an orchestrated effort. It's not sporadic. They use the internet, mobile phones, and leaflets handed out at mosques. There are lots of clerics asking for liberal writers to be banned and they are lobbying for that. These clerics are terrified. For a long time they had an exclusive franchise, but now they have been shocked that satellite TV, the press and the internet are willing to accommodate other opinions," Shobokshi said.[30]

When London-based dissident Saad al-Fagih called for demonstrations in December 2004, police filled the streets of Riyadh and Jeddah to stop significant protests, and fifteen, who tried, were given subsequently given jail sentences ranging from two to six months and ordered to receive between 100 and 250 lashes apiece (Saudi paranoia about large public gatherings and protest is again reminiscent of the grand but troubled Abbasid caliphs).[31] Saudi Arabia relentlessly sought to connect Fagih to the al-Qa'ida campaign, and, in December 2004, a week after the protests, he was placed on a UN list of al-Qa'ida associates whose assets should be frozen by UN member states, at the behest of Saudi Arabia, the United States and Britain. This happened after the US Treasury accused him of associations with al-Qa'ida since the mid-1990s, including someone linked to the bombings of US embassies in Kenya and Tanzania in 1998. Fagih has said he only knew the man, Khaled Fawaz, because he once visited his rights group, the Movement for Islamic Reform in Arabia, in London and hails from the same tribe.[32]

The eventual ascendancy of King Abdullah has created a new political playing field. Saudi Arabia now appears to bear witness to the odd phenomenon of a liberal governing elite and conservative society at large. Now the Wahhabi establishment, including the state-backed clerics and the independent cleric reformers, fear that the liberals have gained the ear of the king. His main advisers are thought to be liberals, and the government is seen as plotting how to gradually "secularize" the country and the reduce the power of the Wahhabi clerics – or encourage a new generation of younger, moderate Wahhabi clerics – without stirring open revolt and dissent among its Wahhabi allies. State television was placed in the hands of a liberal Information Minister, Iyad Madani. Al-Arabiya, the Saudi-owned pan-Arab channel that seeks to promote "moderation" in relations with the West and in religion, is ridiculed by the al-Qa'ida supporters as al-Ibriya ("the Hebrew channel").

Popular Saudi attitudes towards America

Popular attitudes towards the United States have soured markedly since September 11, in tune with popular Arab and Muslim attitudes to the United States elsewhere in the region. Society at large was suspicious and resentful of their official "friend". Ordinary Saudis opposed the Iraq war as much as Arabs anywhere else in the region. Saudi newspapers published graphic and gory images of Iraqi civilians hit by US bombings during the war. When a Baghdad market was hit on 28 March, *al-Riyadh* daily proclaimed in its frontpage headline: "Yet another massacre by the coalition of invaders." Saudis, especially those with business interests in the United States where they may have sent their children, sensed the hostility to them in the United States from almost every corner of society bar the White House. Around a third of the al-Qa'ida suspects held at Guantanamo Bay were Saudis. Families of September 11 victims filed a $100 trillion lawsuit in 2002 against Saudi banks, Islamic charities and prominent members of the Saudi royal family. A capital flight began, as Saudis began to pull out some of the $500–700 million of overseas investment held in the United States, encouraged by the government to place it in the Saudi stock market that took off from late 2002.[33] In June 2004, the al-Qa'ida insurgents kidnapped and killed an American citizen who lived in Riyadh, citing his work for defence contractor Lockheed Martin on the manufacture of Apache helicopter gunships as justification. "This act is to heal the hearts of believers in Palestine, Afghanistan, Iraq and the Arabian Peninsula," the group said.[34] "This is so that he can taste what Muslims have suffered from Apache planes and their rockets. The slain American parasite was working on their maintenance and developing their systems in Saudi Arabia." The group called themselves the "Falluja Brigade" of al-Qa'ida in the Arabian Peninsula, in reference to the Iraqi city which was at the forefront of the Sunni Arab insurgency against the US occupation in Iraq.

Yet Saudi Arabia still offers a confusing picture of America love and hate. Until the 1970s, most Saudis probably felt deep respect and gratitude for the United States for having helped them turn a vast, diverse desert land into a modern country through their development of the oil fields. As the country became more wealthy and political consciousness became more discernible, attitudes began to change. Since the 1970s, the religious establishment became more powerful and the general discourse of political Islam since that time has been no less anti-American in Saudi Arabia than elsewhere in the Arab world. The government partly encouraged this after the 1979 seizure of the mosque in Mecca by Wahhabi zealots. Commentators have noted that Saudis of the generation preceding the 1980s were far more pro-American than those who followed, when the syllabuses developed a marked xenophobic and anti-Western slant.

The signs of American cultural influence are everywhere. Americana dominates even in the holy city of Mecca, where Western fast-food chains, malls and other real estate development are the order of the day. "Mecca and Medina are the most disturbed cities in the world in every sense. They are totally out of balance. New buildings are coming up and the skyline of Mecca will be like the skyline of New York," architect Sami Angawi says.[35] Mecca also has an exclusive hotel called Burj Zamzam – towering over the central mosque and heavily advertised on al-Arabiya – where you pay the world for a view of the *Kaaba*, the large cuboid structure in the middle of the Grand Mosque in Mecca towards which Muslims round the world turn in prayer. The history of the fledgling state's development means that for Saudis modernity is America and America is modernity. Many have surmised that wealthy Saudis, even perhaps royals, were knowingly channelling charity money to bin Laden before September 11 to salve their consciences for their American lifestyles, American education for their children, American business partners, American protected government, and so on. Now more Saudi tourists prefer to go to Lebanon, Cairo, Damascus or Malaysia than the United States, where the stories of trouble are legion in the Arab world. American-style consumerism is Saudi Arabia's top pastime, next to obsessive puritanical religion.

Many Saudis wonder what has happened to them with the sudden modernization and Americanization of recent decades, and tell stories of how their parents and grandparents reminisce over how much easier or healthier or morally appropriate their lives were before. Some say they even feel envy for people living in the poor distant mountainous south. A young driver called Fahd from a desert area north of Riyadh says of people's eating habits: "I have five brothers and sisters and at least once a week we say let's order something. Kudo's my favourite, I have to eat at Kudo every day. But in Jazan and Abha people are more healthy, they eat honey, yoghurt and dates. Here it's all fast-food, even at home. A lot of people are saying that things aren't the same anymore."[36] Riyadh is a city of concrete-and-glass shopping mall monotony. Jeddah contains an old district, a true residential area, where the buildings run in narrow alleys running north-south and east-west to make the most of the sea winds. Within each alley the houses jut out at an angle to create shadows that further lessen the effects of summer heat and sun. Wooden windows boxes with intricate woodwork called *mangour* (*mashrabiya* in Egypt) lets in enough sun to light up the inside of houses without overheating them and allows women to see the street without themselves being seen.

The buildings are constructed with large stone slabs for natural cooling. It is a self-contained world that attained the highest levels of civilization in pre-industrial times.

In the space of a few decades this world had its appointment with modernity. Its soaring population and army of six million expatriate workers, Saudi Arabia needed pristine apartment blocks and villas with the lastest aircon technology, and no one cared anymore about the direction the building faced, the materials used to build it or the styling of the windows. "We eat from a freezer, we live in a freezer, we write in a freezer, we ride in a freezer," Sami Angawi says.[37] To the Saudi mind, this is America, America's way and America's doing. A writer on an Islamist website pined about the country's rulers in July 2005: "Have they put an end to the Western view of us as a consumerist people that sells them oil that it did not toil to produce in order to buy things created by the West and the Far East? Did they really improve our education so that we invest what we have in order to be better and not just richer? Did they create a strong army that can protect the country and defend its borders? After all this time all they have managed is crude propaganda ... and a country that has not achieved anything to be proud of."[38] This brutal assessment, offered by a user calling himself "someone Saudi", could equally have come from a liberal or an Islamist.

Saudi Arabia is the main target audience for the Arab television channels offering American entertainment, and many of them, such as MBC, Orbit, ART and Rotana, are owned by Saudi royals and Saudi entrepreneurs close to powerful royals. Wahhabi clerics have not stopped warring against these developments in viewing habits. They condemned the Saudi winner of the Arab version of *Pop Idol*, called *Star Academy*, and all those who watched him or voted for him in 2005. Sixty-three preachers issued a statement describing the show as "young Arab men and women together in an abominable state of mingling of sexes ... exposing themselves, singing and dancing". It went on: "Women's bodies have been commercialized through dancing, sexual provocation, showing body flesh and exploiting adolescence for the sake of making huge amounts of money at the expense of young men and women, and this is against Islamic Sharia law."[39] But the young man, Hisham Abdel-Rahman, twenty-four at the time, received a hero's welcome on his return to Saudi Arabia in April 2005. Newspapers reported that in shopping malls admirers would touch his hands or kiss him, prompting the religious police to put him on a plane to the Sodom and Gomorrah of Jeddah. During the show, a group of young musicians from across the Arab world shared a house and were filmed twenty-four hours a day as they competed for a recording contract. Drawing huge audiences across the region, the programme was aired jointly by Lebanon's LBC and the Saudi-owned Rotana.

According to young Saudi novelist Rajaa al-Sanie, Saudi Arabia is schizophrenic. "Society lives some form of 'paraphrenia' and the conflict between traditions and modernity is the cause," she says.[40] It is a similar schizophrenia to that seen at the level of foreign policy. Saudi Arabia is the homeland of fifteen of the nineteen men who carried out the attacks in New York and Washington of 11 September 2001, not to mention their mentor Osama bin Laden. Yet it has been in intimate alliance with the United States since the 1940s and has done next to nothing to challenge American foreign policy, which since 1967 has been seen uniformly all over the Arab world as against Arab and Muslim interests. During the uproar over Danish cartoons of the Prophet Mohammad in early 2005, Saudi bloggers were scathing about the government's motives for stoking the fire by withdrawing its ambassador from Denmark. "I don't recall such a reaction when Afghanistan and Iraq were invaded. More importantly, I haven't seen anything done for the Palestinian cause besides financial support," one called Jo wrote.[41] Another calling himself Opinionated Voice said: "It is absurd that we are now known to become more outraged over these cartoons than we do over poverty, occupation, terrorism, war and oppression."[42]

The Arab view of the US-Saudi relationship

"The people of Palestine better know their own valleys," the founder warrior-king Abdel-Aziz once famously said in a phrase (actually a twist on a Quranic verse) which has long fashioned Arab views of the Saudi commitment to Palestine.[43] Ibn Saud did not want any problems in challenging the wider Western-imposed order in the region, and similarly the kingdom was happy to back the Palestinian Liberation Organization as the representative of the Palestinian people and nationalist struggle because it kept the problem of Palestine at a distance, a problem that could be dealt with through generous handouts of cash but little at the level of policy. It also neutralized Egypt's Nasserist-era role as defender of the Palestinian cause, and all that that entailed in terms of tensions with the West and pressure from the street. The Al Saud are viewed among their Arab critics as using two elements to maintain their realm: an intimate alliance with the United States, based on access to oil in return for protection, and an alliance with the followers of the radical Wahhabi school of Sunni Islam who are free to make of Saudi Arabia their vision of a puritanical and Utopian Islamic state. The country's leadership has constantly improvised and crisis-managed the various challenges to this decades-old system that its inherent contradictions have thrown up. Clerics resented Westernization with its inevitable American taste for Saudis, as it resented the leadership's open resort to US military power to protect the kingdom in the decade following 1990–1991 and facilitation of US military plans for Iraq after September 11. The US alliance produced a violent Saudi backlash that ultimately led to September 11. September 11 led to American pressure on the government to loosen up the religious alliance, allowing the clerics to decry a new and more sinister wave of infidel culture, its secular-liberalism and plans for democracy.

Saudi Arabia has made a considerable effort to limit potentially destabilizing criticism of the country within the Arab world through domination of the pan-Arab media. Whereas Egypt's leadership of the Arab nationalist period of anti-colonial resistance was marked by Egypt's domination of the Arab media, the period of accommodation and alliance with the West has been marked by the ascendancy of the United States closest Arab friend, Saudi Arabia. The dozens of prominent columnists from around the Arab world who appear regularly in *al-Hayat* or *Asharq al-Awsat* will avoid strong criticism of Saudi foreign or domestic policy. Close links with the Egyptian government, as well as the Muslim Brotherhood, and the gradual spread of religious conservatism since the 1960s, have relegated serious criticism in Egypt of Saudi state and society to the pages of opposition newspapers where liberals in the 1990s helplessly decried the Saudization of Egypt. When in 1996 Egypt's highest court ordered the divorce of Cairo University professor Nasr Abu Zeid from his wife on the grounds that his writings on the Quran proved he was an apostate from Islam and therefore could not be married to a Muslim, Egyptian state television refused Abu Zeid's call for a public debate with his adversaries. Abu Zeid's chief lawyer, Abdel-Aziz Mohammed, said at the time: "The judiciary is not isolated from what's happening in the country. Conservative currents are dominant in society and growing, and they have the power to influence ... the winds of fundamentalism are blowing from Saudi Arabia and the Gulf."[44]

Many of Egypt's senior judges spent time in Saudi Arabia during the oil boom in the 1970s and sunk much of their earnings into Islamic investment banks when they first appeared in the late 1980s. Palestinian writer Said Aburish's book *The Rise, Corruption, and Coming Fall of the House of Saud* is a good expression of the considerable resentment "urban Arabs" in particular feel towards the Saudi Arabia, over its wealth, its fundamentalism, and its apathy towards Arab nationalism – it is a scathing attack on profligate spending, feudal dictatorial rule and moral corruption.[45] Late Egyptian diplomat Tahseen Beshir no doubt had Saudi Arabia in mind in his famous description of the Arab countries as little more than "tribes with flags", manufactured states based on families and tribes lacking any real ideological convictions or cohesion beyond that of survival.

The great son of this resentment is Osama bin Laden. In one of his video tapes, aired on al-Jazeera and posted on Islamist websites in October 2004, bin Laden taunted George Bush over the number of people killed in Iraq. "More than 15,000 of our people were killed and tens of thousands wounded and more than 1,000 of your people (Americans) were killed and tens of thousands wounded. Bush's hands are sullied with the blood of those on both sides just for oil and to employ his private companies." Then, consciously or unconsciously, he used a phrase made famous in Arab political parlance by Gamal Abdel-Nasser: "Remember that for every action, there is a reaction."[46] Again, the employment by Islamists of Nasserist language: "what has been taken by force can only be got back by force" is a well-known phrase coined by Nasser, often cited in public life and instantly recognizable to any educated Arab. Before bin Laden's offer to Saudi royals to defend the oil fields, an offer made at a time when bin Laden had hero-like status with many Saudis because of his role in fighting the Soviets in Afghanistan where they eventually left in 1989, he had already turned against America. Buoyed by their success, at some time circa 1989 a group of Arab mujahideen in Afghanistan decided to take the jihad beyond that country. American and Pakistani military advisers helped train the mujahideen, the three most prominent of whom were Zawahiri, bin Laden and a Palestinian religious scholar named Abdullah Azzam. America's backing of the Islamists should come as no surprise. It was in fact an extension of CIA backing, with Saudi support, for the Muslim Brotherhood against Nasser in the 1950s and 1960s.

All three mujahideen leaders were politically dislocated and disenfranchised individuals with reason to resent America. One was a Palestinian from a country that was no longer his own, living in Saudi

Arabia, another was an Islamist idealist tried and tortured after the Sadat assassination. Bin Laden, the man with the money, status and means in Saudi Arabia, broke with his country after it chose foreigners to defend it. His citizenship was revoked in 1994 when he was in residence in Sudan. Using his pulpit on al-Jazeera, which had no editorial line opposed to airing messages from him after September 11 and during the subsequent Afghanistan invasion, bin Laden for a time appeared convincingly, to many Arabs, in the manner of a popular hero – Robin Hood cum Che Guevara – standing up to the imperialist West, speaking in warrior robes with a Kalashnikov by his side from inside a cave while a dapper Bush spoke from his White House office. An extensive opinion poll of views across Arab and Muslim countries found in 2003 that 55 percent of Jordanians expressed confidence in bin Laden, 49 percent in Morocco and 14 percent in Lebanon (the figures in 2005 were 60 percent for Jordan, 26 percent for Morocco and 2 percent for Lebanon).[47] Most Saudi commentators and preachers agree that general "emotional support" for bin Laden among the public at large was substantial until radicals claiming allegiance to bin Laden began their campaign to bring down the Saudi royals by targeting residential compounds seen as "Western" in Riyadh in May 2003 and in fact killing Saudis, Arabs and Muslims. The February 2006 attack on an oil-processing plant at Abqaiq also played badly to public opinion.

Alarmed by al-Jazeera's influence and concerned that Saudi-owned channels MBC and Orbit did not offer enough hardcore news to a wide enough audience challenge al-Jazeera, influential Saudis set up al-Arabiya in 2003, just in time for the Iraq invasion when a certain amount of anti-Saudi sentiment was bound to follow in the footsteps of anti-American feeling around the Arab region. Aware of the widespread rumours that ideas of breaking up the kingdom or occupying the Eastern Province were once again being discussed inside in Washington, Saudi Arabia wanted also to present a Western-friendly vision of moderation in the Arab world to counter al-Jazeera's hip rejectionism. Al-Jazeera was free to air criticism and "normal" news coverage of the kingdom because of its essentially independent editorial remit, because its Qatari owners had no desire to do Saudi Arabia special favours and because they were in fact independent of Saudi financial pressure through Qatar's enormous natural gas reserves, placing it almost uniquely in the Arab world outside a dependency relationship with Riyadh. Other channels, be they state operations or belonging to business entrepreneurs or political parties, were minded to play by the rules of the vast *cordon sanitaire* that Saudi Arabia had managed to establish around itself in the Arab media.

This policy in fact began after the 1991 Gulf war. During the following decade, Saudi royals and businessmen launched Orbit, MBC and the ART network. Orbit and the BBC World Service Arabic radio scuppered plans to set up an Arabic television station in 1995 over coverage of Saudi dissidents in London. Those BBC Arabic journalists went on to form the core of the al-Jazeera team when it was launched the following year.

Whenever there was criticism, Saudi influence would swing into action. In June 2003, Lebanese authorities cut the international transmission of NTV, owned by businessman Tahseen Khayyat, to stop a planned programme on the effect of the invasion of Iraq on Saudi domestic politics. NTV resumed broadcasts days later, after it agreed not to air the programme. This happened when the late Rafiq al-Hariri, who made his fortune in Saudi Arabia, took nationality and maintained close links with the royals, was Lebanon's Prime Minister. When an Egyptian doctor was imprisoned in Saudi Arabia in 1994 for complaining to the authorities that his son had been raped by his Saudi school teacher, most Egyptian newspapers avoided the story for fear of offending the kingdom. Saudis who appear on al-Jazeera criticizing the country risk punishment. One Saudi opposition figure was prevented from leaving the country in 2002 after he criticized Saudi Arabia's position on the Iraqi crisis in an appearance on the channel. In 2002, Saudi Arabia recalled its ambassador to Doha, one of many Arab countries to do so at some stage since al-Jazeera began in 1996. Saudi companies do not advertize on al-Jazeera because the authorities view it as anti-Saudi – a major loss since Saudi Arabia's 24 million population with a sizeable per capita income (over $14,000 in 2005 and rising with world oil prices) makes it the default market for most TV channels seeking pan-Arab appeal, more important than Egypt with its over-70 million population.[48] Preacher Said bin Zuair was sentenced to five years in jail in 2004 after he spoke on an al-Jazeera show discussing bin Laden's offer of a truce to European countries. When Saudi Arabia jailed three reformers in 2005, there was no special in-depth discussion of their case on al-Arabiya, MBC or other Saudi channels, but there was on al-Jazeera. The measured Arab nationalist critiques of veteran Egyptian journalist Mohammed Hassanein Heikal – the magnifying glass he puts over Arab history since the Second World War – are a running embarrassment for the Saudi regime. Al-Jazeera airs the shows, called *Ma' Heikal (With Heikal)*; al-Arabiya would not dare.

Saudi Arabia, like Kuwait, has shown more trust for its American friends than any Arab state or ruler. It fears the designs of "urban" Arab polities such as Egypt on their oil. The memory lingers in Saudi Arabia of how Egypt's ruler Mohammed Ali put a bloody end to the first Saudi state in 1818. The state feared falling to Egypt again when Nasser was in power, Nasser whose famous slogan declared that "Arab oil is for the Arabs". Starting with the "tripartite aggression" of 1956, when Britain, France and Israel launched military action to retake the Suez canal and bring down Nasser, Western powers engaged in numerous schemes to end Nasser's rule because of his promotion of independence and rejection of regimes and rulers who he viewed as kowtowing to the West against the wishes of their people.

As oil wealth transformed the country in the 1970s, fear of its envious Arab neighbours continued to place limits on the willingness of Saudi Arabia to involve itself in any meaningful political alliance with Arabs who had a more revolutionary approach to the Israeli-Palestinian conflict. The kingdom backs the United States in its efforts to make sure Iran does not acquire nuclear weapons capability, despite the generally positive feeling among Arabs around the region, and it would like to see Lebanese Shi'ite movement Hizbollah defanged. Officials say plainly that they consider Iran, not Israel, a threat, and they hope and trust that the Arab-Israeli conflict can be ended satisfactorily via negotiations. The idea of Shi'ite Islam becoming the new vanguard of Arab resistance to the West is even more anathema to the Wahhabi state, and many Saudi clerics were torn during the fighting between Hizbollah-Israel fighting in 2006 over which party they detested the most, exorting Muslims to understand that Iran's hand was surely moving Hizbollah for its own selfish reasons. Such attitudes have been a painful pill to swallow for Islamists and Arab nationalists. Saudi Arabia is the centre of the Muslim world, the birthplace of Islam and the home of its two holiest shrines, it has the largest economy in the Middle East, the largest stock market in the region and it is the world's biggest oil exporter, with 25 percent of the world's total proven reserves. One thing it has done, however, is offer money. Saudi aid to the Palestinians from 1970 to 2005 is estimated at 20.83 billion riyals, or $5.55 billion, and since 2000 it has given $500–550 million a year, making Saudi Arabia the largest single donor country. On average, Saudi Arabia gives $1–1.5 billion a year to Muslim countries around the world.[49] Saudi aid to the Palestinians has, however, made it a particular enemy of the Israeli Right-wing and a target of pro-Israeli lobby groups in the United States.

This fundamental difference of approach explains Saudi Arabia's bad ties with not only Nasser, but Muammar Gaddafi, Hafez al-Assad and Saddam Hussein. While most Arab governments acquiesced in the Bush administration's decision to prosecute a war on Iraq in 2003, Saudi Arabia's rulers were widely suspected of being secretly delirious that the United States was ridding them of an arch-foe, a revolutionary as well as an ideological enemy (Saddam's secular nationalist Baathism versus Saudi's Islamist Wahhabism). An Egyptian journalist writes bitterly of "the biggest act of looting in history, taking place in the Gulf petrol deserts of the Arabs": "These mini-states, emirates and kingdoms suffer from a crisis of development because their resources have been aimed at developing the United States, on the one hand, and warring a phantom called Saddam Hussein, on the other."[50] Novelist Abdel-Rahman Munif wrote more thoughtfully: "The oil which was found by chance in parts of the Arab region became the basis on which the victorious countries in the First World War dealt with the region. It set the geographical and political form of the states they set up, the nature of the regimes that ruled them, the nature of the relations between them and between each state and the rest of the world. Thus, oil became an instrument of destruction and rivalry, a reason for controlling the region's peoples and even blocking the way to their future development."[51]

Saudi Arabia has been a powerful player in Arab and Islamic politics, but its influence has been "moderate" and "peaceful", in Western political terms, meaning it has been to accommodate American influence in the Middle East. As regional leader, Saudi Arabia over the last generation continued not from the point where Nasser left off, but from the tradition of the Baghdad Pact led by Hashemite Iraq. Most Arab states have come to believe this is the more prudent path. Saudi Arabia was always there; Egypt joined not long after. Former Iraqi Prime Minister Nuri Said, brutally murdered in 1958 for his pro-Western policies, considered the folly of resistance in these comments on Nasser: "He failed to understand that the West would not grant the Arabs the luxury of neutralism, that this area is too decisively vital for that sort of foolishness. He failed to understand that the Middle East is inextricably tied to the West economically – there is no other bigger market for Arab oil, for example. Despite a soldier's background, Nasser overlooked the military reality of Russia's incapacity to defend the Arabs if they made an enemy of the West."[52]

After September 11, Americans not surprisingly felt betrayed by their friendship with Saudi Arabia. They had not realized how dishonest its leadership had been in failing to use its leverage and amicable ties with the White House to openly and fairly challenge US foreign policy, whether in public or in private. Instead, the regime chose to be America's friend and hide the fact that its people were fuming. It was a classic gap between ruled and ruler that has plagued the Arab region during much of the decolonization period: pro-US leaders, anti-US public – but anti-US for reasons that their leaders were too timid, arrogant or incompetent to explain.

Chapter 7
The Sudanese Card

Sudan: Straddling Africa and the Arab World

Sudan has become a poster child country for Arab opponents of American policy and has provided perfect fodder for intellectuals who talk of a Western attempt, led by American politicians, journalists and activists, to deconstruct the Arab world. Sudan has been rent by divisions between its Arab and its African identity since independence and the United States became a factor in this wider struggle after political Islam came to dominate in Sudan, championing its Arab-Muslim identity, and to develop policies deemed as contrary to American interests. Today, the United States government is seen as opposing the spread of Arabic and Islam in Sudan and promoting black African power because it is not based in either Islam or Arab identity, which are capable of mobilizing against American influence. In the view of Islamists and Arab nationalists, Washington preys on Sudan as the achilles heel of the Arab world, and they compare American championing of black African rights at international forums with American disinterest in backing Palestinian rights. On the other hand, democrats in the Arab world consider the Sudanese as classic victims of the anti-imperialist rhetoric that simply serves to cover up brutality and authoritarianism at home. These divides concerning Sudan have never been sharper than they are today because of the conflict in the vast and barrent West Sudanese territory of Darfur. America says Arab tribes have committed genocide against black Africans in a campaign of murder, rape and pillage to force them off the land in a fight for scarce resources. The mainstream media in the Arab world has grappled with these accusations while placing them in a wider context of aggressive, interventionist American policy in the Arab world.

The United States develops ties with post-independence Sudan

Sudan lies at the very heart of the difficult relationship between America and the Arab world. Straddling the Arab world and black Africa, it occupies that tortured zone where different views on identity, ethnicity and nationality collide – the different perceptions of those living in the country itself, those living in the Arab region and those living in the West who also seek to help shape its destiny. As was the case with other countries of the Arab world, when Sudan claimed its independence – in 1956 – it did so from one of the old European powers. The United States came to take on the colonial mantle from Great Britain, as the Western power which developed close relations with Sudan, but it was viewed positively as a country that promoted freedom and independence for the developing world from its traditional colonial masters.

Sudan's situation was complicated by its relations with Egypt. The two countries had close cultural relations but Egypt was technically a party to the British occupation of Sudan, maintaining troops there and traditionally held that the two countries were one, "from Alexandria in the north to Juba in the south", as the unity phrase has it. Unity for Egypt and Sudan was a banner borne by many Egyptian and Sudanese politicians in the decolonization period after the Second World War. Egypt's first republican president Mohammed Naguib was half Sudanese and enjoyed widespread support in Sudan. But unlike the situation with Morocco when Spain withdrew from the disputed Western Sahara in the 1970s, Egypt relented on its hold over Sudan. Naguib signed an agreement with Sudan in 1953 that would allow Sudan self-determination after three years. However, Nasser, the rising star of the Egyptian revolution who was to eclipse Naguib in 1955, earned the opprobrium of many of the Sudanese political class because of a crack down on both communists and Islamists in Egypt. Both groups had a strong presence in Sudanese politics.

In 1955, Sudan's parliament demanded that both Egyptian and British troops quit the country. They did so, leaving parliament to declare the country a sovereign democratic republic by the end of the year. Relations with Egypt were to remain tetchy because of Egypt's large demands on Nile water and a lingering sense in Egypt that the revolutionary leaders had botched the Sudan file and let Sudan suddenly go its own way. In the south of Sudan, where black African tribes had long resisted both Arabization and Islamization, there was a sense of betrayal felt towards the British for not protecting them from the new Arab-Islamic Sudanese state that rose with Britain and Egypt's swift departure. During the colonial period, earlier in the century, Britain had placed southern education in the hands of foreign missionaries in an effort to promote Christianity and Western influence in the face of the wider historical march of Arabization and Islamization. After 1956, the independent authorities in Khartoum quickly set about undoing Britain's work; in 1964, they expelled all of the missionaries.

By 1963, a southern guerrilla movement was already operating against the northern authorities, in response to the perceived status as second-class citizens that southerners found themselves in and the lack of resources placed there by the central government. An agreement signed in the Ethiopian capital Addis Ababa put an end to the fighting and established southern federal rule. But squabbling among southern politicians, rash intervention by Khartoum and a continued sense of marginalization led to a second, more infamous round of bloodletting – the civil war that erupted in 1983. It lasted all of twenty-two years to 2005. The war began as a dispute over the split of power and resources between the Arab-Islamic centre that continued to dominate political and economic life and the deprived black Africans led by a Christian elite in the far south, who felt that Sudan in its current framework could never be their country unless they signed up to its Arab-Islamic ideology. However, during the course of the war, the southerners were to find that they now possessed a number of advantages they had not previously enjoyed: Sudan's developing oilfields were mainly in the south, the southerners' plight became a cause celebre in American society, winning them key political and economic backing, and the Khartoum government's dabbling in radical Islamic politics during the 1990s lost it significant African, Arab and European support. The peace agreement of 2005 accorded the southerners, who make up roughly 10 million of a population of over 30 million people, the right to vote on whether to secede from Sudan in 2011 and form an independent state.

The war began in the era of President Jaafar al-Nimeiri. Nimeiri came to power via a military coup in 1969 espousing a similar secular-nationalist line to Nasser. When he was ousted from power in 1985, his regime reflected the new religious nature of the times in the wider region. Political Islam was the new paradigm of choice in Arab politics, and Sudan was no less affected by this than any other part of the region. The spark for the civil war was in fact Nimeiri's decision to impose Islamic Sharia law, including its harsh hudud punishments, on all Sudan including the largely non-Muslim southerners. To mark his new shift in ideology, Nimeiri famously had Khartoum's whisky dumped in the Nile. Nimeiri was removed in a coup in 1985 by officers alarmed by the course of the conflict in the south, but four years later another military coup brought to power an Islamist regime of an altogether different calibre. Under the National Front government, Islamist ideologue Hassan al-Turabi was the brains behind the brawn of coup leader, General Omar al-Bashir. In the intervening period, Sudan had been ruled by a government led by Sadeq al-Mahdi, a liberal democrat who leads a political movement with origins in the Islamic redemption movement that fought British colonial control a century before and famously killed Britain's General Gordon in 1885. Its leader, Mohammed Ahmed ibn Abdullah claimed to be the Mahdi, the "rightly-guided one" (*al-mahdi*) who will be chosen by God to lead mankind at the end of time. The Mahdist movement later developed into a political party – the Umma ("Islamic nation") Party – and Sadeq al-Mahdi, a descendant of the first Mahdi, has been its leader since the 1960s.

The war was incredibly destructive, killing over two million people and displacing over four million. It was Africa's longest war in modern times and became more complex with time, as oil fields were developed, as Khartoum became a redout of political Islam, and as the United States acquired more of an interest in the conflict. Under Turabi's direction, Sudan in the early 1990s attracted the leading lights of the radical Islamist movement as well as secular Third World revolutionary forces. Osama bin Laden lived in Khartoum for some five years, Ayman al-Zawahiri was a regular visitor, and Egyptian Islamists used Sudan as a staging post in their war against Mubarak's American-backed, secular government. Turabi scored his political colours as the leading light in the Sudanese branch of the Muslim Brotherhood, the Egypt-based group at the centre of political Islam in the Arab world. Possibly annoyed by his playboy lifestyle, Sudan handed over Carlos the Jackal to France in 1994, the pro-Palestinian Venezuelan guerrilla who had found refuge there in 1991. Palestinian guerrillas who were of the leftist, secular-national persuasion were also at home in Khartoum. Many of these people congregated at a conference organized by Turabi in 1994 under the aegis of his Popular Arab and Islamic Congress. This organization was the vehicle for Turabi's Islamist dream of making real what neither the Organisation of the Islamic Conference or the Arab League had managed to do: be a vigorous, developing world magnet that could rally forces against Western influence. It attracted people as disparate as the old leftist Palestinian George Habash, members of Hamas, Algerian Islamists challenging the government and Iraqi Baathists, not to mention bin Laden and Zawahiri. Turabi set about turning Sudan into the playground of political Islam that Islamist groups throughout the Arab world had long wished they could have in their own countries, but, because of their US-allied governments, could not get. Egyptian Islamist leaders such as Adel Hussein of the Labour Party, Maamoun al-Hodeiby of the Muslim Brotherhood and intellectual Fahmy Howeidy were regular visitors to Khartoum during this time.

A radical Islamist force straddling the Arab world and Africa was exactly what Washington did not want Sudan to be. This put any northern victory in the civil war in a different light and raised political interest in the southerners, support for whom then Secretary of State Madeleine Albright made no secret of showing in the late 1990s. She lavished praise on John Garang, the English-fluent American-educated economist who led the southerners in the war since 1983 as head of the Sudan People's Liberation Army (SPLA). After a meeting in Nairobi in October 1999, she described the former Sudanese army officer in gushing terms: "He is sophisticated and dedicated and determined ... He is a very dynamic leader who has a goal (southern independence) that is difficult to fulfil because he is a leader without international recognition."[1] Following that, the Clinton administration decided to give food aid directly to the rebel movement – the United Nation's Operation Lifeline Sudan had for a decade taken charge of providing sustenance to both sides in the conflict areas – and Sudan's government regularly accused Washington of arming the SPLA.

At the same time, lobby groups based mainly in the United States – ranging from black rights activists, shocked by reports of slavery, to Christian fundamentalists, keen to support their co-religionists in the African continent's war of the faiths with Islam, to pro-Israelis who saw more Arab dirty laundry with which to deflect international attention from the problems in its own backyard – sought to make Sudan an administration foreign policy priority. The number of these groups has increased with the Darfur crisis which broke out in 2004. The list includes: the Congress-funded United States Institute of Peace, Christian Solidarity International (Swiss-based), International Christian Concern, the American Anti-Slavery Group, Samaritan's Purse (run by Christian fundamentalist Franklin Graham), the Save Darfur Coalition, Lutheran World Relief (LWR), Action by Churches Together, the American Jewish Committee (AJC), the Central Conference of American Rabbis, the New York Board of Rabbis, the Rabbinic Assembly, the Rabbinical Council of America and the Reconstructionist Rabbinical Association. Of course, well-known international human rights groups have also taken great interest in Sudan.

Rights groups managed to influence Western oil companies hoping to work in Sudan. Several American oil companies wanted to join their rivals from other countries around the world in exploiting Sudan's new oil riches, which came on tap in 1999. Canada's Talisman Energy, Sweden's Lundin Oil and Austrian oil group OMV were all under pressure from rights groups to pull out of Sudan. All three did between 2001 and 2003, but China's National Petroleum Corporation and Malaysia's Petronas were safe. Sudan was not a political issue in either country. China sees a country that like itself suffers attempts by foreigners to meddle in its domestic affairs, and Malaysia is keep to boost all manner of political, economic and social links with fellow Islamic countries. India's Oil and Natural Gas Corp, ONGC, even bought its way in, as the Westerners sold out.

Arab concern in the country was often cursory throughout the long years of the war. Though it has been by far the most bloody conflict in the Arab world over the last six decades in terms of sheer numbers of lives lost, public interest in the suffering of Sudan's civil war was low. Palestine and conflicts connected to it have always received the lion's share of Arab media interest. When Sudan became independent in 1956, Syria even objected to it acquiring membership in the Arab League, arguing Sudan was not sufficiently Arab. The Islamist military regime that came to power 1989 clothed Sudan in a strident Arab-Islamic identity that was wilfully Arab, and, moreover, outwith Egyptian, and American, control – its Islamist colours almost seemed designed specifically for that purpose. The regime was successful in appealing to the wealthy Gulf Arab countries for financial support but appeared to delight in alienating its American allies to the north. Egypt, backed by the United States, was active in getting UN sanctions imposed on Sudan after a failed assassination attempt on Hosni Mubarak in Ethiopia in 1995 which Egypt immediately blamed on Turabi and Bashir. A border dispute then flared up at the time between the two countries. Overriding this angry sideshow, Egypt was as concerned as the Gulf Arab countries that Sudan should stay part of the Arab club and feared that an independent south Sudan, which would likely be in the American and Israeli political orbit, would threaten its access to Nile water.

Similarly, when the Darfur crisis entered world consciousness in 2004, there was less concern in Arab media and government over the suffering of black Africans, who looked little like the rest of the Arabs, than over the political leverage it offered the United States against Sudan. The Arab world saw a stark contrast to Washington's lack of interest in the plight of the Palestinians and Israel's nonchalant attitude towards UN resolutions regarding Palestinian rights – the World Court ruled Israel's "security barrier" illegal (because it is not built along the path of the Israel's border before the 1967, but on occupied Palestinian land) – in the same year that Darfur became an international question, commentators noted. Despite that ruling, Washington made sure that no action could be taken over the wall. Sudden interest in Sudan was yet another example of the blatant double standards the Arab world had seen since the era of bare, uncoded colonialism some five decades before.

In this typical comment, an Egyptian columnist says the United Nations has acceded to an American agenda on Sudan, as it did on Syria, where Washington was instrumental in obtaining a United Nations resolution in September 2004 to force Syria to withdraw troops from Lebanon. "Although Syria has withdrawn its troops from Lebanon before the scheduled time at the end of April, UN Secretary-General Kofi Annan said in his report that some commitments in the international resolution 1559 have not been implemented. Then he called on the international community to intervene in Sudan to stop the brutal and inhuman practices against people in Darfur," Mohammed al-Farsi writes in *al-Wafd*.[2] "But it is not acceptable to focus on situations in Sudan and Lebanon and ignore the crimes of the Israeli government against Palestinians and the American violation of the rights of Arabs and Muslims in Iraq and Afghanistan. In my opinion, UN resolution 1559 aims at disarming Hizbollah for the sake of Israel." When the United States helped broker the preliminary Sudanese peace deal in 2002, there was much irritation in the Arab world over the right to self-determination for the south that it guaranteed. "Everyone agrees that the oil of the Sudan was the real motive behind the agreement between the SPLA and the government. We can all predict that American companies will devour the lion's share of Sudanese oil, and these companies are waiting for the green light from the American administration," columnist Salah Attiya wrote in Egypt's state-owned paper *al-Gomhouriya*, reflecting the widespread cynicism towards American intentions in the region.[3] When President George W. Bush froze the assets of a dozen Sudanese companies and threatened sanctions in 2002 during the talks at Machakos in Kenya which produced an interim peace agreement, the UAE's *al-Khaleej* saw "an American campaign against all things Arab and Muslim".[4] The sanctions threat was an unconcealed attempt to force Khartoum to back down to the SPLA in the talks, the paper said – which was in fact largely true.

Many northerners in Khartoum reflected the prevailing cynicism about US motives at the time. "We don't know what's it about, what they will talk about tomorrow. It took time before the government published details about this agreement, and most people feel they don't know what's going on. Sudanese don't feel happy about this peace because they feel it was pushed by the Americans," said Muzammil, a 38-year-old hotel receptionist from the far north. Abdel-Hadi, 40, a tribesman from north Sudan who had religious leanings, said: "This peace is dangerous.[5] America wants to divide Sudan. Political life should be according to religion." Other northerners felt it was no more than a deal between two men, Bashir and Garang, that ensured continued power for their political groupings to the detriment of wider societies, but southerners seemed more enthusiastic about the agreement, that it could bring the conflict that had devastated south more than north to an end.

Arabization and Islamization

In the five decades since independence, Sudan has experienced a fundamental cultural shift that has underlined its political development throughout the period, a shift which explains the underlying reasons behind the problems Sudan has had with the United States. Though verging on the racist, the Syrians back in 1956 had put their finger on something – the country's identity was indeed borderline Arab, not because of colour, but because of language and culture. Like Morocco, where some 50 percent of the population are in fact Berbers, Sudan was another of the Arab world's sordid secrets, in that only some 50 percent of the population spoke Arabic. How things have changed. Sudan has been engaged in a process of language switching, or Arabization, over the last fifty years of statehood, a process which continues to this day and seeks to complete the Arabization that has in fact been underway for some 1,000 years. By "Arabization" is meant the spread of the Arabic language and the identity transformation that comes with it, whereby new generations of non-Arabs grow up speaking Arabic and consider themselves Arabs. Arabization has usually been accompanied by the concomitant process of "Islamization", the spread of the Islamic religion among individuals and communities who previously described themselves in other terms, albeit Christian, animist, etc. The cultural depth and diversity, in the widest sense, of the Arab world stems in large part from the mix of previous identities, or "lesser traditions", with the Arab-Islamic "greater tradition" that holds the Arab world together.

Power in Sudan is monopolized by ethnic-tribal groups living in the north around the River Nile which are all essentially Nubians, the most prominent of which are the Shayqiyya and Ja'liyya tribes, who consider themselves ethnically "pure Arab". The Nubians are an old ethnic group, stretching into south Egypt where they vied historically for power with Egypt's Pharaohs, sometimes taking over, but in the centuries since they converted to Islam they have largely lost their language to Arabic. With their Islam and their Arabic they form the backbone of the modern Sudanese state. Veteran Sudanese Foreign Minister Mustafa Osman Ismail speaks fluent Dongolawi, the Nubian language of the Dongola area he hails from, yet he has been a central figure in the Arabist-Islamist regime for which Islam and Arabic mean unity and progress. Modern Sudan is in many ways a Nubian state – but, like Egypt, Arabized. The term "Nubian" itself carries little prestige or resonance in Sudan today.

Sudanese linguist Amin Abu Manqa estimates that at least 65 percent of Sudanese today speak only Arabic, compared to 51 percent in 1956.[6] Since Arabic is the language of God's revelation in Muslim theology, speaking that language is regarded as a desirable goal by all Muslims, even to the extent of disregarding one's own tongue. This process has been going on throughout history, even in the modern age of nation states, modern media and global interaction, and many smaller languages are thought to have disappeared in Sudan over the last five decades or are threatened with extinction. Abu Manqa cites the example of the Gule people, who reside in a mountainous area southeast of Khartoum. Their language is no more, though they were in fact the founders of the Islamic Funj Sultanate of the sixteenth century CE. "Now they say they are Arabs. It's a social aspiration to be from the Arabs and the Prophet's house," he says.[7]

Arabic and Islam have been the great unifiers for post-independence governments in Sudan, in the way that English and Protestantism were for the British authorities after union between Scotland and England in 1707. The ideology of Arabism has clearly brought with it a price, particularly for those in the south or those caught in the grey area in-between north and south. The Nuba Mountain people, for example, are Muslim but do not speak Arabic. "Any language has an ideology but with Arabic it is systematic," says Ismail Ali Saadeldin, state minister for Nuba Mountain Affairs.[8] "It's now a psychological problem, because we feel inferior and they think being Arab makes them superior. The first step is a political agreement to build our confidence about who we are. That's the base line. It'll take a generation to change people who now think they are Arab." The Islamist regime has periodically persecuted Sufi orders and the *zaar* cult – a traditional healing ceremony based on the belief in spirits which is regarded as superstition – in its drive to homogenize through Islam and Arabic.

This homogenization is regarded as key to the process of nation-building not just in Sudan, but virtually in every Arab country. (Lebanon has traditionally promoted diversity as an adjunct to its multi-confessional system which seeks to mediate power among myriad Christian and Muslim sects.) American support for diversity and heterogeneity is regarded with suspicion. American policy in Iraq and its promotion of a sectarian federalist system is judged negatively for this very reason – it is viewed as a formula for weakening, dividing and deconstructing a political and cultural unity for its own selfish interests. Sudan's Islamic government has in fact succeeded in making Arabic the lingua franca of southerners where it vies with English as the language of the southern elite – a policy first promoted by independent government in 1956. Today's south Sudanese are not the same south Sudanese who took up arms in 1983, in large part because some three to four million southerners have lived as communities of the displaced in shantie towns ringing the capital. Rights activists in Khartoum say there is even some evidence that the practice of female circumcision is spreading from Muslim communities in the northern cities to neighbouring southern non-Muslim communities, as the southerners adopt the customs of the dominant social caste.[9]

This Sudanese experience is part of a wider historical development in the Arab world. The battle to Arabize the region continues today as it always has done since the days of the first Arab conquests over 1,300 years ago. The concept of the Arabs being the original people of Islam, to whom God made his final and complete revelation – a chosen people in the fashion of the Jews – has been around since the Arab conquerors first sought to legitimize their vast empire encompassing the Middle East and North Africa. Modern scholars of Islam argue that Islam was originally conceived of as the religion of the Arabs and only in time did it became a religion for all people, regardless of race or caste. Eventually, classical Islam during the period of the Abbasid caliphate in Baghdad settled on the idea of Arabic as the chosen language of God, as opposed to the idea of the Arabs as the chosen people of God. If it had not been for this theory of *i'jaz*, or the "perfection" of the uncreated Quran in Arabic whose text is an indivisible part of the divine being since the beginning of time – an idea developed in Abbasid times which effectively blocked any ideas to translate the book into other languages – the Arabs might not today be the Arabs. Still, Arabization took centuries to make serious inroads among the conquered peoples after the Arab conquests of the middle seventh century AD. Records show that people of the conquered communities in those early decades often became nominal members of Arab tribes and that membership of the new religious community of Islam was attractive in that it meant avoidance of paying many taxes levied on Christians, Jews, Zoroastrians and others. There were other key factors in the spread of the new religion. Its theoreticians were to present it as the completion and perfection of the same Judaic and Christian faith of most of the conquered peoples, and the Arab rulers switched the language of administration to Arabic in the conquered provinces.

Today, modern communications, entertainment, media, politics and business have facilitated more linguistic unity and mutual understanding than ever. Arabic dialects are being standardized within individual Arab countries around the prestigious dialects of their capital cities, and these national dialects are in turn being affected by other dialects and formal Arabic. Formal and colloquial Arabic are interacting in popular culture and politics in the Arab world today in a manner critical to the final victory of Arabization in "the Arab world". Since independence, a synergy of cultural reaffirmation in dealings between countries of the region themselves and between individual countries and the rest of the world has emphasized similarity, homogeneity and a greater sense of something, identified as Arabness or Arab identity (*al-huwiyya al-arabiyya*) or Arabism (*al-'uruba*). Modern media and communications have increased the sheer volume of those shared cultural elements and further marginalized those parts of the region's cultural profile that do not fit into the wider picture. A greater tradition of Arab identity exists alongside ancient little traditions of local, non-Arab identities, but over the last fifty years more and more of these smaller traditions are assuming the lofty title "Arab", as the historic process of Arabization of the Middle

East, begun with the Arab conquests in the seventh century AD, reaches some point of cultural closure. It is against this background that Arab evaluations of Western policies on Middle East minorities must be judged.

Sudan's deteriorating relations with the United States

The United States gave the appearance of taking on the role from Britain of Western power and benefactor in Sudan almost immediately upon independence. The government accepted US aid at the same time as popular attitudes towards America began to sour because of Egypt's troubled relations with Washington during the Nasser era. Diplomatic links were severed for five years after the 1967 Arab-Israeli war. When three US diplomats including the ambassador were killed by Palestinians in 1973, Nimeiri's government refused to hand them over to the United States even after a trial convicted them. But as Egypt moved closer to the United States and away from the Russians in the 1970s, so did Sudan under the same Nimeiri, who was concerned about the Soviet-backed regimes in neighbouring Ethiopia and Libya. Nimeiri backed Egypt's peace with Israel and in 1985 collaborated in transporting Ethiopia's Falasha Jews to Israel, though Khartoum had no relations with the Jewish state. This US-Egyptian alignment produced a backlash that lasts to this day, since, away from Nimeiri's maneuverings, Sudan had quietly grown more Islamist, just like the rest of the Arab world, and the Islamists eventually took power.

Relations with America deteriorated rapidly after 1989. The United States included Sudan on its list of "states supporting terrorism" in 1993 and imposed sanctions in 1997, by which time Osama bin Laden had left the country for Afghanistan. In August of 1998, the Clinton administration ordered the bombing of a pharmaceutical factory just outside Khartoum which the CIA said it was in fact manufacturing materials for use in chemical weapons since a soil sample collected near the plant had revealed the presence of a chemical used in the manufacture of VX nerve gas. The attack came in response to the suicide bombing of the US embassies in Nairobi and Dar es Salaam and was accompanied by a similar attack on al-Qa'ida training camps in Afghanistan. The embassy bombings were in fact the opening shot in al-Qa'ida's war against the United States and its interests in the region. The American attack on Sudan, though, engendered an intense debate in the West about the moral and political implications of American policies, while in the Arab world the attacks more confirmed what everyone already thought. Media scrutiny subsequently revealed that the factory was not involved in illicit activity but the attack against it had provided respite for the administration from its problems over President Clinton's affair with a Whitehouse intern, Monica Lewinsky. The incident resembled the Hollywood movie *Wag The Dog* of the same year where the administration uses the media to manufacture the impression of a war in a distant land in order to distract the public's attention from a sex scandal involving the president. Clinton had claimed that the el-Shifa factory was owned by bin Laden himself. Left-wing American intellectual Noam Chomsky described the attack as an atrocity that "destroyed half the pharmaceutical supplies of a poor African country and the facilities for replenishing them, with an enormous human toll", which was comparable to the September 11 attacks, or worse since the administration gave no thought to the consequences.[10] Other Western commentators slammed the Sudan attack but did not see in it evidence that the United States was anything other than a benign power, albeit one that sometimes makes mistakes: they cited the hundreds of thousands of African deaths caused by the Islamist regime in Khartoum during the civil war as evidence that Third World dictatorship was worse.

Arab reactions at the time almost invariably placed Sudan in a wider context of American policy towards the region and rarely looked at Sudan as a case study in its own right. Posters of bin Laden were carried by Palestinians marching in protest in the West Bank town of Nablus, as the Islamist dissident became widely known to the public in Arab and Islamic countries for the first time. There were days of violent protests in Khartoum in response to the attack, during which the US and British flags were pulled down at their embassy buildings, and Bashir bolstered his image as an Arab, Muslim leader standing up to Washington with strident public appearances where his audience held up copies of the Quran and held banners saying things like "Clinton, screw Monica, not Sudan". In an interview on al-Jazeera, Bashir said he did not expect much support from Arab leaders because they were frightened of offending the United States. He also talked of a "Zionist-Crusader alliance" in Washington – the language of the radical Islamist movement that was then taking shape and which the attacks were meant to bring down. "The truth is that we say that Arab reactions are weak. However, we received many telephone calls from many Arab leaders, expressing support for Sudan and denouncing this aggression. We appreciate these brothers' stances. Many sides do not want to anger the United States, although we know that they are convinced that what was carried out by the United States is terrorism. If terrorism is throwing a bomb to destroy an installation and kill innocent people, then terrorism will be more serious when it is carried out by a state, a superpower that is a permanent Security Council member and morally responsible for maintaining international security and peace," he said.[11] He added: "There is a great deal of hostility towards Sudan in the US administration. We know that the United States is currently leading a Zionist-Crusader alliance, and that the US administration and the US policy-making bodies are now entirely controlled by Jews." On the same theme he told a news conference in Morocco: "The American aggression was made because the United States is under the full domination of Zionist forces ... In fact, the Jews control all decision-making centres in the United States. The Secretary of State, Defence Secretary, National Security Adviser, leaders of the foreign, security and the CIA (Central Intelligence Agency) are all Jews."[12]

Wider media criticism focussed on the fact that this was a pharmaceutical factory in a Third World country and Clinton's problems over the Lewinsky affair, though on the latter issue in particular the Arab media was more following trails it picked up in the Western media. These reflected two common themes in the Arab media's vision of the West – that it wants to stop the developing world catch up with them, and that it has ulterior motives for its dabblings in the region, other than the publicly stated justifications. "The United States has made a mistake – they have applied the law of the jungle, snubbing the views of the international community. By bombing the sites in Sudan and Afghanistan, the United States hasn't realised that it is replicating terrorist acts with yet another terrorist act," Qatar's *al-Sharq* said.[13] Egyptian semi-official papers said the government should not have associated with radical Islam though. "Shame on the United States for having reacted with such violence and barbarity, leaving innocent people dead. But shame also on the Islamic nation for not rejecting those who shelter murderers and criminals disguised as fighters for the faith," *al-Ahram al-Messai* said.[14] A more ominous response was that of al-Qa'ida itself. It contacted several newspapers to say they would seek revenge for the double attack on Sudan and an al-Qa'ida base in Afghanistan. Zawahiri himself contacted Pakistan's *The News* to say that: "The war has just started. The Americans should wait for the answer." And the London-based Arabic paper *al-Quds al-Arabi* said it received a call promising to respond with "deeds not words".[15]

After September 11, Sudan was under American pressure to end the war and to cooperate with Washington against the international Islamic radicals it had once hosted. Responsive to the calls of Christian conservatives at home, Bush sent John Danforth, an Episcopal priest and former senator from Missouri, as his special envoy to Sudan in 2000, where he managed to negotiate a local cease-fire between the rebel movement and Khartoum. With that success, Washington pressed for a fully negotiated end to the fighting in its entirety with the stick of repercussions if Khartoum was deemed not serious, leading to an interim peace agreement in 2002 called the Machakos Protocol and a formal end to the war in 2005. The Sudan Peace Act approved by Bush in October 2002 authorized the spending of up to $100 million a year for assistance to areas outside Sudanese government control. The Act also listed various measures that could be taken against Khartoum if it was deemed not to be pursuing negotiations with the SPLA in good faith, including seeking a UN Security Council arms embargo on the Sudanese government, instructing American officials to actively oppose any loans, credits or guarantees for Sudan from international financial institutions, and denying Sudan access to oil revenues and downgrade or suspend diplomatic relations. Washington had had no permanent diplomatic presence in Sudan since 1996 when diplomats were withdrawn on security grounds (a charge d'affaires would move between Khartoum and Nairobi). This US peace effort ultimately won through against similar efforts to end the war led by an East African forum called the Intergovernmental Authority for Development, (IGAD) and a belated Arab attempt to end the war on Arab terms led by Egypt and Libya.

Under Egyptian guidance, Arab countries sniffed at the interim peace deal mainly because it laid down a framework for self-determination in south Sudan which was backed by the United States. The Arab world did not want Sudan broken up and did not want to see a southern state. The Bashir regime had been susceptible to American pressure to bring the war to an end because like its SPLA enemy it was tired and because through peace it hoped to replace Washington's enmity for its favour. Despite the rhetoric of August 1998, Bashir himself had seen the way the wind was blowing and divested Turabi of his considerable powers in a mini-coup within the ruling clique in 1999. It was the sidelining of Turabi that opened the way to rapprochement with Egypt and the United States. The final peace deal signed in 2005 also managed to deflect some of the foreign pressure on the government at the time over the Darfur crisis (see later), and so provided protection to a regime whose ultimate aim and success has been none other than its own survival.

The conclusion of the civil war has in fact maintained the Islamist National Front regime in power, creating what Sadeq al-Mahdi has called a "diarchy" between the southern independence movement and a military regime that had wilfully turned the civil war into a religious conflict when it came to power in 1989.[16] The peace deal divides power up between the government and SPLM, allocating a small number of seats in parliament to other northern and southern parties in a kind of Lebanon-style sectarian system. "What we have arrived at now is almost a failed state. The UN's role in Sudan, now, is almost a protectorate; you must call things by their name. The Sudan is under UN protection now. So a dictatorship took us to this situation, where the country has lost much of its sovereignty," Mahdi says.[17] Indeed, during the Islamist regime, the conflict became internationalized, international sanctions were in force, and communities were placed under UN protection, though the UN's Operation Lifeline Sudan to provide food aid began under Mahdi's government. Khartoum has faced the possibility of the UN Security Council authorizing the use of force against the government over the Darfur crisis, but it accepted the African Union providing troops to monitor a ceasefire between the warring parties in the region of West Sudan, which is as big as France. "The architects of the ethnic cleansing (in Darfur) have retained significant power in the new government of national unity, which thus far remains unwilling to take the military and political steps needed to resolve the conflict: neutralising the Janjaweed militias and establishing genuine power and wealth sharing between Darfur and Khartoum," the Brussels-based International Crisis Group warned in a report issued in October 2005.[18] Before 1989, there was no humanitarian problem of internally displaced people and refugees, as well as war crimes and crimes against humanity, and ethnicity was not as politicized as it is today. Now the Khartoum government is looking for US help to get over its post-war problems, as if this was a quid pro quo for having made peace with the south. "The United States has put an effort into the peace process so now it should lift sanctions and oblige donors in Oslo to meet their promises and obligations and help make peace permanent. There are more than four million displaced southerners in the north," Sudan's ambassador to the United States Khidir Haroun said.[19]

Many argue that the war was needlessly prolonged by the American policy during the 1990s. Driven by ideological opposition to Khartoum, the United States backed the southern rebels with arms and political support, thus discouraging the SPLA from sueing for peace. Sudan found military support from a list of countries with anti-US grievances, including Iran, Iraq and Malaysia. Other funders included France, unique among Western nations, South Africa and former Soviet bloc states.[20] Former US President Jimmy Carter said in April 2001: "For the last eight years, the US has had a policy which I strongly disagree with in Sudan, supporting the revolutionary movement and not working for an overall peace settlement."[21] This support came despite the fact that international rights groups had had equally harsh words for the SPLA, who Human Rights Watch had termed a gross rights abuser. The US policy was viewed in the Arab world as unfairly one-sided and influenced by blatant ideological preference: Christian and African was good, Muslim and Arab was bad.

The "anti-Sudan lobby"

Apart from Khartoum's radical Islam, a key factor in the US policy was the virulent anti-Sudan lobby which was so demonized in the Arab world that Sudan's northern opposition parties avoided all contact with them. This lobby is large and heterogeneous, grouping organizations and pressure groups from across the political spectrum – from conservative Christian fundamentalist groups to liberal and leftist African American organizations. Their voices grew stronger throughout the 1990s in a furious debate in the West over Sudan. Some have lacked credibility. A Sudanese southern independence activist called Kola Boof, author of *Long Train to the Redeeming Sin: Stories of African Women*, achieved media notoriety in the United States with a claim not only that a Sharia court in Sudan had issued a fatwa against her life in 2002 for her campaigning against slavery, posing topless and renouncing Islam (she was born to a Muslim father), but that she was forced into an affair with Osama bin Laden in Morocco in 1996 and at some other stage with Turabi.[22] In one prominent case which won Western media attention, Mende Nezer wrote in her 2004 book *Slave* that she was abducted at the age of 12 from the Nuba Mountains, taken to Khartoum and then on to London where she worked as a maid for a high-ranking Sudanese diplomat.[23] Civil rights groups and the Christian right have vociferously admonished the Sudanese authorities for the persecution and marginalization of southern Sudanese Christians and turning a blind eye to the practice of slavery and other major violations to human rights.

The Arab media has not missed the links between these lobby groups and pro-Israeli and Christian fundamentalist organizations in the United States .The campaign against slavery in Sudan was partly an outgrowth of the pro-Israeli lobby. One such group is the American Anti-Slavery Group (AASG), set up in 1993 by Charles Jacobs who has a history of public support for right-wing Israeli policies. He works closely with the right-wing, Likudist National Unity Coalition for Israel and was chairman of the right-wing American Friends of the Israeli Double Column Plan, which backs annexing lands occupied by Israel in 1967. In 2000, Jacobs became head of The Sudan Campaign, a coalition of anti-government groups that sought to connect events in Sudan in the minds of Americans with images of slave plantations in the nineteenth century, seeking to present the issue in the starkest ethnic and religious terms possible and create the impression of a highly-organized trade directed by the Sudanese state itself. Jacobs also sees a connection between the suffering of non-Arab Sudanese today and Jews in biblical times. In 2004, he was able to say that "... thanks to pressure brought by an unlikely coalition that includes Christian and Jewish groups, the Congressional Black Caucus, black church leaders and secular activists, stopping the horror in Sudan is now American policy".[24]

The charges of slavery and religious persecution caused the government major damage. The Center for Religious Freedom, run by the Washington-based Freedom House, another group at the centre of the campaign against the government, claimed in 2001 that "no place on earth is religious persecution more brutal" than in Sudan.[25] In 2003, the Rift Valley Institute, a British-Kenyan NGO, launched its Sudan Abductee Database, with details of some 11,000 cases of southerners abducted from rebel-held areas. The group said it had documented thousands of cases of liberated slaves who were forced to Arabize and Islamize by their captors.[26] The campaigns worked in gaining public attention. Anti-Sudanese activists including former District of Columbia Congressional delegate Walter E. Fauntroy, radio talk show host Joe Madison and the Hudson Institute's Michael Horowitz chained themselves to the fence in front of the Sudanese embassy in 2001 with the aim of getting arrested in order to bring attention to "slavery in Sudan".

Politically, they contributed to the Bush administration's pressure on Khartoum to come to terms with the southerners. The Swiss-based Christian Solidarity International said in 2005 that in conjunction with the government itself it had returned 880 to their homes in Bahr al-Ghazal region of south Sudan as part of the group's "slave redemption" programme, though these figures were much lower than the tens of thousands it had maintained for several years had been abducted and liberated in total. Sudan is one of fifteen countries where the government and/or rebel groups use child soldiers, according to the United Nations in January 2004, and during the Darfur conflict, abduction and rape against women were used as weapons of war.[27]

Khartoum has tried to strike back. An affiliated lobby group called the European Sudanese Public Affairs Council (ESPAC) has tried to present the image of crazed opponents of Arab and Muslims engaged in a deliberate campaign of exaggeration and manipulation of public opinion in the United States, where slavery as a concept has deep emotional resonances for historical reasons. "Sudan has been wracked by civil war for decades. Since 1983 the war in the south has been fought against the Government of Sudan by the Sudan People's Liberation Army (SPLA). It is a conflict that has been distorted by the deliberate use of propaganda. One propaganda theme has been that of 'slavery'," it has said.[28] It has documented cases of aid organizations being duped into believing they were freeing "slaves" who were actually defrauding them for cash or staging "slave redemptions" with local collusion, where slaves are apparently bought by rights groups who grant them their freedom, in order to get money out of naïve Western donor organizations.[29]

Some rights activists say that the debate between the West – mainly the United States – and the Arab world about human rights in Sudan has become so politicized that some facts about the historical relationship between communities in Sudan have been obscured or forgotten. According to Ahmed Mufti, the Sudanese head of the United Nations and government-backed Committee for the Eradication of Abduction of Women and Children (CEAWC), slavery has been a traditional practice made worse by the proliferation of modern weaponry in the civil war.[30] Abductions have been common for generations among nomadic tribes cutting across the north-south cultural divide in southwest Sudan who compete for cattle-grazing land and water resources in arid desert, he says. "Before 1999, these tribes wouldn't talk to each other, and they wouldn't even recognize this is a problem. If you said to them this is 'abduction' they wouldn't understand ... Our strategy is to tell tribes that if they cooperate with us there will be no legal action. If we had taken the law and order path we would have had big problems. These people are fighters," said Mufti, who hails from Dongola in the north.[31]

The Darfur crisis

In the shadow of war in Iraq, an insurgency began in 2003 in the huge west Sudanese area of Darfur. In response the government raised tribal militias and armed Bedouin tribes. Dividing lines were quickly drawn: the rebel Sudan Liberation Army (SLA) represented the sedentary Darfurans after whom the area is named (Arabic: "the land of the Fur"), the government backed the nomadic Arab tribes. While the SLA was partly fighting over the same forms of poverty and neglect that the southerners had taken arms over, it was also fighting because of an already-existing dispute with the Arab tribes. Desertification had broken a symbiotic relationship between the arable farmers and the migratory tribes, as each group tried to protect their resources to the detriment of the other. A drought in the mid-1980s had sent hundreds of thousands of Darfurans to Khartoum. What was striking about the Darfur conflict since 2003 was the degree of devastation suffered by the sedentary Darfurans and the nature of the suffering – the nomadic tribes were not only well armed but implementing what appeared to be a systematic policy of depopulation, or what in modern parlance has come to be known as ethnic cleansing. These Janjaweed, as their Darfuran victims referred to them, came with "light and medium weapons, communication, internal structure and impunity".[32] It was a repeat of the "scorched earth policy" that rights groups had accused the Khartoum regime of using to clear out African villagers from the areas in the rough boundary line between "north" and "south" Sudan where international oil companies began exploring and drilling oil in the 1990s.

The conflict also reflected the ideology shift in Sudan since the civil war began, where "Arab" and "Muslim" meant more than "African". The Darfur population, both nomad and sedentary, is Muslim but some writers have argued that ethnic Arab chauvinism had been making inroads among the tribes in Darfur since the 1980s, promoted by Libya. Since regional elections in 1981, the Arab tribes had come together in an "Arab Gathering" (*al-Tajammu' al-Arabi*) with the ultimate aim of taking control of Darfur from the numerically stronger village and town dwellers, most of whom are not native Arabic speakers.[33] The tribes used the classic argument in the Sudanese context that since they descend from the Qureish tribe of the Prophet Mohammed in Mecca, they should by right be in charge. Other arguments that have been advanced to explain the government's position include: keeping the military busy and providing new sources of profiteering, weakening Umma party support in Darfur, providing a pretext for maintaining emergency laws and repressive policies in central and north Sudan.

Since 2003, the conflict has killed tens of thousands of people and forced more than two million people to flee their homes. They have been rounded into squalid camps where they have often faced further attack. Estimates for how many died through murder, starvation and disease vary widely – at the end of 2004, a figure of 70,000 was commonly cited; by early 2005, some organizations talked of 400,000 people. The Darfur crisis rose to the top of the global news agenda in mid-2004 and not long after the Bush administration declared that a "genocide" had taken place there. A United Nations commission said in January 2005 that the government was not guilty of genocide but some individuals may have acted with "genocidal intent". It detailed extensive atrocities authorized by the Sudanese government and carried out by Janjaweed militias. "The Commission found that Government forces and militias conducted indiscriminate attacks, including killing of civilians, torture, enforced disappearances, destruction of villages, rape and other forms of sexual violence, pillaging and forced displacement, throughout Darfur. These acts were conducted on a widespread and systematic basis, and therefore may amount to crimes against humanity," it said.[34] In international law, genocide is a crime of specific intent – it requires that the guilty parties intended to destroy all or part of an ethnic, racial, national or religious community. The category came into existence largely through the efforts of a Polish Jew named Raphael Lemkin who worked to frame a law that captured the unique horror of a concerted campaign to deny a specific group's right to exist. He was instrumental in drafting the 1948 Convention on the Prevention of Genocide. But the UN report on Darfur concluded that the various tribes who were subject to attacks and killings did not appear to make up ethnic groups distinct from the ethnic group to which their attackers belonged. An African Union force was sent to Darfur but there was no deployment of international troops and no UN sanctions against Khartoum. In 2005, the US Senate introduced the

Darfur Accountability Act, which calls for increased aid to the African Union force, as well as a military no-fly zone and a tight arms embargo. The Khartoum government subsequently played "the al-Qa'ida card" in an attempt to ward off further internationalization of the conflict. Bashir said such a force would be a return to colonialism, and Islamists outside government said they would fight it. The followers of bin Laden were also apparently readying themselves for the appearance of non-African troops in Sudan. In a videotaped message aired on al-Jazeera, Ayman al-Zawahiri called on Muslims to fight any foreign troops sent to Darfur.

But these measures seemed like sops to public opinion which had been led to believe the US administration would take great steps over Darfur, after the massacre of some 800,000 people in Rwanda and 200,000 in Bosnia during the 1990s. The administration resisted pressure to refer the issue to the International Criminal Court (ICC) because of its opposition in principle to the new entity set up in 1998 for fear that US citizens could be hauled up before it in politically motivated cases. The court was eventually given UN authority to begin investigating war crimes in June 2005. Ironically, from an Arab perspective, these "politically-motivated cases" that Washington has in mind would likely involve the Arab-Israeli conflict or US actions in Iraq. The UN report recommended that unnamed Sudan government officials and militia leaders appear before the ICC. Meanwhile, the UN Security Council has resisted American arguments to impose sanctions on Sudan's oil industry. Conflict has also broken out in east Sudan, where the Beja tribespeople live in poverty despite residing in a region that includes Sudan's only port, its main oil pipeline which carries Sudanese crude exports and the country's largest gold mine.

Sudan has been backed in all of this by the Arab countries and most commentators in the Sudanese media are skeptical of the United States role in the region. In this typical analysis, Ahmed Naqd Idris, a writer in the pro-government *Akhbar al-Youm*, sees a similarity in American policy in Iraq and Sudan – to back minorities that help weaken centralized polities that opposed Washington. "Because the American cowboy has lost the battle on the ground, he has as usual gone for provoking civil strife between the sons of the one united country and one religion, the Shi'ites and the Sunnis, via this disastrous constitution which was written in the White House with unnecessary haste," he says.[35] He then goes on to say that: "American intelligence defines Sudanese society in a manner that undermines its sense of Arab belonging. The

CIA website says that Sudan is 39 percent Arab, 25 percent black, 6 percent Beja, 20 percent foreigner and 10 percent other. But all of the 39 percent that it says are Arab actually came from black origins ... Arabism is a language, however hateful that is to the Americans." Idris said that US administrations have been trying since the 1967 Arab-Israeli war to change Sudan's position in the Arab world. "They want to change our identity, as we can see from this headline in *Akhbar al-Youm* from 12 May 1968: a government spokesman said that Sudan will not return its diplomatic relations with America and accused America of striving for the defeat of the government parties in the last elections in order to change Sudan's position on the Arab question [Israel and the Palestinians]." The writer also says southerners who do not speak Arabic should not serve in key government ministries. "We are giving our south more than it deserves in land, money and authority, without asking for a receipt for the sacrifices, blood and money we have borne in the north while facing advanced American weaponry that the SPLA, America's ally, fought us with." In a similar vein, celebrated Egyptian novelist Gamal Ghitani writes: "Egypt has its own special characteristics, and so does Morocco, Yemen, Iraq, Syria, Sudan, but they are all united by a cultural passion based on language, and this sacred language is now under threat from numerous factors, despite the presence of the Quran which protects it and forms its authority. There are social, economic and cultural circumstances weakening this language, and I fear that one day we'll read the Quran without understanding it, like the Turks and Muslims of southeast Asia."[36] Even Turabi, the man who champions an ideology that many see as having been instrumental in causing the Darfur crisis, told Arab television: "See how the world regards us now, while whether we like it or not we represent Arabness [*al-'uruba*] and Islam. I don't want this to be our image."[37]

Sudanese commentators who write in the pan-Arab media are, while antagonistic to the Islamist regime, wary of opposition movements with foreign support. Abdel-Wahhab al-Effendi writes in the London-based *al-Quds al-Arabi* that the Darfur rebels and the United States have missed their moment, after the government made peace with southerners. "The Darfur negotiators failed to take advantage of the period of intense international pressure on the government and the time when the government's agreement with the south was still early to impose better negotiating conditions. The Darfur negotiators need to realize that the choice of a military option is now over. The international community now will not let them launch a war on a government of national unity and threaten the peace agreement."[38] Political commentator Hassan Sati, who often appears on the Arab satellite channels, writes with similar conviction that Sudan's Islamist government is being targeted by Washington for an ideological overhaul, like the Taliban was. But while both had a lot in common, he suggested Sudan's Islamist project was more deep-rooted than Afghanistan's and so would prove tougher for America to root out. "While the Taliban was a Pakistani creation, the Islamic movement in Sudan was different. It began with the Egyptian Islamist movement then went its own way through several groups, from Muslim Brotherhood, to the Islamic Charter Front, the National Islamic Front and then ruling National Congress ... the Islamic movement in Sudan has its base in the elite and technocrats, not religious schools," he writes.[39] But there will be no shortcut to democratic system, he said. "There is no shortcut to democracy and freedom. The circumstances have to come together to arrive at a level of maturity that allows the situation to take off easily by itself, though sometimes you can speed things up with a catalyst, and this is exactly what Uncle Sam is trying to do, with more and more pressure for political reform and plans like the Greater Middle East Project. So we can dream of democracy spreading in this millennium, either through Uncle Sam's stick or the choice of the peoples involved. We've got the Afghanistan example today, and maybe a Sudanese example tomorrow."

The southern intelligentsia is little represented in the Arabic media in Sudan – the English-language *Khartoum Monitor* is one of their few outlets in the capital, and it has been frequently shut down by government censors. Though Arab nationalism has been cruel to many minorities, the one thing it has offered is integration into the mainstream through the Arabic language, something Copts of Egypt and Christians of Lebanon have done with gusto, allowing them to be the remarkable conveyors of literature. But set outside even the world of literary Arabic, employing English, the worldview of the southern intellectuals offers a sharp contrast to that of the northerners and the rest of the Arab world. Omar Shurkian shoots from the hip in this piece on www.sudaneseonline.com after the death of Garang in August 2005 in a helicopter accident. "Surely, when more than twelve million people have become convinced that they are rejected in a country in which they live, and that there is no longer any basis for unity between them and other groups of people, then unity has already ceased to exist. You cannot kill thousands of people, and keep killing more, in the name of unity. There is no unity between the dead and those who killed them; and, worse still, there is no unity in slavery and domination," he says.[40] "The Sudanese society is infested with countless episodes of social diseases, including racism, tribalism, religious bigotry, sectarianism, exploitation, cultural assimilation, gender discrimination and so forth. In the Northern communities, Garang witnessed a great deal of this manifestly practised misdemeanour in Arab jokes, folklore, neighbourhood relations, mass media, employment opportunities and Government policies."

With intense international attention, words like genocide being tossed around and threats of UN sanctions and trials in The Hague, the Arab media has given the Darfur crisis more serious attention than it perhaps ever gave the civil war. Government officials have faced tough questioning on the pan-Arab satellite channels about conduct that has brought negative world attention not just on Sudan but the entire Arab world and taken attention away from the key issues in Arab-Western relations regarding Iraq and Israel. The general tone is that the Sudanese authorities have irresponsibly "let the side down" and given the enemy a chance to make considerable gains, has been the general attitude. According to the 2004 Amnesty International report "Rape as a Weapon of War", the Sudanese government and the militias it backed "benefited from the support or silence of Middle Eastern countries". Human Rights Watch reporter Julie Flint, who had visited Darfur herself to report on the events there, caught the atmosphere of Arab attitudes towards the Darfur crisis at a seminar at the Press Syndicate in Beirut in July 2004 in the presence of the Sudanese ambassador. In an account of the meeting, she writes: "Ethnic cleansing by government forces in Darfur? An invention of the people who brought you Abu Ghraib and who lied about Saddam Hussein's weapons of mass destruction! (Loud applause.) A conspiracy against the Arabs! (Louder applause.) Rape? What nonsense! Not more than two cases, the ambassador declared – apparently unaware that, under the relentless accumulation of facts, his own government had been compelled to set up committees to investigate accusations of rape in Darfur and help victims through criminal cases."[41] Lebanese journalists and civil society activists present agreed that the Darfur crisis was in essence an American plot against the Arabs, Flint wrote. This was just months after the Abu Ghraib scandal and a year after the American invasion of Iraq. But she saw a pattern of reactions to other Western exposes of atrocity in the Arab world: "The Arab silence on Darfur is reminiscent of the silence that followed the gassing of thousands of Iraqi Kurds by the former regime of Saddam Hussein. Arab states have turned their eyes away while an Arab government working with Arab proxy forces has created what relief officials call the greatest humanitarian disaster in the world today. Their silence is all the more shocking because the victims of this disaster, although not of the same ethnic origin as their oppressors, are, like them, of the Muslim faith."[42]

In fact, the attitude of the Arab audience was no surprise at all; it reflects a society that believes it has no control over its own destiny, a society inured to brutality and a society where the line between information and propaganda has blurred to the point of non-recognition. A small number of commentators have tried to speak out frankly about Darfur, though more often than not they appear in the English-language rather than Arabic media. The *Daily Star* has written: "The government in Khartoum is still in denial. It has dismissed international pressure to address the crisis as a Western assault on Islam and Arab culture. But the fact is that it doesn't take a mufti or a sociologist to explain the world's outrage over the slaughter of innocent civilians. Culture cannot suffice as an excuse anymore; the crimes have gone beyond culture and to the very essence of humanity. The world has simply spoken out because Sudan has been brutally murdering its own children."[43]

Chapter 8
Conclusion

In the decolonization period, America inherited the colonial mantle from Britain and France, establishing strong political and economic relations wherever it could and seeking to check rival Soviet influence in the Middle East. Its first major ally was Saudi Arabia, helping develop the state to serve its oil interest. Israel became central to US foreign policy in the region after the 1967 Arab-Israeli war. Egypt, whose non-aligned policies under Nasser favoured a "horizontal" pan-Arab axis rather than "vertical" links with Western powers, joined the American fold during Anwar Sadat's presidency and was cemented with Egypt's 1979 peace treaty with Israel.

However, the attacks of 11 September, 2001 showed that these elaborate state–state relations were far removed from what was going on inside rapidly expanding Arab societies themselves. Over the decades, and particularly after the humiliating defeat to Israel in 1967, a wide spectrum of Islamist and secular political constituencies had developed a deep resentment of their governments' accomodations of American foreign policy, and those ineluctable state-state relations had themselves helped turn society against the United States. The two main political-intellectual camps in the Arab world today, political Islam and Arab nationalism, are virulently anti-American; only the beleaguered liberal democrats have any sympathy. The Arab media revolution which began in the early 1990s has hugely strengthened the influence of Arab societies vis-à-vis Arab states and governments, compounding the problems of the United States. The invasion of Iraq, which was presented by the US government as part of a wider campaign to spread democracy in the Arab world, has further damaged the American position in the region, despite the fact that they were both intended to improve it.

At the same time, the Arab world is by turns obsessed, mesmerized and repelled by American popular and political culture, and American foreign policy and the world of domestic America are to a large degree treated separately on their own terms. Arab television has gorged itself on American TV, filling the airwaves with chatshows, sitcoms and even real-time news programmes, while music, fashion and other elements of Arab popular culture are doing their level best to ape Americana as much as they can within the surprisingly elastic confines – given the high rhetoric and claims of religion – of Islamic mores.

The Arab world has overwhelmingly come to interpret and respond to the United States through the prism of the Arab-Israeli conflict and the plight of the Palestinians, who live under Israeli occupation in the territories, as second-class citizens in the self-defined "Jewish state" (Israel), or as unwanted refugees in Arab countries (though a large number do live as full citizens in Jordan). In Arab discourse, Zionism is a racist and exclusivist ideology with origins in colonialism that denigrates and disposes the Arab and seeks to establish hegemony over his political and cultural space. Yet, the United States cherishes and idolizes Zionism today as much as it ever did, and arguably more so. In Arab society, among the media and intellectual elites, a realization has in recent years sunk in that the United States and Israel are for many influential Americans cultural soul-mates, and the Arab world is struggling to elaborate strategies to deal with this. Arab political elites consider that since the second Palestinian uprising of 2000 Israel has managed to draft the US government on side for the next, decisive stage of the Israeli-Palestinian conflict, the demographic war. Settlement building and land confiscation continues, while Palestinians of the territories are excluded from work and travel in Israel. Palestinians and Arabs in general are in the process of adjusting their political strategies accordingly, and the two-state solution supported by Washington since 1993 is at risk of becoming obsolete.

Arab governments, opposition and intellectuals have long assumed that a solution to the Israeli-Palestinian conflict would remove the underpinnings of the authoritarian political systems of the Arab world, where security apparatus and army have society held tightly in a vice. Washington's Iraq project turned this thinking on its head. Only when Arab societies became economically open, politically democratic and renounced their challenge to the Pax Americana would the Arabs get a Palestinian state. For the Arab world, the Iraq project is the dawn of a neo-imperial era in which Arab regimes contracted in the independence era to secure US interests are to be swept away if they prove not up to the job. For much of the Arab political class, American-style capitalism wants to vaporize the memory banks of the wounded civilizations, a tool wielded by the West against the Arabs that will help them forget past wrongs and "get with" the future. Furthermore, the Arab view considers that American behaviour in Iraq – the invasion and the attempt to crush the anti-occupation insurgency – is modelled on Israel's brutal treatment of Palestinians in the territories. The Abu Ghraib torture scandal seemed to confirm this. It hardened the dominant image of an arrogant neo-colonial power whose human rights rhetoric is a cover for geopolitic aims. Intellectuals inspired by Edward Said's *Orientalism* thesis said America's treatment of Iraqis was driven by decades of degrading discourse about Arab culture in the United States, fuelled by Zionism.

America's alliance with Egypt succeeded in breaking the back of any meaningful pan-Arab policy to challenge the emerging US-dominated order in the Middle East and to reestablish the Nasserist project of giving paramouncy to regional, not Western, ties. The US alliance also corrupted Egyptian political life, as the country's "crony capitalist" elite sheltered around an undemocratic regime which was both alienated from its increasingly Islamic and Islamist society and bolstered by political and financial support from Washington. Held in this rigid straitjacket, Egypt developed into a deformed political creature as the gap between government and society expanded to bitter proportions but with no one able to do a thing about it. Shackled by its US alliance, Egypt remains deeply troubled and ill-at-ease with itself.

The same is true for Saudi Arabia. A new-fangled polity, the Saudi state has remained heavily reliant on British and then US support for its survival in the face of numerous regional threats, from Nasser's pan-Arab movement to Communism to Saddam Hussein's expansionist Iraq. The kingdom's rulers have been deeply paranoid about the possibility of any disintegration of the country due to foreign meddling or domestic opposition. There remains a fundamental problem of legitimacy for the ruling family, but unflinching American support – despite the hiccup of 9/11 – has helped obviate the need to deal with this issue in a manner consonant with modern state building (representative government, popular participation, elections, etc.). Saudi Arabia's need for US protection came out into the open during the 1990–1991 Gulf crisis when US troops were posted to Saudi Arabia and stayed there until 2003. Resentment in the Arab world runs deep over Saudi Arabia's facilitation of US interests in the region, while punching beneath its weight in foreign policy, especially with respect to the Arab-Israeli conflict.

The Arab world closed ranks to offer political, economic and moral support to the Islamist regime in Khartoum against US backing for southern rebels during the 1983–2005 civil war and to support the regime over the Darfur crisis, despite the huge suffering caused in both cases by regime policy. The United States is generally viewed in the Arab world as backing division, deconstruction and weakening of Sudan's Arab-Muslim identity because it is from pride in that identity that the statederives its ability to resist American influence.

One theme that will have come through in this book is the spirit of independence, whether for good or bad, that pulses through the Arab world. It is perhaps salutory to consider that the evolution of Islam itself is due in no small part to the rejection of foreign influence. For much of the Umayyad period – the first dynasty of Islam that ruled Damascus from 661 to 750 AD – Islam was not in fact clearly defined as a separate religion, neither by their largely Christian subjects nor by the Arab ruling class. Christianity for the Arabs had a distinctly Greek face. Christianity was the state religion of the Byzantine empire that the Arabs had defeated in the conquests of the mid-seventh century, and the Christian church was in any case split into warring factions, sects and polities. Judaism was largely closed off to outsiders. What the Arab empire facilitated, then, was the reworking of the existing monotheistic tradition, of Judaism and Christianity, in an Arabic format and giving the Arabs of the peninsula a central role in the sacred topography of the Semitic world. Judaism and Christianity were both well attested throughout the length and breadth of the Arabian peninsula, but the Arab conquerors were not content to simply choose one over the other – they attempted to submerge them both in a new super-monotheistic religion. It was nothing if not an astounding statement of cultural strength and independence.

The cultural, religious and historical banks that the Arab world has to draw on in the face of perceived threats are vast. Indeed, in both the Sunni and Shi'ite Islamic traditions, it is religious scholars who are heavily steeped in the knowledge and traditions of the past who carry the authority to reinterpret Islam and chart new territory – an in-built conservatism that reflects the tenacity of Arab-Islamic culture. Of course, the beginnings of the Arab world date back to an era nearly 1,400 years ago when tribal control of the desert swathe from the Atlantic board to the foot of the Zagros Mountains in Asia made it possible to consolidate this large political-cultural entity referred to subsequently by historians as Arab-Islamic civilization. In the modern era, technological developments have rearranged the geopolitical map, and North Africa may today find it more logical to develop relationships of whatever nature with the Iberian peninsula, for example, than the Middle East. Similarly, the United States thought that with its invasion project it could nudge Iraq away from the Arab orbit. But one thing that, over the decades, Arab reactions to the Zionist movement as well as to the ongoing Iraq experience have demonstrated is the tough and hardy nature of Arab-Islamic culture – its stubborn and implacable will to resist those who will violate the integrity of the whole.

Chronology

1948 Creation of the state of Israel and the Palestinian refugee problem
1952 Military coup in Egypt ends the monarchy, brings Gamal Abdel-Nasser to power
1956 Nasser emerges victorious from the Suez crisis, becomes a hero figure around the Arab world
1956 Sudan gains independence from Britain and Egypt
1958–61 The merging of Egypt and Syria in the United Arab Republic
1962 Algeria gains independence after seven-year war against the French
1963 The Baath party takes power in Syria
1967 The Arab-Israeli war in which Israel seizes the West Bank, East Jerusalem, Gaza Strip, Sinai and Golan Heights and more Palestinians are made refugees
1968 The Baath party takes power in Iraq
1970 Nasser dies, succeeded by Anwar Sadat who takes Egypt into the Western orbit
1973 The October war, led by Egypt and Syria against Israel; Saudi Arabia embargoes oil to Western countries
1975 The Lebanese civil war begins
1975 Saudi Arabia's King Faisal assassinated by a royal disgruntled with modernization
1977 Sadat makes a sudden trip to Jerusalem where he addresses the Knesset with a call for a comprehensive Arab-Israeli peace
1977 Israel begins its program of settlement building in the occupied territories
1978 Israel invades Lebanon, occupies the south
1979 Egypt and Israel sign a peace treaty
1979 Iranian revolution
1980 The eight-year long Iran–Iraq war begins
1980 Berbers stage protests against marginalization in Algeria
1981 Egyptian President Anwar Sadat assassinated; succeeded by Hosni Mubarak
1982 Israel invades Lebanon
1983 Southern Sudanese launch civil war against northern domination
1987 First Palestinian Intifada against Israeli occupation begins

1987 Zein al-Abidine Ben Ali takes power in Tunisia
1988 Algeria allows political liberalization
1989 Islamist regime comes to power in Sudan after a military coup
1990 Iraq invades Kuwait; UN sanctions on Iraq begin
1990 Lebanese civil war declared over
1991 US-led coalition ousts Iraqi forces from Kuwait, but Iraqi regime survives rebellion
1992 Algerian military cancel parliamentary elections, Islamist rebellion begins
1992 Radical Islamist groups in Egypt begin insurgency against the Egyptian government
1993 Oslo peace accords between Israel and the PLO
1994 Jordan signs a peace treaty with Israel
1996 Israeli Right-wing returnss to power under Netanyahu
1996 Qatar sets up al-Jazeera satellite television channel
1996 Lebanese entertainment channel LBC launches around the region
2000 Mauritania establishes diplomatic relations with Israel
2000 Second Palestinian Intifada begins after Camp David talks fail to resolve disputes between Israel and the Palestinians
2000 Hafez al-Assad dies; his son Bashar takes over
2000 Israel ends twenty-two year occupation of south Lebanon in face of Hizbollah resistance
2001 Right-wing Israeli government led by former general Ariel Sharon comes to power
2001 September 11 attacks in the United States; new war on Islamic extremism begins
2003 A US-led invasion topples the regime of Saddam Hussein; UN sanctions ended 2004 US President George W. Bush says Israeli should be allowed to keep parts of the West Bank
2005 Abdullah ascends the throne of Saudi Arabia, after the death of King Fahd
2006 Israeli wages a thirty-four-day war against Lebanon in an effort to destroy Hizbollah

Glossary

Abbasid
The name of the second major dynasty of Islam, which established itself in Iraq in 750 and lasted until the Mongols sacked Baghdad in 1258 (though a branch survived in Cairo to 1517, when the Ottoman Turks took Egypt).

Abu Ghraib
Iraqi prison which was notorious under the rule of former President Saddam Hussein and where US forces also tortured prisoners after they ousted Hussein in the 2003 invasion.

Al-Ahram
Egypt's leading daily newspaper and the state's flagship paper. Also one of the oldest newspapers in the Arab world.

Al-Arabiya
Leading Arabic news channel, majority-owned by Saudi Arabia's MBC television.

Al-Azhar
A mosque and religious education institution based in Cairo, seen as one of the highest authorities for Sunni Muslims. Al-Azhar runs its own religious school system, separate from Egypt's state education system, with secondary schools and university branches throughout Egypt which are attended by Muslims from around the world. Since 1961, the institution has been officially an arm of the state, since its leader, the Grand Sheikh, is nominated by the Egyptian president and in the pay of government.

Al-Jazeera
Leading Arabic news channel, owned by the Qatari government.

Al-Qa'ida
Loose radical Islamist network headed by Saudi dissident Osama bin Laden and formed in the cauldron of post-Soviet Afghanistan. It is dedicated to fighting the US presence in Arab and Islamic countries.

Al Saud
The Bedouin family which has ruled the country which carries their own name since it obtained UN recognition in 1932.

Andalucia (al-Andalus)
The last of the Arab-Islamic provinces of the Iberian peninsula to fall to the Spaniards, in 1492. Often used as a reference point for the Arab conflict with Zionism.

Asharq al-Awsat
Leading pan-Arab daily newspaper, which is Saudi-owned.

Baath Party
Secular Arab nationalist political party established in Syria and which spread to Iraq, where both movements took power in the 1960s. The Baath, led by Saddam Hussein, was removed from power with the 2003 invasion of Iraq. The Baath in Syria is still in power.

Balfour Declaration
> The document by a British foreign minister in 1917 promising British help to establish a homeland for the world's Jews in Palestine, which at that time had a native Arab population which, as in other regions of the Arab world, hoped to eventually gain independence.

Caliph
> The name of the figure designated by Muslims to rule over the community of believers in the Prophet Muhammad's stead – these rulers termed themselves the "successor/viceregent of the prophet of God" (*khalifat rasul allah*), though there is some debate among scholars of Islamic history over whether some of them were presented as "the viceregents of God" (*khalifat allah*) in the manner of the Shi'ite imams.

Camp David
> The US presidential retreat where Egyptian and Israeli leaders thrashed out the details of a historic peace treaty in 1978 which was signed the next year. Palestinian and Israeli leaders were brought there in 2000 to try to put an end to the Israeli-Palestinian conflict.

Crusades
> Series of medieval-era campaigns led by European nobility with Papal backing to take Jerusalem "back" from the Muslims for Christendom. The wars, which extended to the rest of the Levant and Egypt, have retained a heavy presence in the minds of Arabs throughout the centuries and are used as a reference point for discussion of the Arab experience of Zionism.

Daily Star
> Lebanese English-language daily newspaper.

Darfur
> Large area of Western Sudan where a conflict between pastoralists and nomads developed into a humanitarian disaster in 2004 with tens of thousands of the settled population dying. The Sudanese government had backed the nomadic group, known as Janjaweed, behind the atrocities committed there.

Da'wa
> Iraqi Shi'ite religious party which was based for years in Iran until the 2003 Iraq invasion. Led by Ibrahim al-Jaafari, it is part of the Shi'ite alliance that won elections in December 2005.

Fedayeen
> Term used to refer to guerrilla or resistance fighters. Often used in the past to describe the Palestinian liberation movement, the word has a broadly neutral-to-positive connotation in Arabic.

FIS
> The Islamic Salvation Front that was poised to win Algerian elections in 1992, which the Western-backed military halted, provoking a bloody civil war that killed well over 100,000 people.

Fundamentalist
> Term used to refer to the current of political thought which favors a return to the way of early Muslims in all forms of life, institutional and individual, public and private. Fundamentalists often prefer the term "Salafi", which means going back to the ways of the ancestors, or *salaf*.

Gamaa Islamiya
Egyptian Islamist group whose spiritual leader was Omar Abdel-Rahman and which launched an open war against the government from 1992 to 1997.

Hadiths
Sayings of the Prophet or his close family and companions which have been passed on from generation to generation and collected by hadith scholars some 200–300 years later. Many of these hadiths form a key element in Islamic law, but the various schools of law and sects often differ over favouring and discounting different hadiths.

Hashemites
The ruling royal family in Jordan, which Britain installed as the ruling royal family in Iraq after the First World War but which was deposed in a violent 1958 coup. The family ruled the Hejaz cities for 1,000 years until the armies of the nascent Saudi state overran the area in 1926, with British approval.

Al-Hayat
Leading pan-Arab daily newspaper, based in London. Owned by a Saudi royal.

Hizbollah
Lebanese Shi'ite group that led opposition to the Israeli occupation of south Lebanon that ended in 2000. With seats in parliament and a paramilitary force, it remains a major player in Lebanese politics.

Ijtihad
The idea in Islamic law that in the absence of clear guidance from the Quran or the Sunna, or "way of the Prophet", clerics can build new theories or opinions based on their own intellectual endeavour. Liberals in the Arab world say there should be more *ijtihad* rather than blind adherence to centuries-old custom.

Intifada
The name for two Palestinian revolts against Israeli occupation, one from 1987 to 1992 and the second begun in 2000 which is still ongoing.

Islamic Jihad
Egyptian radical Islamist group set up by Ayman al-Zawahiri and which was merged into al-Qa'ida in 1998. There is a separate, unconnected Palestinian group with the same name.

Jihad
Any effort, including holy war, made for the sake of the Islamic community – similar to "crusade" in English.

Levant
The geographical area comprising Israel, Palestinian territories, Jordan, Syria and Lebanon.

Mandate
The technical term used to describe the political framework through which Britain and France established colonial administrations after the First World War in countries of the Middle East and which were technically held in British trust for the benefit of the local population. "Mandate Palestine", for example, was Palestine under British authority until 1947.

Maronites
The main Christian sect in Lebanon.

Mashreq
The Arabic term for the eastern part of the Arab world.

Maghreb
The Arabic term for the western part of the Arab world, as well as for Morocco specifically. It also refers to the setting of the sun and the prayers that take place at that time of day.

Mufti
A (Sunni Muslim) religious scholar charged with issuing religious opinions, or fatwas.

Mujahideen
Term for those fighting *jihad*. It is used to describe the Arabs who fought in Afghanistan and Islamist insurgents in Iraq describe themselves in the same manner.

Mushrikeen
The term used to mean those who practice *shirk*, or polytheism – attributing the qualities of God to other beings. The term can refer to pre-Islamic worshippers of idols such as stones, trees or talismans, Hindus with their pantheon of gods or Christians for the Trinity.

Muslim Brotherhood
The first group in modern "political Islam" in the Arab world, set up in Egypt in 1928 after the Islamic caliphate had been abolished four years earlier with the collapse of the Ottoman Empire after the First World War.

Nakba
The Arabic term, meaning "catastrophe", for the dispossession of up to one million Palestinians in the fighting that saw the establishment of the state of Israel in 1948.

Naksa
The Arabic term, meaning "setback," often used to refer to the Arab defeat to Israel in the 1967 war.

Nasserism
Term for the strident nationalism – fascistic in many of its methods and symbols – followed by Egyptian President Gamal Abdel-Nasser. Neither "Sadatism" nor "Mubarakism" (in reference to Nasser's successors as president Anwar Sadat and Hosni Mubarak) have taken off as terms of reference for schools of thought in Arab political discourse.

Normalization
Term used to mean the setting up of normal relations with Israel, beyond political relations at the level of the state i.e. trade relations, tourism, cultural exchange, academic mingling, etc.

Orientalism
Term coined by Palestinian-American scholar Edward Said in his 1979 book of the same name to refer to a European intellectual tradition with its roots in colonialism which tended to belittle the non-Western world, in particular Arab-Islamic culture.

GLOSSARY

Oslo peace process
The name given to the secret round of talks conducted mainly in the Norwegian capital between 1991 and 1993, leading to the Declaration of Principles signed by Israel and the Palestinian Liberation Organization in 1993 and the establishment of Palestinian civilian autonomy in the occupied territories through the Palestinian Authority.

PLO
The Palestinian Liberation Organization, set up in 1964 as an umbrella organization for Palestinian groups fighting Israel.

Political Islam
The term referring to the political movement in Islamic societies calling for the Islamization of public as well as private life through the work of political parties.

Prophet
Islam theorizes that God's final revelation, completing the message of the prophets of Christians and Jews, came through his final prophet, Mohamed (or Muhammad, in strict transliteration).

Al-Quds
The Arabic term for Jerusalem, with an inherent religious connotation for Muslims: the word means "the sacred" or "the holy" and is used only to refer to the city.

Quran
In Islam, God's final revelation came in a text referred to as *al-Qur'an*, meaning the reading or the recitation – the term is flexible since Islamic tradition says God revealed His word to Muhammad via asking him to recite the words out loud, but at some stage in early Islam this oral text was codified in book form.

SCIRI
The Supreme Council for the Islamic Revolution in Iraq, a Shi'ite opposition group based in Iran during the rule of Saddam Hussein. It is led by Abdel-Aziz al-Hakim and is a leading player in the Shi'ite coalition that won elections after the 2003 war.

Sharia law
General term connoting the whole of Islamic law, itself a vast and changing corpus. For some it includes the draconian punishments of removing the hand of thieves, stoning adulterers and beheading murderers. More often the term is used as a general call for a more moral, ordered society or ending anarchic situations.

Six-Day War
The phrase often used to describe the June 1967 war between Israel and several Arab states since it lasted only six days.

Suez crisis
The British – French – Israeli invasion of Egypt's Suez canal zone in 1956 after President Gamal Abdel-Nasser announced Egypt was nationalizing the company that administered the key waterway. Britain, France and Israel hoped to see Nasser toppled from power, but American intervention helped forced them to withdraw.

Sumoud
: Arabic term meaning "endurance" often used as a morale-booster by Palestinians to describe their state-of-mind in the struggle with Israel.

Sykes-Picot
: Secret agreement between Britain and France in 1916 to create zones of British and French influence in the Middle East once the First World War was over. The accord ran counter to promises given to the Sherif of Mecca regarding a united, independent Arab state.

Takfir
: Term associated with radical Islamist groups who declare some sections of Arab societies – such as Shi'ites or secular or US-allied governments – to have strayed from Islam's true message to such a degree that they are no longer Muslims, but infidels (*kuffaar, kafara,* or *kafireen*).

Transfer
: Term used in the Israeli media and political life to denote forced removal of some or all of the Palestinian population in Israel and/or the occupied territories.

Umayyad
: The first dynasty in early Islam, named after the Bani Umayya family and based in Damascus, Syria from 661–750.

Umma
: Arabic term meaning a community or nation, normally used with reference to Islam (the Islamic nation, *il-umma il-islamiyya*) and in recent decades the Arab world (*il-umma al-'arabiyya*).

Al-'uruba
: Political term meaning Arabness and the sense of Arab identity (also *al-qawmiyya al-arabiyya*, or Arab nationalism).

Wafd
: Egyptian party of government before the 1952 revolution which came back as an opposition party in 1983.

Wahhabism
: Saudi Arabia's particular version of Sunni Islam, which is rigorously enforced throughout the country. Named after an eighteenth century religious reformer called Mohammed bin Abdel-Wahhab. His ideas on purifying Islam of innovations regarded as having sullied its original monotheistic spirit inspire the Saudi state.

Zionism
: The dominant ideology among Jewish settlers in Palestine since the late nineteenth century, which holds that Palestine (the West Bank of the Jordan river, Galilee and the coastal plain) is a birthright for all Jews and where they succeeded in setting up a state of their own in 1948. Views differed on the extent of the territory that should return to Jews, with some arguing for bits of the East Bank of the Jordan river and others eyeing the Sinai. Views also differed on what to do about the territory's indigenous inhabitants, who numbered over one million before Israel came into existence.

People

Abbas, Mahmoud
Veteran member of the Palestinian Liberation Organization who the Bush administration backed as prime minister of the Palestinian Authority (PA) in the occupied territories against then PA president Yasser Arafat. Abbas was voted by Palestinians as president after Arafat died in 2004.

Abdel-Nasser, Gamal
A leader of the army coup that brought down Egypt's monarchy in 1952 then went on to become president of a military republic from 1954 to his death 1970. One of the most influential, and tragic, figures in twentieth century Arab politics.

Ajami, Fouad
Lebanese Shi'ite scholar who has become a strong proponent of US-led political change in the Arab world.

Akef, Mohammed Mehdi
Leader of Egypt's Muslim Brotherhood, a leading Islamist opposition group, who has taken a more pro-active line in challenging the Egyptian government than his predecessors.

Arafat, Yasser
Leader of the Palestinian national struggle since the 1960s who embarked upon a peace process with Israel in 1993 that saw him return to the occupied territories and head the newly established Palestinian Authority. Arafat was sidelined by the US government after a Palestinian uprising broke out in 2000 when the peace process failed to produce statehood for Palestinians.

Assad, Hafez
Syrian president from 1971 to his death in 2000. He led Syria throughout its conflict with Israel in 1973 and the fifteen years of the Lebanese civil war and was succeeded by his son Bashar.

Bashir, Omar Hassan
Sudanese president who came to power in a 1989 coup. He established an Islamist government that finally made peace with the southerners in 2005, ending a twenty-two-year civil war.

Bin Laden, Osama
Saudi dissident who fought the Soviet Union in Afghanistan and resided in Sudan during the 1990s before returning to Afghanistan to set up an alliance of Arab anti-Western Islamist forces termed al-Qa'ida.

Bin Talal, al-Walid
Saudi billionaire prince who owns hotel and recreation firm Kingdom Holdings and Arabic entertainment company Rotana.

Chahine, Yousef
Egyptian film director who was the only Arab of his era to study directing in America, in the 1950s, but who has been severely critical of US policies in his most recent works. A French-speaker whose work is often feted at Cannes, he is the best-known Arab director abroad.

Al-Hamad, Turki
Saudi novelist whose work has often touched on Saudi Arabia's sudden transformation through oil into a modern society.

Al-Hariri, Rafik
Former Lebanese prime minister who was assassinated in February 2005, prompting domestic and foreign pressure on Syrian troops to leave Lebanon where they had been since the civil war in 1976. Pro-Syrians were thought by many to have been behind the murder, which came after Hariri had given his backing to international efforts to force Syria to reinstate Lebanese independence.

Khomeini, Ayatollah
Iranian cleric who came to power during the Islamic revolution of 1979. Although his was a Shi'ite movement, it invigorated Sunni Islamist groups in the Arab world, as well as provoked Arab government fears of a resurgent Iran promoting anti-US radicalism. Most Arab regimes backed Iraq in the subsequent eight-year long Gulf war.

Al-Mahdi, Sadeq
Leader of Sudan's Umma Party and the last democratically elected prime minister in Sudan, overthrown in the Islamist military coup of 1989.

Makiya, Kanan
Iraqi writer whose exposes of life under Saddam Hussein gained him influence and notoriety in America. He was a proponent of the 2003 invasion of Iraq and the idea of US-led change in the region.

Moussa, Amr
Current Secretary-General of the Arab League and former Egyptian foreign minister, popular in the Arab world for his Arab nationalist politics. He opposed the 2003 invasion of Iraq, where he is not popular among the majority Shi'ite Arabs or Kurds.

Mubarak, Gamal
Son of Egyptian President Hosni Mubarak who has rapidly risen through the ranks of the ruling National Democratic Party.

Mubarak, Hosni
Egypt's leader since his predecessor Anwar Sadat was assassinated in 1981. He has seen Egypt through a number of regional wars and conflicts, including a campaign by Islamists to overthrow his regime.

Munif, Abdel-Rahman
Celebrated Saudi novelist who was banished from his country for his writings depicting the sudden change in Saudi society after Americans developed its oil fields.

Nasrallah, Hassan
The charismatic leader of Lebanese guerrilla group Hizbollah. Nasrallah, a Shi'ite cleric, became a household name and popular hero throughout the Arab world after Israel withdrew from south Lebanon in 2000 and failed to çrush his group in a summer war against Lebanon in 2006.

Nimeiri, Jaafar
Sudanese president from 1969 to 1985. He came to power in a coup and was ousted in a coup. When he came to power he was a leftist, when he left he was an Islamist. The

civil war begun under his rule in 1983, prompted by his decision to introduce Islamic Sharia law.

Nour, Ayman
Egyptian politician seen as one of the leaders of the liberal-secular trend. He came second to Hosni Mubarak in 2005 presidential elections. The government accuses him of being backed by the US government and imprisoned him for alleged fraud.

Al-Qaradawi, Yousef
Egyptian cleric based in Qatar who has a wide audience through his regular appearances on al-Jazeera television and his Web site.

Qutb, Sayed
Egyptian Islamist who was hanged by Nasser's regime in 1966 for allegedly plotting a coup. His writings are regarded as seminal works for today's al-Qa'ida and other groups.

Al-Sadr, Moqtada
Iraqi Shi'ite leader who has led several uprisings against US troops, gaining him support among the Sunni-dominated wider Arab world.

Sadat, Anwar
Egyptian president who fought Israel in the 1973 Middle East war before making peace in 1979, but he was assassinated in 1981 by Islamists angry at the concessions he had made.

Said, Edward
Palestinian academic famous for his seminal 1979 book *Orientalism* which critiqued Western academic work concerning the Arab and Islamic world, interpreting it as an adjunct to government policy.

Al-Sistani, Ali
The most powerful Shi'ite cleric in post-Saddam Iraq. His demand for elections scuppered American plans for local leaders to select delegates to a transitional government by July 2003. He was crucial in holding Shi'ites back from full-out war with Sunni Arabs as Islamist insurgent groups deliberately targetted Shi'ites, who they hated for accepting the US occupation.

Turabi, Hassan
Sudanese Islamist ideologue who rose to prominence under the military regime that took power after a coup in 1989. He was sidelined in 1999, allowing President Bashir to rebuild ties with countries who blamed Turabi for Sudan's radical Islamist policies.

Wadud, Amina
American Muslim woman who led Muslim women at Friday prayers for the first time in 2005, causing an outcry in the Arab world.

Zarqawi, Abu Musab
Jordanian Islamist who led resistance to the American occupation of Iraq after the invasion of 2003 via an al-Qa'ida-affiliated group that included Sunni Arab Iraqis and volunteers from other Arab countries.

Zawahiri, Ayman
Egyptian Islamist who set up the Islamic Jihad group that unsuccessfully fought Mubarak's government before settling in Afghanistan where he set up al-Qa'ida with bin Laden in 1998.

Notes

Preface
1. As witnessed by author in Mecca, January 2004.
2. Transcript of speech, *New York Times*, 6 October 2005.
3. Interview with author, July 2005.
4. Kaplan, Robert D. 1993. *The Arabists: The Romance of an American Elite.* New York: The Free Press.
5. "Taking Arabs Seriously," *Foreign Affairs*, September/October 2003, p. 83.

Chapter 1: America in the Arab World
1. Mackintosh-Smith, Time. 1999. *Yemen, Travels in Dictionary Land*, London: Picador.
2. Abdel-Meguid, Wahid. 1998. *Camp David 20 Years On*. Cairo: al-Ahram Publishing.
3. "Clinton's Words in Gaza: Citing the 'Waste of War'," *Associated Press*, 15 December 1998.
4. Zakaria, Fareed. *Newsweek*, 1 October 2001.
5. *New York Times*, 27 November 2001.
6. Transcript of speech, *New York Times*, 6 October 2005.
7. Commentary on al-Arabiya, 7 September 2005.
8. Forum on "The Arab World: Between the Realities of Today and the Promises of Tomorrow," 14 December 2004.
9. "UAE Urges Radical Arab Reform from Within," *Reuters*, 13 December 2004.
10. "US Troops Fire on Anti-American Protesters," *Associated Press*, 30 April 2003.
11. Commentary, *Daily Star*, 8 February 2005.
12. Said, Aburish. 2001. pp. 297–298. *Saddam Hussein*. London: Bloomsbury.
13. www.salamegypt.org (cited 1 April 2006)
14. "US Senator: Israeli Security US' Top Mideast Priority," *Associated Press*, 21 May 2005, quoting Republican Senator Gordon Smith.
15. al-Arabiya seminar, aired on the channel on 21 May 2005.
16. *Newsweek*, 15 October, 2001.
17. *Al-Ahram Weekly*, 20–26 May 2004.
18. Said, Edward. 1979. *A Question of Palestine*. London: Vintage Books.
19. "The Roots of Muslim Rage," *Atlantic Monthly*, September 1990.
20. Lewis, Bernard. 2002. *What Went Wrong?: The Clash between Islam and Modernity in the Middle East*. London: Phoenix.
21. Commentary, *al-Hayat*, 18 July 2003.
22. Qutb, Sayed. 1973. pp. 29–91. *Milestones*, Beirut: Dar al-Shurouq.
23. "Iraq Qaeda says to Spare Anti-US Sadr Group – Web," *Reuters*, 19 September 2005.
24. Qutb, 8–25.
25. Polk, William. 2005. *Understanding Iraq: The Whole Sweep of Iraqi History, of Outside Rule from Genghis Khan to the Ottoman Turks to the British Mandate to the American Occupation*. New York: HarperCollins.
26. al-Bukhari's hadith collection *Sahih al-Bukhari*, No. 3090, *al-Jihad*.
27. Maalouf, Amin. 1998. p. 74. *Les Identites meurtrieres*, Grasset: Paris.
28. "A Dialogue with Abdul Rahman Al-Rashed," *Transnational Broadcasting Studies*, Spring/Summer 2005: 119.
29. Editorial comment, *Daily Star*, 16 September 2005.
30. "Zarqawi backs killing civilian 'infidels' –Web," *Reuters*, 7 October 2005.
31. Eid al-Adha sermon, www.alhesbah.org (cited January 2005)
32. Programme *al-Mashhad al-Iraqi (The Iraqi Scene)*, al-Jazeera, 29 May 2005.
33. Article, *Akhbar al-Adab*, 8 September 2002.

34. Al-Jazeera, 12 February 2005; the book is *Seize the Moment: America's Challenge in a One-Superpower World*, New York: Simon & Schuster, 1992.
35. *Middle East Times*, December 1995.
36. Lacouture, Jean. 2005. *Gamal Abdel Nasser*. Paris: Bayard.
37. Schivelbusch, Wolfgang. 2003. *The Culture of Defeat: On National Trauma, Mourning, and Recovery*. Trans. Jefferson Chase. London: Granta Books.
38. Polk, 140.
39. Bilal Hassan, in *Thaqafat al-istislam (The culture of defeat)*, examines the writings of Kanan Makiya, Hazem Saghiya, Saleh Bashir, Al-Afif Lakhdar and Amin Al-Mahdi.
40. Mustafa Bakry, *al-Osboa*, 25 September 2000.
41. Commentary, *Asharq al-Awsat*, 26 July 2005.
42. Commentary, *Asharq al-Aswat*, 24 August 2005.
43. "Director's Testimony in Congress," Institute for Gulf Affairs, 20 March 2006.

Chapter 2: Domestic America
1. Article, *al-Qahira*, 13 June 2000.
2. Ibid.
3. *Newsweek*, 1 October 2001.
4. "US public diplomacy falls short of reaching English-speaking Arabs," *Daily Star*, 8 November 2004.
5. Interview with author, July 2005.
6. Clip of Egyptian actor Mohammed Sobhy shown in al-Jazeera promotional slots.
7. Interview with author, July 2005.
8. Press conference, 9 December 2004.
9. Interview with author, July 2005.
10. Interview with author, September 2005.
11. Dhaher was speaking on LBC shows in February 2004; Alabbar revealed his *The Apprentice* plan at a press conference on 27 February 2005.
12. "Look Who's Rocking the Casbah: The revolutionary implications of Arab music videos," *Reason*, June 2003.
13. Commentary, *al-Hayat*, 20 April 2004.
14. Press conference in Dubai, 14 May 2004.
15. Commentary, *al-Hayat*, January 2002.
16. Interview with author, December 1999.
17. Interview with author, July 1999.
18. Ibid.
19. Mursi Attallah, *al-Ahram al-Messai*, 16 May 2004.
20. Ramsay Short, "The six faces of Osama according to Kaabour," *Daily Star*, 23 March 2005.
21. *al-Sharia wal-Hayat (Sharia Law and Life)*, al-Jazeera, 19 December 2004.
22. Interview with author, June 2005.
23. al-Qa'ida in Iraq statement, www.ansarnet.ws/vb (cited 1 February 2005)
24. Forum string, www.yaislah.net (cited 2 February 2005)
25. "The Party's Over," *Al-Ahram Weekly*, 1–7 September 2005.
26. Commentary, *Akhbar al-Khaleej*, 3 August 1998.
27. Article, *al-Khamis*, 23 November 2000.
28. al-Ghaity, Mohammed. 1996. *A Scandal Called Saida Sultana*. Cairo: Dar al-Gumhouriya.
29. al-Fiki, Mustafa. 2002. *Al-Arab, al-Asl wal-Sura (Arabs, the Image and the Reality)*. Cairo: Dar al-Shurouq.
30. Saar, Erik. 2005. *Inside the wire: A Military Intelligence Soldier's Eyewitness Account of Life at Guantanamo*. New York: Penguin Press HC.

31. Ibrahim, Sonallah. 2003. p. 69. *Amrikanli*. Cairo: Dar al-Mustaqbal al-Arabi.
32. Ibid., p. 266.
33. Statement, www.muslimwakeup.com (cited 13 March 2005)
34. "A critique of the argument for women-led Friday prayers," alt.muslim, 18 March 2005.
35. "Erudition as dead-end: Hina Azam and the perils of legal dogmatism," www.muslimwakeup.com (cited 25 March 2005)
36. al-Mesaa, 19 March 2005.
37. Zainab Abdallah, *al-Osboa*, 19 March 2005.
38. Nomani, Asra. 2005. *Standing Alone in Mecca: An American Woman's Struggle for the Soul of Islam*. San Francisco: Harper Collins.
39. "Nourished by the waters of indigenous Islam," www.muslimwakeup.com (cited 18 October 2005)
40. "Our Mission," www.muslimwakeup.com (cited 2 April 2006)
41. "Saudi prince tutors 'noble' Bush on Mideast-paper," *Reuters*, 14 May 2002.
42. Article, Saudi daily *Okaz*, 15 May 2002.
43. Arab Strategy Forum, Dubai, 14 December 2004.
44. "New York mayor rejects Saudi prince's donation," *Reuters*, 11 October 2001.
45. Editorial, *al-Khaleej*, 14 October 2001.
46. al-Jazeera, 14 October 2001.
47. Commentary, *al-Hayat*, 5 January 2001.
48. Samir Ragab, *al-Gomhouriya*, 13 January 2001.

Chapter 3: The Palestinians
1. Raban, Jonathan. 1979. p. 11. *Arabia: A Journey Through The Labyrinth*. London: Picador.
2. Shlaim, Avi. 2000. p. 310. *The Iron Wall: Israel and the Arab World*. London: Penguin Books.
3. Figures compiled by the Jewish Virtual Library using US State Department and United States Agency for International Development (USAID) statistics (www.jewishvirtuallibrary.org).
4. "US sees Arafat, aides hand in arms shipment," Carol Giacomo and Jonathan Wright, *Reuters*, 9 January 2002.
5. "US Anglicans eyeing divestment criticize Israel," *Reuters*, 12 May 2005.
6. "Israeli settlers proliferate in the West Bank," *Associated Press*, 26 August 2005; European Union report on East Jerusalem, 24 November 2005.
7. Pipes, Daniel. 1996. p. 159. *The Hidden Hand: Middle East Fears of Conspiracy*. London: MacMillan.
8. Ibid., p.160.
9. Polk, William. 2005. p. 188. *Understanding Iraq: The Whole Sweep of Iraqi History, of Outside Rule from Genghis Khan to the Ottoman Turks to the British Mandate to the American Occupation*. New York: HarperCollins.
10. "Powell calls US 'Judeo-Christian', then amends," *Reuters*, 23 September 2003.
11. "Under the gun: a Palestinian journey," *The Guardian*, 18 December 2000.
12. Huntington, Samuel P. 2005. p. 54. *Who Are We?: The Challenges to America's National Identity*. New York: Simon & Schuster.
13. Commentary, *Akhbar al-Adab*, 21 April 2002.
14. "Survival of the Fittest? An interview with Benny Morris," Ari Shavit, *Haaretz Magazine*, 9 January 2004.
15. Huntington, 247.
16. Commentary, *al-Hayat*, 3 August 2002.
17. Hroub, Khaled. 2000. p. 248. *Hamas: Political Thought and Practice*. Washington: Institute for Palestine Studies.

18. Israeli human rights group B'Tselem, www.btselem.org (cited 2 April 2006)
19. www.btselem.org; by February 2006, the Palestinian Red Crescent Society reported 3,821 Palestinian deaths, suggesting some 400 suicide bombers, www.palestinercs.org.
20. "World Bank – almost half of Palestinians in poverty," *Reuters*, 23 November 2004.
21. "Foreign investment in Israel hits record $9.7 bln," *Reuters*, 8 January 2006.
22. *Bil-Arabi*, al-Arabiya, 17 July 2005.
23. Hardtalk, BBC World, 9 May 2002.
24. al-Arabiya, 28 May 2005.
25. Commentary, *al-Hayat*, 14 May 2005.
26. Pape, Robert. 2005. *Dying to Win: The Strategic Logic of Suicide Terrorism*. New York: Random House.
27. Ben Gurion's opinions have been studied and quoted in number of works, including those of Israeli historian Benny Morris and Peter Rodgers *Herzl's Nightmare: One Land, Two Peoples*, New York: Nation Books, 2005.
28. "Mubarak voices Palestinian fears of explusion," *Reuters*, 26 March 2002.
29. Morris, Benny. *The Birth of the Palestinian Refugee Problem, 1947–1949*. Cambridge: Cambridge University Press, 1989. First published 1987, revised edition in 2004.
30. "Survival of the Fittest? An interview with Benny Morris," Ari Shavit, *Haaretz Magazine*, 9 January 2004.
31. Commentary, *Al Ahaly*, 7 March 2002.
32. "Survival of the Fittest? An interview with Benny Morris," Ari Shavit, *Haaretz Magazine*, 9 January 2004.
33. *Min Washington (From Washington)*, al-Jazeera, 29 August 2005.
34. Huntington, Samuel. 2002. pp. 20–21. *The Clash of Civilizations and the Remaking of the World Order*. London: Simon and Schuster.
35. "Mubarak voices Palestinians fears of expulsion," *Reuters*, 16 March 2002.
36. Commentary, *al-Ahram*, 5 August 2002.
37. Interview, *Akhbar al-Adab*, 4 June 2000.
38. Ajami, Fouad. 1999. p. 275. *The Dream Palace of the Arabs: A Generation's Odyssey*. New York: Vintage Books.
39. Ibid., p. 287.
40. "Arab report sees little reform, faults U.S. action," *Reuters*, 5 April 2005.
41. "The time has come: A call for freedom and good governance in the Arab world," UNDP, 5 April 2005.
42. *Istithmar al-Fawaz (Utilizing Victory), Kuwait Union of Palestinian Writers and Journalists 1983, (cited in Hroub)*.
43. Interview on ABC's "This Week," 29 May 2005.
44. Commentary, *Asharq al-Awsat*, 30 May 2005.
45. Address to members of Egyptian parliament, reported in *al-Ahram*, 12 December 2000.
46. Interview with author, September 2002.
47. "Egypt official says Arabs should cultivate Europe," *Reuters*, 22 January 2001.
48. Editorial, *al-Ahram*, 18 April 2004.
49. "Abbas says redress for refugees is key to peace," *Reuters*, 15 May 2005.
50. Mouin Rabbani and Chris Toensing, "Mahmoud Abbas' Mission Improbable," Middle East Report, 1 June 2005.
51. "Barghouti at his closing trial: I do not recognize Israel's jurisdiction or court authority over me," www.amin.org (cited 29 September 2003)
52. "Marwan Barghouthi's Scarecrow," www.avnery-news.co.il (cited 4 October 2003)

Chapter 4: The Iraq Project

1. "Iraq strike would 'open gates of hell': Moussa," *Reuters*, 7 September 2002.
2. "Mubarak says Iraq war will produce '100 bin Ladens'," *Reuters*, 31 March 2003.

3. "Briefing depicted Saudis as enemies: Ultimatum urged to Pentagon Board," *The Washington Post*, 6 August 2002.
4. News commentary on al-Arabiya, 9 April 2003.
5. Commentary, *al-Ahram*, 10 April 2003.
6. Commentary, *al-Quds al-Arabi*, 10 April 2003.
7. "A eulogy for the Arab state system," *Daily Star*, 6 October 2003.
8. Cartoon, *al-Wafd*, 31 March 2003.
9. Shafiq Ghabra, "An Arab house, openly divided," *The Washington Post*, 9 March 2003.
10. "Tempers flare as Saudi-Libya spat erupts at summi," *Reuters*, 1 March 2003.
11. London Review of Books, 23 April 2003.
12. Commentary, *al-Hayat*, 18 July 2003.
13. Khalidi, Rashid. 2004. *Resurrecting Empire: Western Footprints and America's Perilous Path in the Middle East*. Boston: Beacon Press.
14. Ian Frazier, "Destroying Baghdad," *The New Yorker*, 25 April 2005.
15. Text of speech, www.news.bbc.co.uk (cited 2 May 2003)
16. Text of speech, *al-Hayat*, 12 June 2000.
17. "US general says met Israeli interrogator in Iraq," *Reuters*, 3 July 2004.
18. Commentary, *al-Hayat*, 8 July 2004.
19. Tahiya Abdel-Wahhab, in live commentary on al-Arabiya, 9 April 2003.
20. Commentary, *al-Watan*, 11 April 2003.
21. Bogdanos, Matthew. 2005. *Thieves of Baghdad*. London: Bloomsbury.
22. Sanaa al-Said, *al-Wafd*, 25 May 2003.
23. Interview with author, November 2003.
24. "Sunni neighbours dread spectre of Shi'ite Iraq," *Reuters*, 19 January 2005.
25. Conversation with author, August 2005.
26. "Ambush kills 15 Iraqi troops north of Baghdad," *Reuters*, 3 December 2005.
27. *Liqaa Khaass (Special Interview)*, al-Jazeera, 4 October 2005.
28. "Iraq's marginalized Sunnis rally for Saddam," *Reuters*, 26 August 2005.
29. "Popstar's love life takes Iraqis minds off war talk," *Reuters*, 13 January 2003.
30. Conversation with author, January 2003.
31. Interview with author, January 2003.
32. Interview with author, November 2003.
33. Interview with author, December 2003.
34. Interview with author, December 2003.
35. Makiya, Kanaan. 1993. *Cruelty and Silence*. London: Jonathan Cape.
36. Ajami, Fouad. 1999. *The Dream Palace of the Arabs: A Generation's Odyssey*. New York: Vintage Books.
37. Wolfowitz speaking via video phone at a special ceremony held in Tel Aviv to honour historian Bernard Lewis in March 2002.
38. Photo caption, www.alshaab.com (cited 21 May 2005)
39. "Indelible images of Iraq abuse leave bitter legacy," *Reuters*, 10 May 2004.
40. *al-Ittijah al-Mu'akis (The Opposite Direction)*, al-Jazeera, May 2004.
41. Article, *Daily Star*, 24 May 2004.
42. Commentary, *al-Arabi*, 23 May 2004.
43. Commentary, *al-Quds al-Arabi*, 20 May 2004.
44. Editorial, *al-Gomhouriya*, 3 May 2004.
45. Commentary, *al-Hayat*, 16 May 2004.
46. Interview with author, 31 August 2003.
47. al-Qa'ida in Iraq posting, forum, www.inn4news.net (cited 20 April 2005)
48. News commentary, al-Jazeera, 8 October 2004.
49. "In their own words: Reading the Iraqi insurgency," International Crisis Group, 15 February 2006.

50. Interview with author, November 2003.
51. Commentary, *al-Osboa*, 28 February 2004.
52. Commentary on www.alshaab.com (cited 22 February 2005)
53. Commentary, *Afak Arabia*, 17 February 2005.
54. "The war in Iraq: civilian casualties, political responsibilities," *The Lancet*, 20 November 2004 (print)/28 October 2004 (online).
55. "39,000 Iraqis killed in fighting, new study finds," *Reuters*, 11 July 2005.
56. Online magazine www.Brandchannel.com (cited 31 January 2005)
57. This account and the quotes contained are based on the author's first-hand experience of the operation on 3 December 2003.

Chapter 5: Peace with Egypt

1. "US discussing aid cuts with Egypt, aid chief says," *Reuters*, 19 March 1995.
2. Ibid.
3. Interview with author, October 1997.
4. Fawzy, Wa'il. 1995. *Hiwarat Mamnu'a (Forbidden Conversations)*. Cairo: al-Khuloud.
5. Coldwell, Dominic. *Egypt's Autumn of Fury: The Construction of Opposition to the Egyptian-Israeli Peace Process between 1973 and 1981*. PhD thesis, University of Oxford.
6. Shlaim, Avi. 2000. *The Iron Wall: Israel and the Arab World*. London: Penguin Books.
7. Henry, Clement and Robert Springborg. 2001. p. 150. *Globalization and the Politics of Development in the Middle East*. Cambridge: Cambridge University Press.
8. "Breaking the silence," *Cairo Times*, 1–14 October 1998.
9. Ibid.
10. Ibid.
11. Ibrahim, Sonallah. 2003. p. 324. *Amrikanli*. Cairo: al-Mustaqbal.
12. Samia Nakhoul, "Moslem militants rule Cairo slum," *Reuters*, 20 November 1992.
13. *The New Yorker*, 22 January 1995; also, "Egyptian Moslems condemn arrests as election ploy," *Reuters*, 23 January 1995.
14. John Walsh, "Egypt's Muslim Brotherhood: Understanding Centrist Islam," *Harvard International Review*, Vol. 24 (4), Winter 2003.
15. *The New Yorker*, 22 January 1995; "Egyptian Moslems condemn arrests as election ploy," *Reuters*, 23 January 1995.
16. Interview with author, August 1998.
17. "Court blow for Brotherhood lawyers," *Middle East Times*, 3 February 1996.
18. "Veiled voices protest at Egypt raids, detentions," *Reuters*, 5 February 1995.
19. Interview with rights activist Hisham Kassem, June 2005.
20. Interview with author, January 1996.
21. Interview with author, September 1996.
22. Interview, al-Arabiya, 26 April 2005.
23. Commentary, *al-Haqiqa*, 22 September 2001.
24. Al-Aswani, Alaa. 2002. p. 139. *Emarat Ya'qubian (The Yacoubian Building)*. Cairo: Madbouli.
25. Fawzy, *Forbidden Conversations*.
26. Interview with author, June 2005.
27. Fawzy, *Forbidden Conversations*.
28. See note 2.
29. Interview with author, October 2001.
30. *al-Arabi*, 12 February 1998.
31. Interview, *al-Arabi*, 27 February 2005.
32. Interview with Hisham Kassem, who was asked to translate the paper.
33. "White House report, June 1: Egypt, Afghanistan, Venezuela, Watergate," US Department of State, 1 June 2005.

34. Interview with author, June 1997.
35. News report on al-Jazeera, 8 May 2005.
36. Headline, *al-Osboa*, 9 May 2005.
37. "In Egypt, the 'thrill of defying tyranny'," *Daily Star*, 7 September 2005.
38. "US sees problems, progress in Egypt elections," *Reuters*, 8 December 2005.
39. "Mubarak says Egypt won over Rice on democracy," *Reuters*, 1 March 2006.
40. "New look, new methods," *Cairo Magazine*, 1 September 2005.
41. "The Egypt Game," *New York Times*, 1 August 2000.
42. Commentary, *Akhbar al-Youm*, 5 August 2000.
43. Interview with author, June 2005.
44. Ajami, Fouad. 1999. p. 243. *The Dream Palace of the Arabs: A Generation's Odyssey*. New York: Vintage Books.
45. *Adab al-Sujoun (Prison Etiquette)*, al-Jazeera, 22 July 2005.
46. Interview with author, June 2005.
47. Interview with author, June 2005.
48. Interview in *Afak Arabia*, 10 April 2005.
49. Samir Ragab, *al-Gomhouriya*, 12 June 2005.
50. "Interview: The Prospect for Democracy in the Middle East," *Logos Journal*, Issue 4.2, Spring 2005.

Chapter 6: The House of Saud
1. Al-Rasheed, Madawi. 2002. p. 100. *A History of Saudi Arabia*. Cambridge: Cambridge University Press.
2. Ibid., p. 116.
3. Interview with author, April 2003.
4. Commentary, www.arabtimes.com (cited 21 February 2006)
5. Conversation with author, April 2003.
6. These themes are discussed in Crone, Patricia, and Martin Hinds. 1986; *God's Caliph: Religious Authority in the First Centuries of Islam*. Cambridge: Cambridge University Press, Crone. *Slaves on Horses: The evolution of the Islamic polity*. Cambridge: Cambridge University Press, 1980.
7. "Khobar Towers," *Air Force Association Magazine 'Air Force,'* 81 (6) (June 1998).
8. Interview with author, June 1996.
9. Interview with author, June 1996.
10. Al-Rasheed, 117.
11. Dawisha, Adeed. 2003. p. 9. *Arab Nationalism in the Twentieth Century: from Triumph to Despair*. Princeton, N.J.: Princeton University Press.
12. Munif, Abdel-Rahman. 1992. pp. 33–34 *Mudun al-Malh (Cities of Salt, part one)*. Beirut: Arab Institute for Studies and Publishing.
13. Al-Rasheed, 96.
14. Al-Hamad, Turki. 2000. pp. 221–223. *Sharq al-Wadi (East of the Valley)*. London: Saqi Books.
15. Al-Rasheed, 140.
16. Glosemeyer, Iris. 2005. "The Saudi Political System," p. 223 in *Saudi Arabia in the Balance*. Edited by Paul Aarts and Gerd Nonneman, London: Hurst.
17. "Saudi Arabia's ambitious al-Qaeda fighter," posted on NBC's website, www.msnbc.com (cited 24 June 2005)
18. Interview with author, August 2003.
19. Interview with author, August 2003.
20. Statement, published on www.hesbah.com (cited 25 February 2006)
21. Prince Turki bin Faisal, quoted in *Arab News*, 7 November 2001.
22. Text of statement, *al-Quds al-Arabi*, 23 February 1998.

23. Editorial, al-Watan, 21 March 2003.
24. "Briefing depicted Saudis as enemies: Ultimatum urged to Pentagon Board," *The Washington Post*, 6 August 2002.
25. "The Future of US-Saudi Relations," FrontPageMagazine.com (cited 11 July 2003)
26. Commentary, *al-Hayat*, 25 June 2003.
27. "Saudi reformers to appeal jailing during Rice visit," *Reuters*, 20 June 2005.
28. Ibid.
29. Mohamed Nabhan Swelam, "A Saudi nemesis in the U.S. Congress," *Daily Star*, 13 July 2005.
30. Interview with author, October 2003.
31. "Saudi to jail, lash 15 for anti-monarchy protests," *Reuters*, 12 January 2005.
32. "UN Council adds two Saudis to al Qaeda list," *Reuters*, 23 December 2004.
33. "Saudis sit tight on US assets, but fear future," *Reuters*, 21 August 2002.
34. "Qaeda beheads American in Saudi then chief killed," *Reuters*, 18 June 2004.
35. Interview with author, April 2003.
36. Interview with author, August 2003.
37. Interview with author, April 2003.
38. Forum, www.alsaha.net (cited 10 July 2005)
39. "63 Saudi preachers say 'Star Academy' is a crime against the Islamic nation," al-Arabiya.net (cited 14 May 2005)
40. Interview with author, January 2006.
41. "Saudi bloggers attack Saudi over cartoon row," *Reuters*, 14 February 2006.
42. Ibid.
43. Al-Rasheed, 103.
44. Interview by author, August 1996.
45. Aburish, Said. 1996. *The Rise, Corruption, and Coming Fall of the House of Saud*. London: Palgrave MacMillan.
46. al-Jazeera, 24 October 2004.
47. Pew Research Center; "Support for bin Laden falls in Muslim countries," *Reuters*, 14 July 2005.
48. Robert Looney, "Development Strategies for Saudi Arabia: Escaping the Rentier State Syndrome," *Strategic Insights*, Volume III, Issue 3 (March 2004).
49. "History of Saudi aid to Palestinians," Saudi National Security Assessment Project, 2005; interview with Nawaf Obaid, managing director of the Project, in Bitterlemons-international.org (cited 2 March 2006), Edition 8, Volume 4.
50. Commentary by Ahmed Taha, *Akhbar al-Adab*, 27 August 2000.
51. Munif, Abdel-Rahman. 2003. p. 26. *Bayn al-thaqafa wal-siyasa (Between Culture and Politics)*. Beirut: al-Mu'assasa al-Arabiyya lil-Dirasat wal-Nashr.
52. Cited in Adeed Dawisha. *Arab Nationalism in the Twentieth Century*. New Jersey: Princeton University Press, 2003: 162.

Chapter 7: The Sudanese Card

1. "Albright Vows to Discourage Ties With Sudan Africa: Secretary of State, meeting with rebel leader, backs sanctions against brutal dictatorship," *Los Angeles Times*, 24 October 1999.
2. Commentary, *al-Wafd*, 28 May 2005.
3. Commentary, *al-Gomhouriya*, 23 August 2002.
4. Editorial, *al-Khaleej*, 24 October 2002.
5. Interviews with author, August 2002.
6. Interview with author, August 2002.
7. Ibid.
8. Interview with author, August 2002.

9. "Sudan peace may help end female circumcision," *Reuters*, 21 August 2002.
10. "Noam Chomsky: Reply to Hitchens," *The Nation*, 1 October 2001.
11. Interview, al-Jazeera, 22 August 2005.
12. "Sudan's Bashir says US dominated by 'Zionists'," *Reuters*, 10 September 1998.
13. Editorial, al-Sharq, 21 August 1998.
14. Editorial, *al-Ahram al-Messai*, 21 August 1998.
15. "War has just begun, says bin Laden," *The Hindu*, 23 August 1998.
16. Interview, www.sudaneseonline.com (cited 10 October 2005)
17. Ibid.
18. "Unifying Darfur's Rebels: A prerequisite for Peace," International Crisis Group, 6 October 2005.
19. Interview, *al-Rai al-Aam*, 8 October 2005.
20. Human Rights Watch report; www.hrw.org/reports98/sudan/Sudarm988-02.htm.
21. "Carter Says Wrong Time for Mideast Talks," *Reuters*, 24 April 2001.
22. See her Web site, www.kolapress.1colony.com (cited 3 April 2006); *Long Train to the Redeeming Sin: Stories of African Women*. California: Door of Kush, 2004.
23. "Sudanese woman rises from slave to author in UK," *Reuters*, 15 January 2004; *Slave*. London: Time Warner Books, 2004.
24. "In Sudan, a modern-day story of slavery," The Forward Forum, www.forward.com (cited 9 April 2004)
25. "Center for Religious Freedom Fact Sheet: Sudan," Center for Religious Freedom, Freedom House, Washington-DC; www.freedomhouse.org (cited 3 April 2006)
26. "880 slaves freed in Sudan but many left, group says," *Reuters*, 4 February 2005.
27. "Rights groups fault UN steps on children in wars," *Reuters*, 20 January 2004.
28. "The Sudan Abductee Datebase: Yet More Questionable Propaganda," ESPAC, 30 May 2000.
29. On Web site: www.espac.org/usa_sudan_pages/raspberry.html (cited 3 April 2006)
30. Interview with author, August 2002.
31. Ibid.
32. Flint, Julie and Alex de Waal. 2005. *Darfur: A Short History of a Long War*. London: Zed Books.
33. Ibid.
34. Executive summary, "Report of the International Commission of Inquiry on Darfur to the United Nations Secretary-General," 25 January 2005.
35. Commentary, *Akhbar al-Youm*, 30 August 2005.
36. Commentary, *Akhbar al-Adab*, 31 December 2000.
37. *al-Ain al-Thalitha (The Third Eye)*, al-Arabiya, 17 March 2006.
38. Commentary, *al-Quds al-Arabi*, 20 September 2005.
39. Commentary, *al-Rai al-Aam*, 20 September 2005.
40. Article, http://www.sudaneseonline.com/earticle2005/sep15-82069.shtml (cited 15 September 2005)
41. "A conspiracy of silence on Darfur ... in Beirut," *Daily Star*, 23 July 2004.
42. Ibid.
43. Editorial, "The culture excuse for Darfur atrocities no longer holds water," *Daily Star*, 7 June 2005.

Bibliography

Aarts, Paul & Nonneman, Gerd, eds. *Saudi Arabia in the Balance*. London, Hurst & Company, 2005.

Abdel-Meguid, Wahid. *Camp David 20 Years On*. Cairo: al-Ahram Publishing, 1998.

Aburish, Said. *Saddam Hussein*. London: Bloomsbury, 2001.

Aburish, Said. *The Rise, Corruption, and Coming Fall of the House of Saud*. London: Palgrave MacMillan, 1996.

Al-Aswani, Alaa, *Emarat Yacoubian*, Cairo: Dar al-Madbouli, 2002.

Al-Ghuddami, Abdallah. *Fikrat al-Hadatha (The Idea of Modernity)*. Beirut: al-Markaz al-Arabi al-Thaqafi, 2004.

Al-Hamad, Turki. *Sharq al-Wadi (East of the Valley)*. London: Saqi Books, 2000.

Al-Hamad, Turki. *Al-Thaqafa al-Arabiyya fi Asr al-Awlama (Arab Culture in the Age of Globalization)*. London: Saqi Books, 1999.

Ajami, Fouad. *The Dream Palace of the Arabs: A Generation's Odyssey*. New York: Vintage Books, 1999.

Ajami, Fouad. *The Vanished Imam: Musa al Sadr and the Shia of Lebanon*. London: I.B.Tauris, 1986.

Al-Faqih, Saad. *Kayfa Yufakkir Al-Saud: Dirasa Nafsiyya (How the Saudi Family Thinks: A Psychological Study)*. London: Movement for Islamic Reform in Arabia, n.d.a.

Al-Rasheed, Madawi. *A History of Saudi Arabia*. Cambridge: Cambridge University Press, 2002.

Amin, Galal. *Whatever Happened to the Egyptians?* Cairo: American University in Cairo, 2001.

Armbrust, Walter. *Mass Culture and Modernism in Egypt*. Cambridge, UK: Cambridge University Press, 1996.

Armbrust, Walter, ed. *Mass Mediations: New Approaches to Popular Culture in the Middle East and Beyond*. Berkeley: University of California Press, 2000.

Benrabah, Mohamed. "Arabisation and Creativity in Algeria." *Journal of Algerian Studies*, nos. 4 and 5.

Bradley, John. *Saudi Arabia Exposed: Inside a Kingdom in Crisis*. New York: Palgrave Macmillan, 2005.

Brett, M., and E. Fentress. *The Berbers*. Oxford: Blackwell Publishers, 1996.

Carey, Roane, *The New Intifada – Resisting Israel's Apartheid*. London: Verso, 2001.

Carey, Roane, Tom Segev, and Jonathan Shainin, eds. *The Other Israel: Voices of Refusal and Dissent*. New York: New Press, 2002.

Chomsky, Noam. *Rogue States: The Use of Force in World Affairs*. London: Pluto Press, 2003.

———. *The Fateful Triangle: The United States, Israel and the Palestinians*. London: Pluto Press, 2003.

Christison, Kathleen. *Perceptions of Palestine: Their Influence on US Middle East Policy*. Los Angeles: University of California Press, 1999.

———. *The Wound of Dispossession: Telling the Palestinian Story*. Santa Fe, N.M.: Sunlit Hills Press, 2001.

Coldwell, Dominic. *Egypt's Autumn of Fury: The Construction of Opposition to the Egyptian-Israeli Peace Process between 1973 and 1981*, PhD thesis, University of Oxford.

Cole, Juan. *Sacred Space and Holy War: The Politics, Culture, and History of Shi'ite Islam*. London: IB Tauris, 2002.

Cole, Juan, and Nikki Keddie, eds. *Shi'ism and Social Protest*. New Haven, Conn.: Yale University Press, 1986.

Crone, Patricia, and Martin Hinds. *God's Caliph: Religious Authority in the First Centuries of Islam*. Cambridge: Cambridge University Press, 1986.

Crone, Patricia, and Michael Cook. *Hagarism: The Making of the Islamic World.* Cambridge: Cambridge University Press, 1977.
"Culture wars: The Arabic music video controversy," Transnational Broadcasting Studies, Spring/Summer 2005, American University in Cairo Press.
Dawisha, Adeed. *Arab Nationalism in the Twentieth Century: From Triumph to Despair.* Princeton, N.J.: Princeton University Press, 2003.
Delong-Bas, Natana. *Wahhabi Islam: From Revival and Reform to Global Jihad.* Cairo: The American University in Cairo, 2005.
Didion, Joan. "Fixed Opinions, or the Hinge of History." *New York Review of Books,* January 16, 2003.
Eickelman, Dale and Anderson, Jon W. (eds.) *New media in the Muslim world: The emerging public sphere.* Bloomington: Indiana University Press, 2003.
El-Gamasy, Mohamed *The October War: Memoirs of Field Marshal El-Gamasy of Egypt.* Cairo: American University Press in Cairo, 1993.
El-Nawawi, Mohammed, and Adel Iskandar Farag. *Al-Jazeera: How the Free Arab News Network Scooped the World and Changed the Middle East.* Oxford: Westview Press, 2002.
Fawzy, Wael. *Hiwaraat Mamnua (Forbidden Conversations).* Cairo: Dar al-Shurouq, 1995.
Fiqi, Mustafa. *al-Arab al-Asl wal-Sura (Arabs, the image and the reality).* Cairo: Dar al-Shurouq, 2002.
———. *Tagdid al-Fikr al-Qawmi (The Renewal of Nationalist Thought).* Cairo: Dar al-Shurouq, 1993.
Fisk, Robert. *Pity the Nation.* New ed. Oxford: Oxford Paperbacks, 2001.
Flint, Julie and de Waal, Alex. *Darfur: A Short History of a Long War.* London: Zed Books, 2005.
Friedman, Thomas L. *From Beirut to Jerusalem.* New York: Anchor, 1990.
———. *The Lexus and the Olive Tree: Understanding Globalization.* New York: Anchor, 2000.
Gellner, Ernest. *Muslim Society.* Cambridge: Cambridge University Press, 1979.
———. *Plough, Sword and Book: The Structure of Human History.* London: Paladin, 1991.
Gellner, Ernest, and Charles Micaud, eds. *Arabs and Berbers: from Tribe to Nation in North Africa.* Lexington, MA: D. C. Heath and Co., 1972.
Haim, Sylvia, ed. *Arab Nationalism: An Anthology.* Berkeley: University of California Press, 1976.
Halliday, Fred. *Islam and the Myth of Confrontation.* London: IB Tauris, 2003.
———. *Two Hours That Shook The World.* London: Saqi, 2002.
Halliday, Fred. *Nation and Religion in the Middle East.* Boulder, CO: Lynne Rienner, 2000.
Hamouda, Adel. *Al-Nukta al-Siyasiya: Kayfa Yaskhar al-Misriyyun min Zuama'ihim (The Political Joke: How Egyptians Laugh at Their Rulers).* Cairo: al-Fursan Lilnashr, 1999.
Hasan, Sana. *Enemy in the Promised Land: An Egyptian Woman's Journey into Israel.* New York: Schocken Books, 1986.
Hass, Amira. *Drinking the Sea at Gaza.* New York: Owl Books, 2000.
Heikal, Mohammed Hassanein. *Azmat al-Arab wa Mustaqbaluhum (The Crisis of the Arabs and Their Future).* Cairo: Dar al-Shurouq, 2002.
———. *al-Mufawwadaat al-Sirriyya (The Secret Negotiations).* Cairo: Dar al-Shurouq, 1996.
———. *The Wandering Arab.* Cairo: Dar al-Shurouq, 2001.
Heggy, Tareq. *Naqd al-'Aql al-Arabi (A Critique of the Arab Mind).* Cairo: Dar al-Maaref, 1998.
Henry, Clement, and Robert Springborg. *Globalization and the Politics of Development in the Middle East.* Cambridge: Cambridge University Press, 2001.
Hirst, David. *The Gun and the Olive Branch: The Roots of Violence in the Middle East.* New ed. London: Faber and Faber, 2003.

Holt, P. M., and M. W. Daly. *A History of the Sudan: From the Coming of Islam to the Present Day.* Harlow, UK: Pearson Education, 2000.
Horne, Alastair. *A Savage War of Peace: Algeria 1954–1962.* 1977. Reprint. New York: Viking, 2002.
Hourani, Albert. *Arabic Thought in the Liberal Age 1798–1939.* Cambridge: Cambridge University Press, 1993.
———. *History of the Arab Peoples.* London: Faber and Faber, 1992.
Hroub, Khaled. *Hamas: Political Thought and Practice.* Washington: Institute for Palestine Studies, 2000.
Huntington, Samuel P. *The Clash of Civilizations and the Remaking of the World Order.* London: Simon and Schuster, 1996.
Huntington. *Who Are We?: The Challenges to America's National Identity.* New York: Simon & Schuster, 2005.
Ibrahim, Sonallah. *Amrikanli,* Cairo: Dar al-Mustaqbal al-Arabi, 2003.
———. *Warda.* Cairo: Dar al-Mustaqbal al-Arabi, 2000.
Kaplan, Robert D. *The Arabists: The Romance of an American Elite.* New York: The Free Press, 1993.
Kennedy, Hugh. *The Court of the Caliphs: When Baghdad Ruled the Muslim World.* London: Phoenix, 2005.
Kepel, Gilles. *Bad Moon Rising.* London: Saqi Books, 2003.
———. *Jihad: The Trail of Political Islam.* Cambridge, MA: Harvard University Press, 2002.
Khalaf, Samir. *Civil and Uncivil Violence in Lebanon: A History of the Internationalization of Communal Conflict in Lebanon.* New York: Columbia University Press, 2002.
Khalidi, Rashid. *Palestinian Identity: The Construction of Modern National Consciousness.* New York: Columbia University Press, 1997.
Khalidi, Rashid. *Resurrecting Empire: Western Footprints and America's Perilous Path in the Middle East.* Beacon Press, 2004.
Kienle, Eberhard. *A Grand Delusion: Democracy and Economic Reform in Egypt.* London/New York: IB Tauris, 2000.
Kimmerling, Baruch. *The Invention and Decline of Israeliness: State, Society and the Military.* Los Angeles: University of California Press, 2001.
Lacouture, Jean. *Gamal Abdel Nasser.* Paris: Bayard, 2005.
Lavie, Smadar, and Ted Swedenburg, eds. *Displacement, Diaspora, and Geographies of Identity,* Durham, N.C.: Duke University Press, 1996.
Lawrence, T. E. *Seven Pillars of Wisdom.* London: Penguin Books, 2000.
Lewis, Bernard. *What Went Wrong?: The Clash between Islam and Modernity in the Middle East.* London: Phoenix, 2002.
Lynch, Marc. *Voices of the New Arab Public: Iraq, al-Jazeera and Middle East politics Today.* New York: Columbia University Press, 2005.
Maalouf, Amin. *On Identity.* London: P. Harvill, 2000.
Mackintosh-Smith, Tim. *Yemen: Travels in Dictionary Land.* London: Picador, 1997.
Makiya, Kanan. *Cruelty and Silence.* London: Jonathan Cape, 1993.
———. (pseudonym Samir al-Khalil). *Republic of Fear: The Politics of Modern Iraq.* London: Hutchinson, 1989.
Mallat, Chibli. *The Middle East into the Twenty-First Century* Reading, UK: Ithaca Press, 1996.
Masalha, Nur. *The Expulsion of the Palestinians: The Concept of "Transfer" in Zionist Political Thought, 1882–1948.* Beirut: Institute for Palestine Studies, 1992.
Ma'oz, Moshe, and Gabrial Sheffer, eds. *Middle Eastern Minorities and Diasporas.* Brighton: Sussex Academic Press, 2002.
Miles, Hugh. *Al Jazeera: How Arab TV News Challenged the World.* New York: Grove Press, 2005.

Morris, Benny. *The Birth of the Palestinian Refugee Problem, 1947–1949.* Cambridge: Cambridge University Press, 1989.
Munif, Abdel-Rahman. *Mudun al-Malh (Cities of Salt, part one).* Beirut: al-Mu'assasa al-Arabiyya lil-Dirasat wal-Nashr, 1992.
Munif, Abdel-Rahman. *Bayn al-Thaqafa wal-Siyasa (Between Politics and Culture).* Beirut: al-Mu'assasa al-Arabiyya lil-Dirasat wal-Nashr, 2003.
Pape, Robert. *Dying to Win: The Logic of Suicide Terrorism.* Chicago: 2005.
Pappe, Ilan, ed. *The Israel/Palestine Question.* London: Routledge, 1999.
Peres, Shimon. *The New Middle East.* New York: Holt, 1993.
Pipes, Daniel. *The Hidden Hand: Middle East Fears of Conspiracy.* London: MacMillan, 1996.
Polk, William. *Understanding Iraq: The Whole Sweep of Iraqi History, of Outside Rule from Genghis Khan to the Ottoman Turks to the British Mandate to the American Occupation.* New York: HarperCollins, 2005.
Qutb, Sayed *Ma'alim Fil-Tareeq (Milestones).* Beirut: Dar al-Shurouq, 1979 (first published 1965).
Raban, Jonathan. *Arabia: A Journey through the Labyrinth.* London: Picador, 1979.
Redfield, R. *The Little Community and Peasant Society and Culture.* Chicago: University of Chicago Press, 1973.
Rodgers, Peter. *Herzl's Nightmare: One Land, Two Peoples.* New York: Nation Books, 2005.
Said, Edward. *Orientalism.* Princeton, N.J.: Princeton University Press, 1979.
——. *The Question of Palestine.* London: Vintage Books, 1979.
Shahak, Israel. *Open Secrets: Israeli Nuclear and Foreign Policy.* London: Pluto Press, 1997.
Schivelbusch, Wolfgang (tr. Jefferson Chase). *The Culture of Defeat: On National Trauma, Mourning, and Recovery.* London: Granta Books, 2003.
Shlaim, Avi. *The Iron Wall: Israel and the Arab World.* London: Penguin Books, 2000.
Vatikiotis, P. J. *The History of Modern Egypt.* London: Weidenfeld and Nicholson, 1991.
Vidal, Gore. *Dreaming War: Blood for Oil and the Cheney-Bush Junta.* New York: Thuder's Mouth Press/Nation Books, 2002.
——. *Perpetual War for Perpetual Peace.* New York: Thuder's Mouth Press/Nation Books, 2002.
Yapp, M. E. *The Near East since the First World War.* New York: Longman, 1991.

Index

Aaronovitch, David 107
al-Abbar, Mohammed 38
Abbas, Jaafar 95
Abbas, Mahmoud 78–9, 82, 219
Abbasid caliphate 84, 94, 101, 156–7, 189, 213
Abdel-Aziz, Saud bin 152, 158, 171
Abdel-Fattah, 130
Abdel-Hafiz, 105
Abdel-Meguid, Wahid 3, 122, 124
Abdel-Nasser, Gamal 1–2, 3, 19, 20, 26, 27, 28, 105, 119, 130, 134, 145, 147, 153, 158, 160, 173, 177, 205
Abdel-Qaddous, 131
Abdel-Rahman, Hisham 170
Abdel-Rahman, Omar 133
Abdel-Sattar, Abdel-Jabbar 104–5
Abdel-Wahhab, Mohammed ibn 154
Abdullah, King 53, 90, 99, 156, 166–7
Abdullah, Mohammed Ahmed ibn (the Mahdi) 182
Avnery, Uri 85
Abu Ghraib 42, 72, 106–9, 114, 118, 203, 207, 213
Abul-Fotouh, Abdel-Moneim 23–4, 128
Aburish, Said 9, 25, 172
Action by Churches Together 183
Adonis (poet) 74
Afghan Arabs 132
Afghanistan 173, 185, 190, 192
African Muslims 52
al-Ahmed al-Sabah, Emir Sheikh Jaber 17
al-Ahmed, Ali 31
Ahmed, Leila 145
al-Ahram 81, 89, 129, 213
al-Ahram al-Messai 192
Ajami, Fouad 8, 74, 75, 78, 106, 144, 145, 219
Ajram, Nancy 39
Akef, Mohammed Mehdi 113, 138, 148, 219
Akhbar al-Youm 143, 200, 201
Al Ahaly 72
Al Saud family 6, 21–3
Alawites 6
Albright, Madeleine 3–4, 30, 183
Algeria 6, 8, 17, 25, 32
Alhurra Television 5, 16
Ali, Mohammed 144, 154, 175

Ali, Noble Drew (Timothy Drew) 51
Allawi, Iyad 98, 105
Alon, Benny 71
Alousi, Mithal 94
Amer, Abdel-Hakim 27
America, and Arab attitudes toward democracy of 42–5; and Arab entertainment aping America 38–42; Arab obsession with culture of 33–5; Arab visitors to 43; attempts at understanding 52–6; cultural influence of 205–6; foreign policy of 33, 36; future of alliance with Egypt 146–9; oil/business interests in Iraq 87–8; political mistakes made by 114–16; politics of 34; relationship with Egypt 119–20, 124, 124–5, 136–7, 146–9; support for Israel 57, 58–9; television on Arab TV screens 35–8; treatment of Iraqi civilians by 116–18; and views on promiscuous culture of 45–8
American Anti-Slavery Group (AASG) 183, 196
American Friends of the Israeli Double Column Plan 196
American Jewish Committee (AJC) 183
American Muslims 48–52; and Black Islam 51–2; and woman imam controversy 48–51
American-Arab Anti-Discrimination Committee (ADC) 30
American-Israeli Public Affairs Committee (AIPAC) 30
American-Saudi relationship, Arab view of 171–7; and Aramco 151–2, 159–60; effect of 9/11 on 161–4; popular Saudi attitudes toward US 167–71; and Saudi reform movement 164–7; and suicide bombers 157; and US military presence in Saudi Arabia 155–8
Amin, Gamal 146
Amnesty International 203
Andalucia (al-Andalus) 161, 213
Annan, Khofi 185
anti-Americanism 14, 16, 77, 88, 117, 174, 205
Anti-Semitism Law (USA, 2004) 11
Arab League 10, 53, 90, 141, 182, 184
Arab League Media Commissioner 53

237

Arab nationalism 2, 7, 8, 12–13, 15,
    17–18, 25–8, 74, 103–4, 106, 109, 113,
    121, 145, 146, 158, 172; and conflict
    with Israel 26–7; and culture of defeat
    26, 27–8; development of 25; and Iraq
    26, 27; shift to political Islam 25–6
Arab states 1; American interests 3; British
    interests 2; and drawing up of borders/
    boundaries 2–3; and need for change 8;
    and problem of Iraq war 7; transnational
    sentiments/resentments 2–3
Arab Strategy Forum (Dubai, 2004) 6, 8
Arab Writers Union 74
Arab-American Institute 30
Arab-American relations, and Arab
    opinion/media 14–17; before 9/11
    1–4; and democracy 5, 7–10; and the
    Islamists 18–25; and Israeli-Palestine
    conflict 3–4, 10–14; and leading Arab
    political trends 17–18; and Liberal
    Democrats/minorities 28–32; and the
    Nationalists 25–8; and Palestine 6;
    post 9/11 4–7; and raprochement
    with Israel 5; and US commitment
    to Israel 3–4
    see also America
Arab-Americans 42, 62
Arab-Israeli wars 3, 33, 57, 58, 158, 205,
    217
al-Arabi 108
al-Arabiya 14, 16, 21, 36, 42, 78, 89, 106,
    115, 166, 169, 174, 175, 213
Arabization 180, 186–90
Arafat, Yasser 4, 46, 78, 82, 91, 102,
    141–2, 143, 219
Aramco 151–2, 159–60
al-Arees, Ibrahim 39
Armstrong, Eugene 111
ART television 170, 174
Asfour, Mohammed 129
Asharq al-Awsat 15, 29, 172, 213
Ashrawi, Hanan 53
al-Assad, Hafez 73, 90, 91, 176, 219
Assyrian Christians 32
Aswan High dam project 2, 26, 119,
    158
al-Aswani, Alaa 131
Ataturk, Mustapha Kemal 144
Atwan, Abdel-Bari 90, 108
al-Awajy, Mohsen 110
al-Awdeh, Salman 165
Azam, Hinza 49

Al-Azhar 213
Azzam, Abdullah 173

Baath Party 91, 94, 97, 101, 104–5, 182,
    213
Badr Brigades 100
Badrakhan, Abdel-Wahhab 93
Baghdad Museum 95–6
Baghdad Pact (1955) 3, 88
Bahrain 2, 7, 38, 72, 155
Baker, james 58
Bakr, Hilmy 39
Bakry, Mustafa 113
Balfour Declaration (1917) 12, 93, 214
Balfour, Lord 12
Baquba 104, 118
Barazani, Massoud 98
Barghouthi, Marwan 85
Bashir, 191–2, 193
al-Bashir, Omar Hassan 182, 219
Bashir, Tahseen 74
Baz, Sheikh Abdel-Aziz bin 165
BBC World Service 17, 174
Bedouin 145, 152, 153, 156
Begin, Menachim 122
Ben-Gurion, David 70, 71
Benjadid, Chadli 133
Berbers 32
Berg, Nicholas 107
Beshir, Tahseen 172
Bigley, Kenneth 111–12
Bin Laden, Osama 16, 20, 22, 24, 29, 31,
    109, 110, 121, 163, 165, 169, 171,
    173–4, 182, 190, 191, 195, 200, 219
al-Bitar 24
Boof, Kola 195
Boutros-Ghali, Boutros 122
Bouzid, Nouri 26
Brahimi, Lakhdar 109
Bremer, Paul 109
Brown, Mark Mallock 76
Brumberg, David 164
Bush, George H.W. 4, 157
Bush, George W. 4, 5, 6, 16, 19, 30, 53, 58,
    66, 79, 81, 82, 88, 92, 137, 148, 193

Cairo conference (2005) 99
Cairo International film Festival 41
Caliph 214
Camp David 3, 58, 82, 119, 123, 125–31,
    140, 143, 144, 214
Carlos the Jackal 182

Carter, Jimmy 3, 122, 195
Central Conference of American Rabbis 183
Central Intelligence Agency (CIA) 3, 20, 21, 80, 105, 173, 190, 200
Chahine, Yousef 26, 41–2, 121, 219
Chalabi, Ahmed 98
Charbel, Ghassan 108
Chomsky, Noam 191
Christian fundamentalism 45
Christian Solidarity International 183, 197
Churchill, Winston 158
cinema 26, 36, 37, 40–2, 68, 134–5
Clinton, Bill 4, 46, 55–6, 107, 140, 143, 183, 190, 191, 192
CNN television 17
colonialism 87, 95, 205
Committee for the Eradication of Abduction of Women and Children (CEAWC) 197
Communism 2, 18, 112–13, 158, 207
Convention on the Prevention of Genocide (1948) 199
Coptic Christians 31–2, 129, 202
Crusades 214
Cruz, Angelo de la 111
culture 204; ambivalence of views 34–5; American influence 168–71, 205–6; and Arab youth 34; and cinema 26, 36, 37, 40–2, 68; Coca-Cola-ization, McDonaldization, Newsweekization 33; denigration/disregard for Arab culture 106–7, 114; distinction with politics 34; Egyptian 144; icons of 34; Israeli view of Arab culture 75; obsession with 33; and pop music 34, 38–9, 38–40, 39–40; as promiscuous 45–8; and television 15, 16–17, 35–8

Daily Star 34, 43, 108, 214
Danforth, John 193
Darfur 31, 179, 183, 184–5, 194, 198–204, 214
Darfur Accountability Act (2005) 199
Da'wa Party 20, 214
Dayan, Moshe 122
Declaration of Principles (1993) 4
al-Degheidy (film director) 40
democracy 1, 5, 6, 7–10, 28, 29, 33, 136; admiration for 42–3; Arab attitudes toward 42–5; arguments concerning 44–5; and Christian fundamentalism 45; and education 43; in Egypt 143–4; and elections 8–9; and Iraq 87, 88; and softness of America 44; and state/religion separation 43–4
Dhaher, Pierre 38
Diab, Amr 41
al-Douri, Ezzat Ibrahim 116
Druze 31, 61
Dubai 8, 35, 37, 43, 72
al-Durra, Mohammed 143

Ebeid, Nabila 42
al-Effendi, Abdel-Wahhab 201
Egypt 1–2, 3, 5, 6, 8, 9–10, 12, 13, 15, 16, 18, 25, 27, 28, 29, 37, 44, 57, 73, 79, 80, 89, 90, 108, 110–11, 113, 172; and Arab nationalism 144–5; changing position in Arab world 140–6; and cinema 134–5; decay/corruption of society 147; and Egypt first-ism 143–4; ejected from Arab League 141; elections in 137–40, 138–40; extremist groups in 126–7; and first Intifada 141–3; future of US alliance 146–9; and Israel as gateway to Washington 119–25; mass arrests in 122; militarization of politics in 122–3; multi-party democracy in 120–1; Muslim Brotherhood in 125–6, 128–31, 138–9, 144; and peace with Israel 120, 121, 122, 142–3, 190, 205; political detainees in 127–8; and political Islam after Camp David 125–31; political opposition in 137–8; relationship with Soviet Union 158; relationship with Sudan 180–1, 184; relationship with US 119–20, 124–5, 136–7, 207; use of media in 134–5; violence of 1990s 131–5; and war in Iraq 135–40; year of protests in 138
Eisenhower Doctrine (1957) 158
Emara, Mohammed 114
Emirates airline 37
Erbakan, Necmettin 149
Erdogan, Tayyip 149
al-Erian, Essam 128
ethnic cleansing 69–74, 85, 203
European Sudanese Public Affairs Council (ESPAC) 197

al-Fagih, Saad 166–7
Fahd, King 153, 163, 165
Faisal, King 153, 160, 161

al-Faisal, Prince Turki 11
al-Faisal, Saud 108
al-Faisal, Turki 89
Fakhreddine, Jihad 35, 37
Falluja Brigade 168
Fandy, Mamoun 29
Farrakhan, Louis 51–2
al-Farsi, Mohammed 185
Fatah movement 22
fatwas 29–30
Fatyan, Yusri 108
Fauntroy, Walter E. 196
Fawaz, Khaled 167
Fedayeen 102, 214
Feith, Douglas 94
al-Fiki, Mutafa 47
FiS *see* Islamic Salvation Front
flint, Julie 203
Freund, Charles Paul 39
Friedman, Thomas 4–5, 8, 37, 72, 143
fundamentalist 214

Gaddafi, Colonel Muammar 9, 90, 176
Galal, Ashraf 39
Gamaa Islamiya 121, 125, 128, 132, 133, 215
Garang, John 30, 183, 202, 203
Garner, Jay 116
Gaza Strip 3, 13, 38, 60, 71, 81, 82, 83
Gebin, Menachim 58
Gellar, Sarah Michelle 37
Gemayyil, Amin 31
Gemayyil, Bashir 61
al-Ghad Party 136, 137
al-Ghanouchi, Rachid 114
Ghazala, Abdel-Halim Abu 125
al-Ghitani, Gamal 64, 201
al-Gomhouriya 56, 108, 185
Gordon, General George 182
Graduate Institute of International Studies 115
Graham, Franklin 183
Greater Middle East project 202
Group for Tawheed and Jihad 109
Guantanamo Bay 47, 107, 168
Guilani, Rudolph 54
Gulf Arabs 58, 77
Gulf states 7
Gulf War (1990–91) 4, 7, 41, 126, 132, 143, 153, 155, 158, 160, 164, 207

Habash, George 182
Habib, Rafiq 130
hadiths 215
Hafez, Abdel-Halim 26
al-Hakim, Abdel-Aziz 98, 100
al-Hakim, Tewfik 75
Halabja 9, 103
Al-Hamad, Turki 159–60, 220
Hamas 66–7, 69, 79, 182
Hamed, Wahid 134
Hanafi, Hassan 23
Hannibal 32
al-Hariri, Rafik 8
al-Hariri, Rafiq 31, 175, 220
Haroun, Khidir 194
Hasan, Sana 74
Hashemites 97, 153, 215
al-Hassan, Bilal 29
al-Hawali, Safar 165
Al-Hayat 15, 55, 66, 108, 164, 172, 215
Heikal, Mohammed Hassanein 27–8, 88, 145, 175
Hensley, Jack 111
Herzl, Theodor 11
Higher Council for Culture 126
Hizbollah 5, 20, 22, 31, 42, 44, 59, 87, 112, 176, 185, 215
al-Hodeiby, Maamoun 183
Howeidy, Fahmy 183
Hroub, Khaled 66
human rights 108, 157, 165, 184, 197
Human Rights Watch 127, 195, 203
Huntington, Samuel 64, 65, 72, 77
Hussein, Adel 125, 183
Hussein, King 16
Hussein, Saddam 3, 7, 9, 26, 27, 88, 89, 90, 94, 97, 101–2, 117, 134, 155, 163, 176, 177, 203, 207
Huweija 118

Ibdaa 126
Ibish, Hussein 49
Ibrahim, Saadeddin 29, 128, 148
Ibrahim, Sonallah 48, 80, 124
Idris, Ahmed Naqd 200
al-Idrissi, Ibrahim 108
Ijtihad 215
Ikhwan (Brotherhood) 152
Imam, Adel 134, 138
Intergovernmental Authority for Development (IGAD) 193
International Christian Concern 183

International Criminal Court (ICC) 200
International Crisis Group (ICG) 112, 194
International Religious Freedom Act (IRFA) 32
internet 44–5, 111, 156, 164, 171
Intifada 25, 36, 53, 67, 74, 79, 80, 84, 141–2, 143, 215
Iran 24, 59, 90
Iraq 1, 4, 17, 19–20, 23–4, 25, 32, 33, 41, 44, 53, 75–6, 84, 153; and Abu Ghraib scandal 106–9; as act of colonialism 87; and alienation of Iraqis in the new Iraq 114–18; American interests in 87–8; American treatment of civilians in 116–18; and Arab perception of neo-colonialism 91–6; Arab resistance to 87–8; body count in 115; British interests/interventions in 92, 93, 151; construction programmes in 101–2; democracy/human rights in 88; Egyptian reaction to war in 135–40; and encouragement of radical Islam 88; and end of pan-Arab Iraq 103–6; and fall of Baghdad 94–6; and fears over sectarian/ethnic divisions 93; as infamously divisive people 105–6; invasion of 206–7; Iraqi views on war 96–101; liberation of 92–3; oil/business interests in 87–8, 94, 151; particularism in 103, 106; political psychology of region 99–100; post-invasion state 100; and post-war reinvigoration of political Islam 109–14; problematic for Arab leaders 7; and pulling down of Saddam's statue 94–5; as rallying call for Islamists 114; and regime fears 88–91; situation on eve of US invasion 101–3; Sunni, Shi'ite, Kurd groupings/beliefs 96–101; as test case 6; unpopularity of 87
Iraq Body Count group 115
Iraq-Iran war (1980–88) 98
al-Iraqiya 5, 16, 106
Islam 2, 208–9
Islamic Charter Front 202
Islamic Group 147
Islamic Jihad 69, 133, 147, 215, 125
Islamic Salvation Front (FiS) 131, 133, 214
Islamists 12–13, 17, 18–25, 68, 74, 134, 148; and al-Qa'ida 22, 23–4; American involvement in 21; anti-American feelings 20; ideology 18–19; and Iraq 23; and jihadism 22; and Palestine issue 22–3; and resistance to the West 21–2, 24; roots 18; Shi'ite groups 19–20; terminology associated with 19; and use of the internet/modern technology 24–5; violence of 19–20, 23
Islamization 180, 186–90
Islamo-fascism 5
Ismail, Mustafa Osman 187
Israel 2, 44, 46–7, 91; American reliance on 93–4; American support for 57, 58–9; attitude towards Palestinians 93; borders/boundaries 60; and cultural soul-mate of America 61–6; dialogue with 74–5; as Egyptian gateway to Washington 119–25; and ethnic cleansing 70–4; and house demolition 68; and interest in Iraqi war 88; invasion of Lebanon 61; and killing of Palestinians 68; and oil link with Iraq 94; and peace with Egypt 122, 190, 205; and possible Israeli-Jordanian-Turkish axis 88; and removal of Palestinians 65; settlement plans 124–5, 141, 206; and two-state solution 60, 82–5; as war society 69
Israeli Arabs 84
Israeli-Palestinian conflict 1, 27, 76, 107, 176, 206; American attitude towards 10–14; American involvement in 3–4, 10–14; Arab attitude towards 10–13; British attitude towards 12, 13; and granting of Jewish national home 2; and US backing of Israel 57
Issa, Salah 20

al-Jaafari, Irahim 98
Jacobs, Charles 196
Jahine, Salah 26
Janadiriya (cultural festival) 156
Janjaweed militias 194
al-Jazairy, Mufid 113
Al-Jazeera 5, 14, 15–17, 23, 28, 36, 42, 50, 53, 69, 72, 88, 94, 101, 108, 111, 115–16, 165, 174, 175, 191, 200, 213
Jerusalem 13, 14, 60, 65, 82, 83, 122–4
Jihad 215
Jihad/jihadism 5, 20, 22, 109, 110, 132
Jordan 2, 7, 13, 16, 61, 72, 73, 89, 142, 151, 153, 160
Jubran, Salem 72

Justice and Social Development Party (Egypt) 149

Kamal, Mohammed 140
Kamel, Ibrahim 122
Kandil, Hamdy 4
Karpinski, Brigadier-General Janis 93
Kassem, Hisham 44, 132
Khader, Samir 43
Khaldoun, Ibn 124
al-Khaleej 54, 185
al-Khalidi, Rashid 92
Khartoum Monitor 202
Khayyat, Tahseen 175
al-Khazen, Jihad 69
Khobar 157–8, 162
Khomeini, Ayatollah 24, 128–9
Kim Jung II 102
Kissinger, Henry 3, 58
Kurds 30, 87, 94, 96, 97, 98, 103, 203
Kuwait 2, 4, 7, 132, 135, 152, 157, 175

Lancet, The 115
Laqtaa, Abdel-Qader 40
Lebanon 6–7, 8, 13, 31, 37, 41, 44, 60–1, 112, 141, 176, 202
Lemkin, Raphael 199
Levant 215
Lewinsky, Monica 45–6, 191, 192
Lewis, Bernard 14, 107
liberal democrats 17–18, 28–30
Libya 9, 25
Likud Party 70, 72, 122, 124, 196
Lundin Oil 184
Lutheran World Relief (LWR) 183

Maalouf, Amin 21
Machakos Protocol 185–6, 193
Madani, Iyad 167
Madi, Abul-Alaa 130
Madison, Joe 196
Maghreb 216
Mahdi Army 112
al-Mahdi, Sadeq 182, 194
Maher, Ahmed 108
Al-Mahfi, Sadeq 220
Mahfouz, Naguib 74
Mahgoub, Rifaat 132
Makiya, Kanan 74, 106, 220
al-Maktoum, Sheikh Mohammed bin Rashid 8
Mami, Cheb 40

al-Manar 5
mandate 215
Manqa, Amin Abu 187
Maronites 31, 216
al-Mas'ari, Mohammed 163
Mashreq 216
Matar, Gamil 45
Maude, General Stanley 92
Medani, Abbasi 133
Medani, Abdel-Harith 127–8
media 14–17, 89–90, 101, 107–8, 192, 205
Middle East Broadcasting (MBC) 16, 35, 38, 41, 170, 174, 175
Miller, Judith 134
Mirazi, Hazem 72
Mohammad, Prophet 20, 97, 171, 199
Mohammed, Abdel-Aziz 172
Moledet Party 70
Moorish Orthodox Church 51
Moqtada al-Sadr movement 27
Morocco 32, 40, 45, 72, 174
Morris, Benny 64, 71, 72
Mossad 94
Mossadegh, Mohamed 20
Mosul 103
Moussa, Abdel-Halim 133
Moussa, Amr 9–10, 87, 220
Movement for Islamic Reform in Arabia 167
Mubarak, Gamal 9, 136, 140, 149, 220
Mubarak, Hosni 8, 9, 10, 27, 31, 73, 80, 81, 88, 90–1, 120, 126, 127, 128, 131, 133–4, 136–41, 143, 184, 220
Mufti 216
Mufti, Ahmed 197
Mujahideen 216
Al-Mulhem, Mohanned 35
Munif, Abdel-Rahman 75, 159, 177, 220
Murooshid, Rashid 36
Mushrikeen 216
Muslim Brotherhood 12, 18, 21, 24, 44, 45, 113, 125–6, 128–31, 137, 138–9, 144, 147–8, 162, 182, 183, 202, 216
Muslim WakeUp! 52
Muslim Women's Freedom Tour 50
9/11 1, 4, 11, 22, 23, 33, 42, 43, 52, 79, 87, 102, 108, 109, 133, 161, 162, 168, 171, 177, 193, 205, 207

Nafaa, Hassan 5, 11
Nafie, Ibrahim 89, 129

Naguib, Mohammed 180
Nakha 216
Naksa 216
al-Nasr, Hamed 128
Nasrallah, Hassan 220
Nasser, Gamal Abdel *see* Abdel-Nasser, Gamal
Nasserism 97, 121, 216
Nasserist Party 135
National Democratic Party (NDP) (Egypt) 9, 121, 136, 138–40, 147, 149
National Islamic Front 202
National Petroleum Corporation 184
National Unity Coalition for Israel 196
Nayef, Mohammed bin 162
Nayef, Prince 162
Nazif, Ahmed 138
Nazmy, Wamidh 98
Nemat, Selama 66
neo-colonialism 91–6
Netanya 69
New York Board of Rabbis 183
New Yorker, The 128
Nezer, Mende 195
al-Nimeiri, Jaafar 181, 190, 220
Nixon, Richard 23–4
al-Nogaidan, Mansour 162–3
Noh, Mokhtar 128
Nomani, Asra 50
normalization 216
Nour, Ayman 136, 137, 139, 147, 221
NTV 175

Oil and Natural Gas Corp (ONGC) 184
Oman 27
OMV oil group 184
One TV 36, 41
Orbit 170, 174
Organisation of the Islamic Conference 182
Organization for Monotheism 20
Orientalism 207, 216
Oslo peace process (1993) 4, 46, 142, 194, 217
Osman, Maher 55
Ottoman Empire 98, 144, 157
Ottoman Iraq 92

Palestine 23, 53–5; and America-Israel as cultural soul-mates 61–6; and appeasement of 'Amerisrael' 79–82; Arab interest in 6; and Arab views of America 57–61; and attempts at influencing America 74–9; and cult of suicide bomber 66–9; and ethnic cleansing 69–74; and fear of extermination 70; and Israeli occupation of territories 4; and massacre of refugees 61; and media revolution 15; refugees from 13; and right of return 65; and self-rule 122; setbacks for 141; and suicide attacks 4; and support of non-Anglo-Saxon Americans 77–8; and two-state solution 60, 82–5; and uprooting of citizens 13; US lack of interest in 185 *see also* Israeli-Palestinian conflict
Palestinian Liberation Organization (PLO) 22, 58, 61, 91, 141, 171, 217
Palestinians 2
Pan Arab Research Center 34
pan-Arabism 145
Partition Plan (UN, 1947) 12
Pax Israelicana 88
Peel Commission 70
Perle, Richard 94
Persian Empire 98
Petronas 184
Philippines 111
Pipes, Daniel 62, 164
political Islam 20–1, 130–1, 135, 168, 217; effect of Camp David on 125–31; post-war reinvigoration of 109–14; rise of 20–1
see also Islamists
Polk, William 62
Popular Arab and Islami Congress (1994) 182
Popular Front for the Liberation of Palestine *see* Palestinian Liberation Organization (PLO)
Powell, Colin 10, 63
Progressive Muslim Union 49
Prophet 51, 217

al-Qa'ida 5, 16, 19, 22, 23–4, 29, 35, 44, 47, 54, 80, 89, 93, 94, 98–9, 100, 107, 110–11, 147, 162, 163, 164, 166, 168, 190, 213
al-Qa'ida Organisation for Jihad in the Land of the Two Rivers 109–10
Qandil, Abdel-Halim 157
al-Qaradawi, Yousef 24, 43–4, 50, 68–9, 77, 221

Qasim, General Abdel-karim 97
al-Qasim, Sameeh 69
Qatar 2, 72, 155, 192
al-Quds al-Arabia 90, 193, 201, 217
Quran 44, 49, 51, 101, 191, 201, 217
Qureishi, Salma 51
Qutb, Sayed 19, 20–1, 39, 47, 221

Raban, Jonathan 57
Rabbinic assembly 183
Rabbinical Council of America 183
Rabie, Gamal 121
Rabin, Yitzhak 141, 142
Radical Islam 5, 34, 80, 110, 126–7, 162, 195
Radio Sawa 5
Rand Corporation 164
al-Rashed, Abdel-Rahman 21–2
Al-Rasheed, Madawi 152, 160
Readers' Digest 33
Reconstructionist Rabbinical Association 183
Red Arabs 64
Rice, Condoleezza 139, 166
Rift Valley Institute 196
Roosevelt, F.D. 158
Ross, Dennis 3–4
Ruby (singer) 39
al-Riyadh 167

Saada, Ibrahim 143
al-Saadawi, Nawal 69
al-Sabah 5
Sabra 61
Sadat, Anwar 27, 119, 120–3, 124, 126, 129, 173, 205, 221
al-Sa'dawi, Nawal 122
Al-Sadr, Moqtada 20, 112, 221
Safavid dynasty 97–8
al-Saher, Kazem 102–3
al-Sahhaf, Said 95
al-Said, Abdel-Moneim 30
Said, Edward 64, 91, 107, 207, 221
Said, Nouri 93, 177
Salafi 110
Salameh, Ghassan 6
Saleh, Adel 116–17
Saleh, Ali Abdullah 80
Salem, Ali 74
Samaritan's Purse 183
al-Sanie, Rajaa 170–1
Sati, Hassan 201–2

Saud, King 153
Saudi Arabia 2, 5, 6, 7, 8–9, 18, 21, 24, 28, 31, 32, 35–6, 38, 44, 53–4, 57, 63, 87, 89, 90, 93, 107, 110, 147; American protection for 155–77; and Arab view of US-Saudi relationship 171–7; British interests/involvement in 151, 158; elections in 165–6; formation of 151–5; and Hejazi separatism 153; morality police in 165; oil in 151–2, 155, 157, 158–60, 172, 176; popular attitudes toward America 167–71; post-9/11 crisis in 161–4; as powerful Middle East player 177; protest/dissent in 165–7; provinces of 152; rebellion in 153, 154; reform movement in 164–7; and regional politics 160–1; relationship with America 207; and Saudi-Wahhabi Bedouin alliance 154–5; and setting up of Najdi state 154; as Sunni Islamic state 152
Save Darfur Coalition 183
Sawt al-Jihad 24
Sawt al-Khilafa 24
Schivelbusch, Wolfgang 26
Seale, Patrick 90
September 11 *see* 9/11
al-Shaab 107, 125
Shadi, Abu 41
Shadi, Ali Abu 40
Shalah, Ramadan 69
al-Shara, Farouk 93
Sharabi, Hisham 17, 91
Sharawi, Sheikh 121
Sharia law 128, 163, 181, 195, 217
Sharon, Ariel 36, 61, 69, 70, 73, 74
al-Sharq 192
Shatila 61
al-Sheikh, Abdel-Aziz 50
Sheikh-Shabab, Tarek 38
Shenouda III, Pope 32
Sherif, Omar 74
Shi'ites 6, 7, 19–20, 27, 30, 31, 61, 87, 94, 96–101, 109, 112, 153, 176, 200, 208
Shlaim, Avi 58
Shoboskhi, Hussein 166
Shurkian, Omar 202
al-Sibai, Hani 19
Sinai 123–5, 141
al-Sistani, Ali 100, 221
Six-Day War (1967) 3, 33, 57, 58, 158, 205, 217

slavery 195–7
Slivers, Laura 51
Solagh, Bayan Jabr 100–1
Soueif, Ahdaf 63
Soviet Union 3, 18, 158
al-Sowayan, Saad 154
Stalin, Joseph 158
Sudan 6, 25, 32, 207–8; and anti-Sudan lobby 195–8; Arab-Islamic ideology in 181; and Arabization/Islamization 186–90; background 179; British/Egyptian interests in 180–1; and charges of slavery against 195–7; civil war in 181–3, 208; and Darfur crisis 198–204; deteriorating relationship with US 190–8; historical development 187–8; human rights in 197; oil in 184, 200; persecution/marginalisation of Christians in 195–6; power in 187; relationship with US 179–86; southern guerrilla movement in 181; US activist groups interested in 183–4; and US bombing of pharmaceutical factory 190–1
Sudan Abductee Database 196
Sudan Liberation Army (SLA) 198
Sudan Peace Act (2002) 185–6, 193, 194
Sudan People's Liberation Army (SPLA) 30, 183, 185, 197, 201
Suez Canal 7, 175–6
Suez crisis (1956) 1–2, 14, 59, 217
suicide bombers 42, 66–9, 77, 102, 110, 157, 161–2, 190
Suleiman, Omar 137
Sultan, Essam 130
sumoud 218
Sunnis 6, 18–19, 20, 31, 87, 92, 96–101, 109, 112, 116, 161, 171, 200, 208
Supreme Council for the Islamic Revolution in Iraq (SCIRI) 20, 100, 217
Sykes-Picot agreement 2, 93, 104, 218
Syria 2, 3, 6, 8, 13, 25, 31, 37, 57, 87, 91, 93, 185

Tagammu (Socialist Rally) party 126, 135
Taif Accords (1990) 8
Takfir 218
Talabani, Jalal 98
Talal, al-Walid bin 219
Taliban 202
Talisman Energy 184
Tamil Tigers 70
Tawfik, Saleh 26
Tawheed 109
terrorism 5, 29, 69, 190
Tikrit 118
al-Tilmissani, Omar 44
transfer 218
Tunisia 8, 27, 41, 43, 141
al-Turabi, Hassan 182–4, 193, 195, 221

Umayyad 84, 218
Umma 218
UN Security Council Resolution 1559 31
United Arab Emirates (UAE) 2, 7, 8, 27, 35, 90, 93, 151, 185
United Arab Republic 18, 145
United Nasserist Nationalist Party 103
United Nations 2, 55, 57, 151, 167, 185, 199, 200
United Nations Arab Human Development Reports 29, 37, 75–6
United Nations Development Programme (UNDP) 76
United Nations Middle East Reports 83
United Nations Operation Lifeline Sudan 183, 194
United Nations Security Council 76, 77, 81, 193, 200
United States *see* America; Arab-American relationship
United States Institute of Peace 183
al-'uruba 218
US Commission on International Religious Freedom 32
USS Cole 80

Vincent, Major Doug 117

Wadud, Amina 49, 50, 221
al-Wafd 90, 96, 185
Wafd Party 135, 136, 137, 144, 218
Wahhabis/Wahhabism 6, 18, 19, 152–3, 161, 171, 176, 218
al-Walid bin Talal, Prince 54
al-Wasat 130
al-Watan 164
Weizmann, Chaim 123
Welfare Party (Egypt) 149
West Bank 13, 58, 59, 60, 65, 71, 76, 81, 82, 83, 122, 191
Wolfowitz, Paul 94, 107
women, cultural provocativeness of 39, 40, 170; and elections 8–9; as prayer

leaders 48–51; as prison interrogators
  47; and right to vote 165; rights of 166
World Court 185
World Economic Forum (Jordan, 2005)
  10–11
World Islamic Front for Jihad against Jews
  and Crusaders 163

Yalta conference (1945) 158
Yamani, Mai 9
Yemen 25, 80, 93, 152, 160
Young, Colonel Mark 118
Young Turk movement 144
Yousra (actress) 40

Zafarani, Khaled 149
al-Zakaria, Fareed 8, 11, 37, 53
Zakaria, Fouad 4
al-Zarqawi, Abu Musab 19–20, 22, 44,
  98, 107, 109, 221
al-Zawahiri, Ayman 121, 132, 163, 173,
  182, 192, 200, 221
Zayat, Montasser 121, 128, 132, 133–4
Zayed, Maali 40
Zeevi, Rehavam 70
Zeid, Nasr Abu 172
Zewail, Ahmed 72
Zionism 2, 4, 11, 12, 13, 14, 32, 53, 57,
  62, 63, 64, 66, 69, 70, 71, 73, 75, 78,
  84, 132, 144, 206, 207, 218, 830
al-Zoghby, Nawal 39
Zuair, Said bin 165, 175